Victor Hugo

Twayne's World Authors Series

French Literature

David O'Connell, Editor
Georgia State University

TWAS 883

VICTOR HUGO IN 1880.
Carjat. Photograph courtesy Bibliothèque Municipale de Tours.

Victor Hugo

Laurence M. Porter

Michigan State University

Twayne Publishers
New York

Twayne's World Authors Series No. 883

Victor Hugo
Laurence M. Porter

Copyright © 1999 by Twayne Publishers

Twayne Publishers
1633 Broadway
New York, NY 10019

Library of Congress Cataloging-in-Publication Data

Porter, Laurence M., 1936–
    Victor Hugo / Laurence M. Porter.
        p.   cm. — (Twayne's world authors series : TWAS 883. French literature)
    Includes bibliographical references and index.
    ISBN 0-8057-1652-1 (alk. paper)
        1. Hugo, Victor, 1802–1885—Criticism and interpretation.
    I. Title.   II. Series: Twayne's world authors series ; TWAS 883.
    III. Series: Twayne's world authors series.   French literature.
    PQ2301.P67   1999 c. 2
    848'.709—dc21
                                                                    98-55426
                                                                    CIP

This paper meets the requirements of ANSI/NISO Z3948-1992 (Permanence of Paper).

10 9 8 7 6 5 4 3 2

Printed in the United States of America

Contents

Preface:
"Hugo . . . hélas!" The Icon of an Age

Today in the United States, as 130 years ago in France, Victor Hugo has become an icon of popular culture. André Gide's lament "Hugo—alas!" when asked who was the greatest poet of nineteenth-century France reflects Hugo's irresistible fascination even for fastidious intellectuals.[1] A master of the lyric poem, the novel, the theater, and the essay, deeply committed to social reform, and the major symbol of resistance to Napoleon III's empire, Hugo became a national monument during his lifetime. Unlike the stereotypical self-pitying romantic, he was an eternally buoyant man who loved sex, food, and the outdoors. Moderate and paternalistic in politics, he staunchly opposed the death penalty and advocated benevolence toward the poor as a form of enlightened self-interest for the well-to-do. As a professional writer, he vigorously defended freedom of the press and of the stage. An optimistic peace-maker, he advocated reconciliation and eventual union of France with Prussia, even at the height of the Franco-Prussian War of 1870 to 1871.

Without neglecting his political career, I emphasize the richness and subtlety of his creative work. Hugo's mastery of poetic form rivals that of Goethe or Shelley. *Les Misérables* may be "the great French novel" of the nineteenth century. Its digressions form a meditative constellation of reflections similar to those in Melville's *Moby Dick,* arguably "the Great American Novel." The poem cycle *La Légende des siècles* is the most successful verse epic produced in nineteenth-century France. And *Les Contemplations* is a spiritual autobiography as imposing as Baudelaire's *Fleurs du Mal.*

Built on sharp contrasts, suicides, and starkly simplified character portrayal, Hugo's melodramatic imagination lost its appeal after 14 years on the French stage (1830–1843). It has found new, more appropriate homes in experimental theater, in opera (e.g., Verdi's *Rigoletto*), and on Broadway ("Les Miz"). Hugo was a screenwriter born before his time.

We would be mistaken, however, to limit Hugo's vision to an elemental struggle between symbolic Light and Darkness, like the neo-

Jungian classic *Star Wars*. He sought to reconcile enemies without sacrificing integrity. His career reflects France's desperate search for political equilibrium throughout the nineteenth century. The country vacillated between despotism and anarchy. To simplify, you could say that the government cycled twice from a divine-right monarchy to a constitutional monarchy, to a republic, and then to a despotic empire.

Kings of the absolute monarchy in France (987–1789) supposedly ruled because God wanted them to. The man might be depraved, but the office was sacred. The Déclaration des droits de l'homme et du citoyen (Declaration of the Rights of Man and Citizen, 26 August 1789) marked the beginning of a precarious compromise between royal authority and the rule of an elected representative assembly. The First Republic began when Louis XVI fled France with his family and was arrested on 10 August 1792. Napoleon I acquired increasing influence during the 1790s and finally crowned himself emperor in 1804. When his foreign wars overextended his power and led to his defeat and exile (in April 1814 and again in June 1815), Louis XVIII took over as king. He was restrained by La Charte, a constitution that instituted parliamentary government. When he died in 1824, his brother Charles X took power but was forced to abdicate in 1830 after his ham-handed attempts to restore a more conservative government failed. The "citizen-king" Louis-Philippe (1830–1848) allowed greater freedom of the press, but his regime preserved a bicameral parliament consisting of an appointed Chamber of Peers, and a Chamber of Deputies elected by only a few wealthy voters. In February 1848, France's Second Republic adopted universal manhood suffrage (in practice, about half the adult males could vote), making France the most liberal country in Europe at the time.

The appearance of liberalism was deceiving: within four years, the president, Louis-Napoléon, readily persuaded the restricted electorate to accept a new hereditary empire. This Second Empire ended with the humiliating defeat of France in the Franco-Prussian War (September 1870). The country was then torn apart by the popular front movement of the Commune, which occupied Paris for three months in 1871 before being defeated by government forces. The Third Republic was formed. Monarchists outnumbered Republicans by two to one in the new Constituent Assembly (in which Hugo served) that was formed after the war, but they were divided among different pretenders to the throne. Nevertheless, the constitution that restored the universal manhood suffrage of 1848 passed by only one vote in 1875. Since then, L'Action française (1899–1937), Vichy (1940–1944), and Le Pen's Front National with 15 percent of the vote today perpetuate reactionary chauvinism—and pretenders to the throne of France can still be found.

As a child, Hugo lived the experience of painfully divided loyalties. To explain to himself his parents' separation and strong mutual hostility, he unwittingly personalized the political: he believed that his mother was a passionate supporter of La Vendée, the royalist counterrevolution in Western France (in fact, she and her family were Republicans).[2] His father, a general under Napoleon, was charged with suppressing the Vendée revolt, and later with exterminating freedom fighters in both Spain (El Empecinado) and in Italy (Fra Diavolo) (see Robb, 20–21, 31, 35). Hugo's lifelong opposition to capital punishment probably began at ages five and nine when he went to Spain and Italy to visit his father. He saw the rebels' severed heads nailed to trees or over church doors in both countries. He mainly lived with his mother, who became a monarchist of convenience after 1815, and he was passionately devoted to her. After her death and his own marriage, Hugo learned to appreciate and admire his father—an experience recollected in the portrait of young Marius of *Les Misérables* (The Underclass).

Hugo's essential message is a call for reconciliation and nonviolence. He points to a spiritual order that subordinates the battles between political factions to a higher truth. Near the end of the preface to Hugo's poetic masterpiece, *Les Contemplations*, he exclaims in a concealed alexandrine verse, "Ah! insensé, qui crois que je ne suis pas toi!" [Oh! You are mad if you think I'm not you!].[3] At first he had hoped to achieve such harmony through the restored monarchy, then through a republic; finally, in exile during the 1850s, he elaborated a mystical narrative according to which all created beings will eventually be reabsorbed into their divine source, and all evil will end.

Hugo's dualistic rhetoric of light versus darkness suggests a simplistic imagination for which he has often been belittled. But the simplicity is ours if we consider as ultimate (fictional) reality Hugo's Manichaean dramas on a chiaroscuro stage. He challenges us to recognize that they are delusional temptations to despair. He finds some potential good and some potential evil in everyone. In his novels, poems, and polemical essays, he repeatedly implies a cosmic vision deeper than the limited visions of his characters. Hugo finds a hidden God revealed not through the rites of a church but through nature and the human heart. I deliberately use some peculiar spellings to reflect Hugo's worldview. Hyphens reinforce the impression of a superficial clash of good and evil (anti-hero, counter-revolution). Capitalization (*He* or *Him* denoting God or Christ, *Inversion* referring to the sudden revelation of a hidden good) suggests the presence of the numinous behind the veil of appearances. Because Hugo believes that heaven will absorb hell at the end of time, these two words are not capitalized.

To treat a monumental author in a short book requires sacrifices. Whenever possible, I have avoided brief summaries of each work. Instead, I blend original overviews with close looks at the textual details that confirm them, offering wide-ranging but accessible readings of the major works. All the translations are mine. Briefer discussions are provided for the early verse and novels, the great poems of the 1830s, the unfinished visionary epics *(Dieu, La Légende des siècles, La Fin de Satan)*, and Hugo's political career. Aside from *Hernani* and *Ruy Blas,* much of the theater is treated only by discussing its enduring impact as a source of stories for stage, film, and TV.[4]

I am indebted to *Nineteenth-Century French Studies* and to the *Romance Quarterly* for permission to publish reworked studies of the visionary poetry, and to French Forum Monographs for permission to reuse, from *The Renaissance of the Lyric in French Romanticism* (1978), scattered quotations and comments on individual poems. The Bibliothèque Municipale de Tours, France, has kindly authorized reproduction of the frontispiece, a portrait of Hugo by Carjat, in 1880. Marion Risser and Cheryl Rye offered helpful suggestions. Elizabeth Manukian deserves thanks for her enthusiastic help as graduate research assistant in fall 1996, a post funded by the College of Arts and Letters at Michigan State University. I thank the college and its former dean, John Eadie, for the extra support that allowed me to accept an NEH Fellowship for College and University Teachers during 1998. My best reader, Marjorie Porter, greatly contributed to making the whole book clearer and more interesting.

This volume is dedicated to my colleague Eugene F. Gray, in grateful acknowledgment of 30 years of unstinting friendship. Our many projects together have enriched my life. His courage, integrity, and unfailing competence have always provided me an inspiring example of what it should mean to be a teacher-scholar.

Chronology

1797   Hugo's parents, Joseph-Léopold-Sigisbert Hugo and Sophie-Françoise Trébuchet, marry.

1798, 1800   Hugo's brothers, Abel and Eugène, are born.

1802   Victor-Marie Hugo is born in Besançon on 26 February. In 1803 his father takes a mistress. Mme Hugo becomes the lover of General Lahorie, a Republican conspirator against Napoleon.

1803–1812   Madame Hugo and her children, sometimes with their father, travel intermittently in Corsica, Elba, Italy, and Spain.

1809   Major Hugo is named count and promoted to general. On 30 December 1810, Lahorie is arrested in Mme Hugo's house. A firing squad executes him for treason on 29 October 1812.

1816   Victor Hugo writes in his diary: "I want to be Chateaubriand [then the most prominent romantic writer, and a leading political figure] or nothing."

1817   Hugo receives honorable mention in a poetry contest sponsored by the Académie Française. As a child prodigy, he becomes an instant celebrity.

1818   Hugo's parents are legally separated.

1819–1820   Hugo wins two annual prizes for odes submitted to the Jeux floraux de Toulouse. He and his older brothers found a literary magazine, Le Conservateur Littéraire (The Literary Conservative, until 1821). In 16 months, Hugo publishes 112 articles and 22 poems there.

1821   Hugo is greatly influenced by the priest Félicité de Lamennais, who stresses the social utility of Christianity. Mme Hugo dies on 27 June. Less than a month later, Hugo's father marries his longtime mistress, Catherine Thomas. Hugo becomes secretly engaged to his childhood playmate Adèle Foucher.

1822   Hugo's first volume of poetry, *Odes et Poésies diverses* (Odes and Various Poems). Because the poems celebrate the monarchy and display great technical virtuosity, King Louis XVIII awards Hugo a *pension* (annual subsidy, often given to writers and artists). This regular income allows him to marry Adèle on 12 October. Hugo's brother Eugène, who also loves Adèle, goes permanently insane during the wedding.

1823   *Han d'Islande (Hans of Iceland* or *The Demon Dwarf)*, a "frenetic" novel with much bloodshed and melodrama, is the first French historical novel. Hugo and other young writers found *La Muse Française* (The French Muse). He becomes close friends with Charles Nodier, then leader of the romantic movement in France.

1824   *Nouvelles Odes* (New Odes). Hugo's oldest surviving child, Léopoldine, is born.

1826   *Odes et Ballades.* With *Bug-Jargal (The Slave King),* a novel of a black slave revolt in the Caribbean, "Western literature acquires one of its first wholly admirable Black heroes" (Robb, 123). Hugo's son Charles is born on 2 November.

1827   Charles Augustin de Sainte-Beuve, later the most famous literary critic of the century, becomes Hugo's best friend. Hugo's literary salon eclipses Nodier's. *Cromwell,* a historical drama, is published but not performed. Its famous preface advocates a new aesthetics inspired by Shakespeare, combining the sublime with the grotesque. Hugo breaks with the *ultras* (supporters of an absolute monarchy).

1828   General Hugo dies suddenly on 29 January. Hugo's second son, François-Victor, is born on 21 October. Hugo becomes disaffected with the monarchy owing to Charles X's extreme conservatism. A new verse collection, *Odes et ballades,* shifts from supporting the monarchy to depicting the exotic and picturesque.

1829   *Les Orientales* (Oriental Poems) further exploit the exotic and display extraordinary prosodic virtuosity. *Le Dernier Jour d'un condamné à mort* (The Last Day of a

Condemned Man) argues passionately against capital punishment—a lifetime preoccupation for Hugo. In August the play *Marion Delorme* is banned by government censors for presenting an unflattering portrait of the dissolute sixteenth-century king François I.

1830   The play *Hernani* marks the triumph of romanticism in French theater after vehement battles between the neoclassic and romantic factions in the audience. On 28 July, Hugo's second daughter, Adèle, is born. Exhausted by continual pregnancies, his wife will from then on sleep in a separate bedroom. Sainte-Beuve confesses his love for her.

1831   The historical novel *Notre-Dame de Paris: 1482 (The Hunchback of Notre-Dame)* glorifies the cathedral and anticipates the rise of democracy. The novel's appeals for architectural conservation inspire the formation of a Commission of Historical Monuments. *Les Feuilles d'automne (Autumn Leaves)*, one of Hugo's greatest verse collections, announces his visionary bent. The love affair between Sainte-Beuve, Hugo's best friend, and Adèle Hugo begins. It will inspire all Sainte-Beuve's creative writing. The Hugos stay together but will never again be more than friends.

1832   The play *Le Roi s'amuse (The King's Diversion)* is promptly banned for disrespect to the monarchy. Hugo moves to La Place Royale, today La Place des Vosges, where he lives until 1848.

1833   The plays *Lucrèce Borgia* and *Marie Tudor* are performed. The first is a great success. On 16–17 February, Hugo begins a lifelong affair with the untalented actress Juliette Drouet. She abandons her acting career and spends the rest of her life sequestered as Hugo's secretary, making fair copies of his manuscripts.

1834   *Littérature et Philosophie mêlées* (Literature and Philosophy Together), essays. Definitive break with Sainte-Beuve. *Claude Gueux* blames society for creating criminals.

1835   *Les Chants du crépuscule* (Songs of Dawn and Twilight), poems.

1837   *Les Voix intérieures* (Inner Voices), poems. Eugène Hugo dies in a padded cell in the Charenton asylum.

1838   *Ruy Blas,* Hugo's greatest play, is performed. The subject, a valet in love with a queen who loves him in return, scandalizes the monarchists.

1840   *Les Rayons et les Ombres* (Rays and Shadows), poems.

1841   Hugo's election to the Académie Française consecrates the militant romantic movement.

1843   The critical failure of the historical drama *Les Burgraves (The Robber Lords of the Rhine)* effectively marks the end of romantic drama. Hugo abandons the theater. His daughter Léopoldine marries; soon afterward, she is drowned with her unborn child and her husband in a sailing accident. In death, she becomes the major inspiration for the *Contemplations* (1856), Hugo's finest poetry.

1844–1851   Affair with Mme Léonie Biard.

1845   Hugo becomes a *pair de France* (comparable to a member of the British House of Lords). Ten weeks later, Mme Biard's outraged husband and a police officer catch Hugo and Mme Biard in flagrante delicto. She goes to prison. Hugo's status as peer makes him immune to prosecution.

1848   Hugo is elected to the Assemblée Constituante (constitutional convention) of the Second French Republic (1848–1851). He and his son Charles found and coedit the liberal newspaper *L'Événement* (The Event).

1849   Presiding over the International Peace Conference in Paris, Hugo gives the first known speech advocating the creation of a "United States of Europe."

1849–1851   Elected to the Legislative Assembly as a conservative, Hugo soon breaks with the Right and formally declares himself a Republican (i.e., a liberal) on 18 July 1851.

1851   Hugo's sons are arrested and jailed in June for publishing seditious articles in their paper. After a political coup by Louis-Napoléon transforms the French Republic into an empire (2 December), Hugo is pursued by the police. He leaves France under an assumed name nine days later. First he takes refuge in Belgium, next on the Channel Islands of Jersey (1852–1855) and Guernsey (1855–1870).

1852 Vehement political tract against Napoleon: *Napoléon le petit* (Napoleon the Little), "a brilliant, precise description of a modern police state" (Robb, 309). Hugo becomes the spiritual leader of the exiles. He refuses amnesty.

1853 *Les Châtiments* (Chastisements), satirical poetry inspired by the Roman author Juvenal. Initiated by his visitor Delphine de Girardin, Hugo and his family conduct seances from 1853 to 1855. They interview many spirits living or dead; Hugo believes that their replies reveal the ideas of punitive reincarnation and universal redemption that will dominate all his later visionary poetry.

1856 *Les Contemplations* (Contemplations), Hugo's most famous poems. Their great success allows Hugo to buy Hauteville House on Guernsey. Today the place is a museum.

1858 Appeal against the execution of John Brown, the American abolitionist.

1859 Part 1 of *La Légende des siècles* (The Legend of the Ages), an epic poem cycle reminiscent of Browning.

1861 Hugo's wife begins spending December through March in Paris, where she secretly sees Sainte-Beuve.

1862 *Les Misérables* (The Underclass), Hugo's greatest novel, has since inspired a Broadway rock opera as well as many films. Hugo starts offering a Tuesday dinner to as many as 50 poor children a week.

1863 In June his daughter Adèle, hopelessly infatuated with a Lieutenant Pinson, follows him to England, Malta, and Halifax only to find him married. She writes home the false news that she has married Pinson.

1864 *William Shakespeare*, a diffuse essay on genius.

1865 *Chansons des rues et des bois* (Songs of the Streets and Woods), virtuoso, sensuous pastoral poetry.

1866 *Les Travailleurs de la mer (Toilers of the Sea)*, a major regional novel dedicated to the Guernsey fishermen and their island.

1867 A triumphant revival of *Hernani* for the Exposition Universelle (Hugo's plays had been banned in France since 1851).

1868 On 27 August, Adèle Hugo, who since the mid-1860s had chosen usually to live apart from her husband, dies suddenly in Brussels after an affectionate reunion. Hugo's grandchildren Georges (16 August 1868) and Jeanne (29 September 1869) are born to his son Charles.

1869 *L'Homme qui rit (The Man Who Laughs* or *By Order of the King)*, a historical novel. Hugo presides over the European Peace Conference in Lausanne.

1870 The Second Empire ends with Napoleon III's surrender to the Prussians at Sedan. After 19 years in exile, Hugo returns to France the day after the Third Republic is proclaimed. He has come to personify international democratic ideals.

1871 Elected to the National Assembly, Hugo becomes opposition leader of 50 liberals against 700 Bonapartistes. He resigns when his proposals go unheard. On 13 March, his son Charles dies suddenly from apoplexy.

1872 Hugo is defeated in elections because of his support of amnesty for the Communards, popular front rebels who had taken over Paris for three months in 1871 after the city had surrendered to the Prussians. In February, Hugo's daughter Adèle returns from Barbados and is committed to a mental institution, where she will die in 1915.

1873 Death of Hugo's second son, François-Victor.

1874 *Quatrevingt-treize* (Ninety-Three), Hugo's most readable novel, treats the Vendée royalist rebellion against the French Revolution and examines the disastrous political divisions among the French that led to the Terror.

1876   Elected to the Senate of Paris, Hugo again vainly urges amnesty for former Communards.

1877   *La Légende des siècles, Deuxième Série* (part 2). *L'Art d'être grand-père* (How to Be a Grandfather), poems. In his finest hour in politics, Senator Hugo leads effective opposition to Marshal MacMahon, who nearly takes over as dictator. Republicans finally achieve a strong majority over the divided royalist factions.

1878   After a minor stroke, Hugo can no longer create. Pious disciples assemble and publish volumes from his manuscripts nearly every year thereafter.

1880   Hugo obtains amnesty for the Communards.

1881   Hugo's 79th birthday (26 February) is declared a national holiday. Six hundred thousand people march past his window throughout the day. In July the Avenue d'Eylau (a street starting at the Place de l'Étoile) where he lives is permanently renamed "Avenue Victor-Hugo."

1882   *Torquemada* is performed (play written in 1869). It will be brilliantly produced for television in 1976. Hugo is reelected senator.

1883   *La Légende des siècles (série complémentaire).* Juliette Drouet dies on 11 May.

1885   Hugo dies of pneumonia on 22 May. His last words are said to be "Je vois de la lumière neuve" [I see a new light]. Two million people march past the Arc de Triomphe, where he lies in state. The first of June is proclaimed a day of national mourning. Hugo is buried in the Panthéon after rushed legislation to reconvert it to a shrine for national heroes. As Hugo had wished, his manuscripts go to the Bibliothèque Nationale.

1886   *La Fin de Satan* (unfinished epic poem, written in 1854).

1888, 1893   *Toute la lyre* (All the Lyre), poems.

1891   *Dieu* (unfinished epic poem, written in 1855).

1902   The Maison de Victor Hugo museum in his former apartment on the Place des Vosges is inaugurated for the centenary of Hugo's birth.

1905   *Les Misérables* is the first full-length feature film to be produced in the United States.

1912–1918   Albert Capellani of Pathé and André Antoine of Le Théâtre-Libre produce a noteworthy series of silent films with a naturalistic flavor: *Les Misérables* (1912), *Marie Tudor* (1912), *Quatrevingt-treize* (1914), and *Les Travailleurs de la mer* (1918). Hugo acquires an international reputation.

1924   Celebrated performance by Lon Chaney as Quasimodo in W. Worsley's *The Hunchback of Notre-Dame de Paris.*

1926   The Cao Dai Buddhist sect, venerating Hugo, is founded in Vietnam. Today it has 1,000 temples and three million followers.

1947   *Ruy Blas* is adapted with dialogue and screenplay by Jean Cocteau. Danielle Darrieux and Jean Marais play the romantic leads.

1968   A fine television version of *Les Burgraves.*

1975   *Adèle H.,* directed by François Truffaut and starring Isabelle Adjani, recalls the tragic life of Hugo's younger daughter. The film wins the Grand Prix du Cinéma Français.

1980   Inspired by the rock opera *Jesus Christ Superstar,* *Les Misérables* by Alain Boublil and Claude-Michel Schoenberg eventually eclipses the record number of international productions of a musical, previously held by *Cats.*

1996   Walt Disney Corporation's playful animated version of *The Hunchback of Notre-Dame* distorts the plot beyond recognition.

Chapter One

The Divided Self:
Royalist Odes and Frenetic Novels

The Early Verse

Hugo's career began under the aegis of the monarchy his parents had opposed.[1] He started publishing under the Restoration only a few years after Napoleon's exile, writing conventional royalist odes. Skilled at self-promotion from the beginning, at age 15 Hugo secured the patronage of Comte François de Neufchâteau of the Académie Française, allowing the older man to publish Hugo's brilliant scholarly essay on Lesage's *Gil Blas* under his own name (Robb, 64–67). Soon he received a "pension" (a regular government subsidy) in recognition of his literary support of the regime. Indeed, in April 1825 he was appointed as the official poet for the coronation of the reactionary Charles X—a new post that Hugo had invented and then solicited (Robb, 114).

As a lyric poet, Hugo seemed to the manner (manor) born. From an early age, he wrote alexandrine (12-syllable) verse with extraordinary grace and facility.[2] He sometimes dreamed in it and could recall entire poems from his dreams.[3] Within a few years, his virtuosic control of a great variety of verse and stanzaic forms would be rivaled in Europe only by Shelley and Goethe.

The young French romantics distinguished themselves mainly in three lyric genres. Lamartine's elegiac *Méditations poétiques* in 1820 was the first noteworthy example of French romantic verse. He depicted mourning and melancholia.[4] Vague spiritual aspirations in Lamartine, molded from a combination of Christian mysticism and Platonism, compensated for isolation and for the death of the lyric self's beloved. Vigny's short "Poëmes" combined solemn historical subjects with the narrative fluidity of the folk ballad. In such poems, he either proposed a neoclassic "exemplum virtutis" (a model of heroic resolve) or sympathized with the victims of history. Hugo's odes conformed variously to any of three traditions: the Anacreontic (celebrating the joys of love and

1

wine and the pleasures of the country), the Horatian (conversational poems, rather like a letter to a friend), and the Pindaric (moral exhortation, poetic and religious inspiration, exalted expressions of patriotism, and reflections on the destinies of dynasties and nations).[5] The elegy reacts to loss with grief or consolation; the ode responds joyfully to victory or achievement.[6] To this repertory, Hugo added satiric verse, vehement personal attacks modeled on the work of the Roman poet Juvenal.

Hugo's early odes, written between 1816 and 1828, are primarily Pindaric. Their essence is to reaffirm the temporal sublime (human values transcending death). The spatial sublime reveals vistas where the world is the house of the gods. In the *Iliad,* Homer says that all Olympus trembles when Jupiter nods, and that Neptune's horses can leap across the ocean in a single bound. Heroic resolve to sacrifice one's life for a higher moral value (as Homer's Achilles did by remaining to fight in the Trojan War, knowing he would be slain) illustrates the temporal sublime, crystallized in a privileged moment of self-sacrificial moral insight.

To fill the void left by the departure of classical pagan deities from literature in other than ornamental roles, the eighteenth century invented the "moral ode." There the poet displayed imaginative power by personifying the virtues that are our immortal part. Hugo follows this tradition in his very early "Ode à l'Amitié" of 1816. He addresses the goddess of friendship, tells two exemplary stories of how people are willing to lay down their lives for their friends, and concludes by addressing the goddess again. Often the moral ode embodies human weakness in an episodic, illustrative anti-self (a "horrible example"), ritually expelled from the poem just before the concluding movement of heroic resolve. At that climax, the poet often appeals for divine inspiration to maintain him in virtue. Hugo follows the convention existing since Pindar, according to which the lyric or epic poet has the power to grant or to withhold the verbal immortality of fame.

As early as 1818, Hugo abandoned the subjects of the traditional moral, allegorical ode (with personified vices and virtues) and turned to current events relating to the fate of the French monarchy. He deplored crimes against the monarchy (the Vendée massacres, during which the king's rebellious supporters in Western France were slaughtered, 1793–1795; the assassination of the Duc de Berry, the second son of Charles X and the Legitimist heir to the throne, in 1820). And Hugo celebrated "Le Rétablissement de la Statue de Henri IV" (The Re-erection of the Statue of King Henry IV), which to this day stands prominently on the western end of L'Île de la Cité in the Seine:

Un jour (mais repoussons tout présage funeste!)
Si des ans ou du sort les coups encor vainqueurs
Brisaient de notre amour le monument modeste,
    Henri, tu vivrais dans nos cœurs;
Cependant que du Nil les montagnes altières,
    Cachant cent royales poussières,
    Du monde inutile fardeau,
Du temps et de la mort attestent le passage,
Et ne sont déjà plus, à l'œil ému du sage,
    Que la ruine d'un tombeau.[7]

(OP 1, 312–13)

[Some day (but we reject that baleful thought!)
If the victorious blows of time or fate
Should smash this modest monument of love,
    Henri, you'd live on in our hearts;
While the haughty pyramids of the Nile,
    Hiding a hundred kings' remains,
    A bootless burden on the earth,
Would bear witness to passing time and death,
And show no more, to sympathetic eyes,
    Than dusty debris of a tomb.]

The vague eternity of loyal memory in the poet's and his readers' hearts survives both the end of an individual life (symbolized by the tombstone) and the end of history (symbolized by the pyramids). The poem itself becomes not just a monument but a monument to a monument. Thus Hugo transcends the *exegi monumentum* topos (the traditional theme, taken from Horace's odes, that a work of art is more enduring than bronze), freeing the poem itself from the risks of deterioration and oblivion. Instead of merely expressing regret for what has passed (as in the *ubi sunt* topos of the elegy—"where are the snows of yesteryear?"), Hugo's ode affirms the eternity of both the loyal subjects' reverence and the poetic vision.

The stanza just cited illustrates the two devices Hugo relies on most in his odes to create an effect of grandiosity and immense visionary scope. The first, *adunaton,* is commonplace in popular culture as well as in formal literature. The word ("disuniting") means that one dissociates two events: for example, "rivers will run dry, day turn to night, crows will turn white, and rocks melt in the sun before I stop loving you" (*OP* 1, 265).[8] In Hugo's poem: "Even if the statue of Henri IV is destroyed, he'll live on in our hearts." Thus feelings seem stronger than death, an attitude typical of the temporal sublime. Contrast with the self-assurance of the ode, the tentative attitude of the typical love song: "Bury me beneath the willow, / . . . / When she hears her love is sleeping, / Maybe then she'll think of me."

The other device, typical of the spatial sublime, has no commonly used name. It is a compound comparison: A is as much bigger than B as B is bigger than C. Compare Milton's description of the fallen Satan in *Paradise Lost:* he walked with a staff that made the mightiest mast you could ever find on a ship look like a frail reed (reed is to mast as mast is to staff). In Hugo's poem, a monument (a glorious memorial) is in proportion to a tomb (an obscure memorial) as a tomb is to its rubble (the pyramids, imagined eons from now as having crumbled into the debased and meaningless fragments of a tomb).

By itself, the compound comparison glorifies the poet indirectly: it asserts a poetic vision (such as Satan's walking stick) that transcends in vastness anything we ordinary people could imagine. Hugo applies the device directly to depicting his anticipated fame, in "Le Désir de la Gloire—Ode" (The Desire for Fame, 1818). After describing the seven planets revolving around the sun, he continues:

>Et peut-être cet astre immense
>Ressent lui-même la puissance
>D'un astre plus immense encore.
>. . . . .
>Astres, dont le feu nous éclaire,
>Parlez, avez-vous un Homère
>Dont le nom vive plus que vous?
>   (*OP* 1, 144–45)

>[And perhaps that vast star
>Itself feels the power
>Of a star vaster still.
>. . . . .

Stars whose fire gives us light,
Speak, have you a Homer
Whose fame outlasts your own?]

Here Hugo surreptitiously imagines his fame becoming as much greater than Homer's as a galaxy is greater than a solar system.

In early 1821, Hugo had already begun to emphasize religious, more than royalist, inspiration in his odes. At first he had served as the major poetic voice of the ultraroyalists—those who wanted to restore a monarchy based on a mandate from God, confirmed by heredity, and needing no endorsement from the people the king served. "La Charte" (the Charter) under the Restoration (1815–1848) stipulated two chambers of government representatives. The king appointed one (the Peers), and the other (the Deputies) was popularly elected—although since suffrage was limited to well-to-do men, initially only one adult in a hundred could vote. The *ultras* (ultraroyalists) would have liked to revoke this charter, to institute severe censorship, and to return to the divine-right monarchy of the ancien régime. When they became increasingly vituperative after the assassination of the Duc de Berry, heir to the throne, in 1820, their cause came to seem less attractive to Hugo.

In the same year, he became acquainted with the widely influential religious writings of the Breton priest Félicité de Lamennais, whose *Essai sur l'indifférence en matière de religion* (Essay on Religious Indifference, 1817, 1821, 1823) defended Christianity as the religion of common sense and social justice and urged that the French church be ultramontane, that is, entirely under the authority of the pope. Because the French monarchy had traditionally succeeded in maintaining "Gallican liberties" (the quasi independence of the French church from Rome, where ecclesiastical appointments, local administration, and the king's right to power were concerned), to admire Lamennais was indirectly to be disloyal to the monarchy. Hugo met Lamennais in the spring of 1821, and when Hugo's mother died in June 1821, his meditative tendencies deepened as they were to do again after the death of his daughter Léopoldine in 1843. He wrote a review article on Lamennais's work.[9] A progressive reconciliation with his father beginning in late 1821 also prepared Hugo to become a less ardent royalist. In the ultimate development of this tendency, after 1870 Hugo called himself "God's civil servant" rather than the government's.

For the time being, Hugo preserved a delicate equilibrium between temporal and spiritual power by not examining their often opposing claims. His 1822 preface to the *Odes* reaffirms the traditional reactionary viewpoint of the ancien régime: "Human history can be poetical only when judged from the elevated perspective of monarchical ideas and religious beliefs" (*OP* 1, 265). Again in the 1823 preface he echoes Chateaubriand's *Le Génie du Christianisme* (The Spirit of Christianity), affirming that the pagan mythology of neoclassicism (of the eighteenth century) must be replaced by Christian dogma in order to heal and sustain a French monarchy "still stumbling away from the orgies of atheism and anarchy" (267).

"Le Poète" (1823; *OP* 1, 402; *Odes* 4, 1) anticipates a decisive move toward ideological independence by standing the ode on its head. Neoclassic odes, like those of classical antiquity, often began by invoking a muse, a spirit who would dictate to the poet preestablished, orthodox messages supporting throne and altar. These messages were conformist and predictable. But here, inspiration and the message from the beyond appear at the end of the poem. It starts by describing the poet's solitary life; he then complains that he must live amid the frivolous crowd; he tells the crowd to leave him in peace, because he is divinely inspired. In the fourth section, he reappears among other humans, bearing revelation: "Son front porte tout un Dieu!" [his brow bears God entire]. Superficially, this statement means that the poet is divinely inspired; by implication, it means that the poet's countenance has been transfigured, shining with divine radiance as was the face of Moses or Christ. Implied by the notation "pale brow," this motif will often recur in Hugo's works (e.g., in "Spes" of the *Contemplations*).

In the preface to his *Nouvelles Odes* (February 1824) Hugo reflects his new apolitical orientation, saying that "he will never be the echo of any word, unless it be the word of God." He begins to see history as a spiritual evolution toward a still mysterious future (*OP* 1, 277). His vision is no longer centered in the French monarchy: it becomes syncretic, combining traditions from all over the world. In July 1824, an early ballad, "La Fée et la Péri," for example, mixes Gothic, Chinese, ancient Celtic, and Indian motifs in a story in which the Fairy of the West and the Elf of the East vie for the soul of a dead child (*OP* 1, 545–49; cf. Robb, 110). The device of the compound comparison communicates this vision neatly in the third stanza of "La Bande noire" (The Vandals), "vieux monuments d'un peuple enfant" [ancient monuments of an infant race] (*OP* 1, 341). As the lifetime of an individual is brief in comparison to the length of time a medieval church of stone endures, so the life span of those churches is brief in comparison to the odyssey of salvation, which humanity has as yet barely begun.

Hugo refines the use of the compound comparison to imply a visionary future in "Aux ruines de Montfort-L'Amaury" (At the ruins of Montfort-L'Amaury [a chateau near Paris]):

> Je médite longtemps, en mon cœur replié;
> Et la ville, à mes pieds, d'arbres enveloppée,
> Etend ses bras en croix et s'allonge en épée,
> Comme le fer d'un preux dans la plaine oubliée.
>
> (OP 1, 475; Odes 5, 18)

> [Long I ponder, withdrawn into my heart;
> And the town at my feet, shrouded by trees,
> Extends its arms, crosslike, and seems a sword,
> Forgotten by a warrior on the plain.]

As greatly as the size of the town surpasses the size of any inhabitant, so the town (an element of organized material history) is surpassed in size by the mythical hero who could pick it up and wield it like a sword in a militant spiritual struggle combining sacrifice (suggested by the cross) with heroic resolve. Cross and sword together imply a holy crusade. The soldierly gesture of taking up this sword would be only a prelude to the drama of redemption in a theater unimaginably vaster than the physical world. Hugo will explore this theater in his visionary poetry of the 1850s.

More explicitly, Hugo once again evokes and transcends individual, historical military valor in his celebrated ode "À la Colonne de la Place Vendôme" (To the Column of the Vendome Square) (OP 1, 395–400; Odes 5, 18). One hundred fifty feet high, this monumental column was forged from the bronze of twelve hundred cannons that Napoleon's Grande Armée took from the vanquished enemy in 1805. By comparing this column itself to a warrior, Hugo suggests a scale even vaster than the Napoleonic empire. The giant warrior would form part of an army of the spiritual imagination, making conquests for God.

If Hugo were to express his poetic vision of humanity's spiritual future only by alluding to a previously unsuspected dimension of vastness, however, he would bind down his vision to the very material order that he wishes to escape. Therefore he suggests transcendence in the

Odes in two other ways as well. First, he employs the archetype of Inversion
in its positive form: what seemed bad, proves good. Material defeat means
spiritual victory.[10] So, for example, in "À M. de Chateaubriand" (*OP* 1, 374;
Odes 4, 2), Hugo praises that minister for resigning from the government in
1824. His material renunciation of worldly fame leads to a moral triumph: "Chacun de tes revers pour ta gloire est compté / . . . / Tomber plus
haut encore que tu n'étais monté!" [Each defeat will contribute to your
fame / . . . / To falling higher yet than once you rose!]. Throughout his later
works, Hugo will shift from the individual vindication achieved through
Inversion—the enlightened revision of values—to a collective meaning:
the necessity of individual sacrifice to redeem humanity.

The second device for achieving transcendence, an implicit glorifica-
tion of the poetic vision, appears in the same ode:

> Il est des astres, rois des cieux étincelants,
>
> Mondes volcans jetés parmi les autres mondes,
>
> Qui volent dans les nuits profondes,
>
> . . . .
>
> Le génie a partout des symboles sublimes.
>
> (*OP* 1, 373)

> [There are stars, monarchs of the sparkling skies,
>
> Volcano worlds strewn among other worlds,
>
> That fly through the deep nights,
>
> . . . .
>
> Genius has sublime symbols everywhere.]

As far as I know, "mondes volcans" is Hugo's earliest use of the *métaphore
maxima,* a juxtaposition of noun with noun that violates conventional
French syntax.[11] (Only the comma prevents "astres, rois" from becoming a second example of the condensed *métaphore maxima.*) Nonconfor-
mity to normal French syntax implies a poetic vision ungraspable by
everyday language. Speaking of "genius" in the abstract, Hugo avoids
blame for being immodest. And the ambiguity of agency in the last line
(is Genius passively embodied in symbols outside itself, or does it
actively find and use them?) tries to shelter the paradoxically humble
superiority of the prophetic poet from our possible suspicions of his self-
aggrandizement.

Hugo's most successful solution for treating his ambivalent feelings about the monarchy was to "bracket" it: to defend the glorious architectural and high-cultural past that the monarchy had supported, but to mention individual rulers only in passing. This is his enterprise in the famous poem "La Bande noire" (1822–1823), condemning those who deface, misuse, or dismantle historic buildings (*OP* 1, 341–44; *Odes* 2, 1). These were particular targets of the mob during the French Revolution; for example, from the facades of churches, rioters broke off the heads of many Old Testament statues they confused with French kings. Hugo's impassioned efforts at architectural preservation might thus be seen as an indirect defense of the French monarchy, a monarchy restored through nonviolent reconciliation.

> O français! [*sic*] respectons ces restes!
> Le ciel bénit les fils pieux
> Qui gardent, dans les jours funestes,
> L'héritage de leurs aïeux,
> Comme une gloire dérobée,
> Comptons chaque pierre tombée;
> Que le temps suspende sa loi;
> Rendons les Gaules à la France,
> Les souvenirs à l'espérance,
> Les vieux palais au jeune roi! . . .[12]
> (*OP* 1, 343–44; *Odes* 2, 3)

> [French people, respect these remains!
> Heaven blesses the pious sons
> Who preserve, in disastrous times,
> The heritage of their forebears,
> As a glory now snatched away,
> Consider every fallen stone;
> Let time pause in its fatal flight;
> Let us restore the Gauls to France,
> Our memories to our hope,
> Old palaces to the young king!]

An important article, "Guerre aux démolisseurs" (Wage War on the Vandals), composed in 1825 and published in the *Revue de Paris* of August 1829, indignantly lists many ruined, reconverted, or demolished churches and royal tombs.[13] But one can detect some doctrinal slippage: as Chateaubriand in *Le Génie du Christianisme* had resorted to an aesthetic, instead of a doctrinal, defense of Catholicism (compare contemporary high-church "smells [incense] and bells"), so Hugo resorts to an aesthetic defense of the monarchy. That most of the buildings he mentions were churches rather than palaces suggests both a "popular" achievement (built by the people for the people) and a divine order higher than that of kings.

The Early Novels

Until the late 1820s, Hugo seemed to be two separate writers. His "frenetic," sanguinary novels of rebellion, *Han d'Islande* and *Bug-Jargal*, may hint at the nascent, still-suppressed political consciousness of a future liberal Republican, safely relegated for the moment to remote locations. More certainly, these novels release Hugo's playfulness, pent by the need for sustained seriousness in the *Odes*.

The extravagant plot of *Han d'Islande* (*Han of Iceland* or *The Demon Dwarf*, 1821), set in seventeenth-century Norway, reveals Hugo's bent for parody and self-parody. The villainous Count Ahlefeld and his secretary Musdoemon have had the former's benefactor, Schumacher, unjustly imprisoned for life with his only child, Ethel. Not yet satisfied, the villains want to dishonor Ethel by having Ahlefeld's son Frédéric seduce her. And they scheme to have Schumacher executed for treason after having him blamed for a rebellion that they themselves will foment against the king. To this end, they try to bribe the supernatural cannibal monster Han d'Islande to lead an insurrection of miners discontented by a new royal tax. Han sees through their hypocrisy and scorns them; he then produces the partly devoured body of Frédéric.

Meanwhile, the hero, Prince Ordener Guldenlew (the name suggests "He who imposes order; golden lion"), raised incognito in the fortress where Schumacher is imprisoned, has fallen in love with Ethel.[14] But his father is one of Schumacher's mortal enemies. To earn forgiveness and to deserve Ethel's love, Ordener tries to prove Schumacher's innocence. Thus the prince seeks a chest of crucial documents supposedly possessed by Han d'Islande. Ordener finds the dwarfish monster and confronts him; their fight is interrupted when Han leaves to save his pet polar bear Friend, beset by hunters.[15]

Next Han disguises himself and tells the royal troops where to trap the insurgent miners, led by a false, giant Han, in a ravine. Then he rains boulders down on the troops from above. Finally, he rushes across the battlefield, slaying indiscriminately with his stone ax.

When the surviving rebels are tried, Schumacher seems sure to be condemned and executed until Ordener takes all the blame on himself. He refuses freedom if it means not marrying Ahlefeld's daughter. So Ethel asks an old priest secretly to marry Ordener and herself.

Han's only son has been killed, and in remembrance of his heir, Han habitually drinks his enemies' blood out of his son's skull. Knowing he cannot perpetuate his race—his line has been carried down by an only son for four centuries—Han surrenders to justice. He then burns himself and the entire garrison of the fortress to death by setting the prison on fire.

Just as Ordener is about to be executed, the bishop arrives to exculpate him. Documents revealing Musdoemon's guilt have been found. Musdoemon is arrested and hung by Orugix, the executioner brother he had rejected. The documents also prove that Musdoemon was the father of Ahlefeld's children. The count goes to punish his wife, but hearing of her son Frédéric's fate, she has gone mad. Schumacher is freed and restored to his former honors as viceroy; Ethel and Ordener announce their marriage.

The motifs of estranged families, illegitimate children, and sons dying unnaturally before their fathers all reflect the political turmoil of the revolutionary era. In the same year that the second edition of Han d'Islande was published, Hugo commented thus on the unfolding of the Revolution: "Enlightened social concern was superseded by that profound bestial blindness that cannot recognize approaching death. Indeed, the rebellion of the limbs [the strife of opposing political factions] quickly leads to the rending of the body, and the decay of the corpse ensues."[16] Kathryn Grossman's conclusion to her inspired reading of the novel helps place its extravagances in perspective: "Analogous to its morally scrupulous . . . hero [Ordener], Han d'Islande only appears then to be criminally linked to the rebellions of its literary contemporaries." As Ordener is vindicated and reintegrated into the social orderliness and justice figured by his grandfather, the king of Norway, so Hugo skips over the corrupted intermediate generations of Voltaire and other Enlightenment sophists to link his effervescent romanticism to the moral integrity of the classical age, achieving a "transgenerational victory."[17] *Han d'Islande* was a great success; starting in 1825, 23 English translations had appeared by the end of the nineteenth century (Robb, 101).

From the first, Hugo recognized two modes of romanticism. Unlike the dominant literary movements of the eighteenth century, he explained, "both [these romanticisms] acknowledge what a mocking [Enlightenment] philosophy had denied: God's eternity, the immortal soul, fundamental verities and revealed truths—but the first Romanticism [that of Chateaubriand] acknowledged these truths in order to worship; the other [that of Byron], in order to curse."[18]

Hugo wrote versions of his second novel, *Bug-Jargal,* in 1818, 1826, and 1832. It was first published in 1820, but the 1826 version is so greatly expanded (to nearly five times as long as the 1818 version) and improved that 1826 is ordinarily considered the canonical date of completion, placing *Bug-Jargal* after *Han d'Islande* in Hugo's artistic evolution. Marking his reconciliation with his father, Léopold, in 1823, the author changed the hero's name in 1826 to Léopold, the name that Hugo also gave to his first child.[19]

Hugo had now become more ambitious; he wished to excel Scott, not merely to emulate him. In his review of Scott's *Quentin Durward* (1823), the tale of a Scotsman at the court of Louis XI (a monarch Hugo would treat in *Notre-Dame de Paris: 1482,* in 1831), Hugo declared: "After Walter Scott's picturesque but prosaic novel, another sort of novel remains to be created, one that we consider more beautiful and comprehensive. It is the novel that is both drama and epic, picturesque but poetic, real but ideal, true to life but great, that will set Scott's gemstone in Homer's ring" (*OC* 5, 131). In other words, Hugo aspires to the combination of local color and world-historical vision characterized in the 1832 preface of *Bug-Jargal*: "Europe and Africa as combatants, America as their battlefield."[20]

The plot of *Bug-Jargal* involves the slave revolt of 1791 in Santo Domingo. Captain Léopold d'Auverney, a recent widower who will be killed in battle the next day, takes his turn telling his adventures to his fellow soldiers.[21] He had gone from France to Santo Domingo to marry his cousin Marie. A character added after the 1818 version, she partially represents the sublime. Another added character, the deformed mulatto dwarf Habibrah, the jester of d'Auverney's cruel uncle, represents the grotesque.

To court Marie, Léopold lays garlands of flowers in the summerhouse where she goes each evening. One day he finds them trampled and replaced by a bouquet of wildflowers. He stands watch to protect her, but is overwhelmed and his dagger taken by a powerful man in the darkness. However, to spare Marie's feelings, the mysterious man does not kill Léopold. The next day, Léopold and Marie hear a Spanish song from Marie's hidden admirer. He describes himself as an enslaved former African king; he warns of troubles to come and advocates mixed-race marriage: "The day needs to couple with the night to give birth to the sunset and the dawn, more beautiful than itself" (188). The unthinkingly racist captain cannot believe a black person could be sufficiently cultivated to compose a love song in Spanish.

Soon afterward, a powerful slave named Pierrot protects Marie from a crocodile. Léopold tells his uncle, who promises to give the man his freedom; but when they find Pierrot, he is intervening to stop another slave from being whipped for a trivial offense. Léopold pleads for Pierrot's life, but the uncle has him thrown in prison for having raised his hand against a white man. Léopold visits Pierrot in prison—from which he could easily have escaped except that "they would think I was afraid"—to offer help. Overcoming his jealousy, for it is indeed he who loves Marie in secret, Pierrot warns Léopold to marry Marie before August 22, and to depart. Pierrot disappears before his official release and does not return to work. Immediately after the marriage, a slave revolt breaks out. Léopold sees Pierrot carrying Marie to safety but thinks he plans to rape her. The uncle has been killed; Habibrah vanishes. The government troops are ambushed, and Léopold is captured by Biassou's forces.

Two rebel leaders figure prominently in the story: the fearsome, cruel mulatto Biassou and the noble, idealistic Bug-Jargal, the African king who is none other than Pierrot. Eventually Pierrot secures the temporary release of Léopold and leads him to a hidden grotto to show him Marie is safe. She does not even know her rescuer loves her. After a touching reconciliation of the two men, Pierrot explains that he has joined the rebellion because his own family, wife, and children were deceived, enslaved, and eventually killed by the Spaniards.

Honor compels Léopold to return to captivity with Biassou, and Pierrot to the whites' camp, so that ten hostages will be freed in exchange for him. As Léopold is being led to his death, Habibrah (in his role as the rebel's *obi*, or high voodoo priest) taunts him, revealing himself as the uncle's assassin. Habibrah also has encouraged Biassou to burn the forest so that Marie will perish in it, wherever she may be hidden. Anticipating both Quasimodo in *Notre-Dame de Paris* and Gwynplaine in *L'Homme qui rit*, Habibrah vehemently exclaims: "So do you think that because I'm a deformed mulatto dwarf, I'm not human? . . . O rage! [as your uncle's jester] I had to mingle my laughter with the laughter my appearance and my buffoonery provoked" (378–79).[22]

Bug-Jargal suddenly appears and twice saves Léopold's life. Offered a post in the colonial army, he refuses with dignity: "Brother, am I suggesting that you enlist with *my* troops?" (395). Biassou, meanwhile, not knowing d'Auverney has been rescued, raises the black flag announcing his captive's death, so that his white adversaries see it. Bug-Jargal returns to captivity to save the ten black hostages. He allows himself to be shot without revealing that the captain is alive. Léopold, wounded by a bullet, is too weak to arrive in time to save his friend.

With comical self-consciousness, the implied author intervenes to say that "investigations have been made" to satisfy readers who want to learn the fate of the remaining characters. He tells of their death. The narrative as a whole leaves one with a mixed impression. It is racist in presenting the mulattoes Biassou and Habibrah as moral monsters; evenhanded in depicting hypocrisy, cruelty, and corruption among both the reactionaries and the revolutionaries; and racist in reverse by taking up the theme, current at the time, of the moral superiority of blacks.[23] Bug-Jargal, a paragon of magnanimity, integrity, and self-control, bears the moral message of the work; Servais Étienne finds that "if the novel's conflicting ethical codes appear to the various protagonists as a series of [mutually unintelligible] foreign languages, each with its own internal logic or 'grammar,' only Bug-Jargal is multilingual. He alone comprehends and incorporates them all into a moral Esperanto" of forgiveness and universal fellowship.[24] By example, he inspires Léopold in turn to be willing to sacrifice his life for a higher value—a perfect illustration of the temporal sublime found in the *Odes*.

A skeptic, however, would observe that the two male lead characters embody a melancholic acceptance of destruction at the hands of others (figured as self-destruction—suicide—in the late novels), an attitude that runs as a constant thread throughout Hugo's work. It reappears in many other novels of revolution in the nineteenth and twentieth centuries, such as André Malraux's *La Condition Humaine* (The Human Condition, usually translated as *Man's Fate*) or Jacques-Stéphen Alexis's *Compère Général Soleil* (Comrade General Sun). The facile explanation is repressed Oedipal guilt—the implied author would allow the symbolic father to kill one or more of his stand-ins to expiate the crime of hating his father. Such a blanket interpretation, however plausible, would tell us more about the human condition, about the "equal and opposite [inner] reaction" elicited by revolt, than about Hugo as a unique genius. Hugo's own declaration of his intentions as a writer, in his early career, is more nuanced: "The art of today should no longer seek only the beautiful, but the good as well . . . when the opportunity arises, [it should] display moral beauty beneath physical deformity . . . teach that there is often a bit of evil in the best of us, and nearly always a bit of goodness in the worst of us, and by so doing, inspire hope in the wicked and indulgence in the virtuous."[25] He failed to achieve such moral complexity in *Bug-Jargal,* but he would attain it in his next novel, *Notre-Dame de Paris.*

Chapter Two
The Cathedral and the Book:
Notre-Dame de Paris: 1482

Notre-Dame de Paris is a polyphonic novel. It presents stories on four levels at once. The individual drama of love and lust describes the fate of a
beautiful young woman, the Gypsy La Esmeralda. She is destroyed by
the love of four men who are drawn to her, and by her love for one of
them. The historical drama, where much of the motivation is implicit,
tells of the dying king Louis XI's attempt to consolidate his political
power and to perpetuate his dynasty. The monumental drama presents
the magnificent Cathedral of Notre Dame, a memorial to an ardent
faith that has waned, outlasting individuals and dynasties even as its
carved symbolic messages become inscrutable in the dawning age of
print culture. And the spiritual drama depicts a world of human blindness and confusion, in which the deformed Quasimodo alone is instinc-
tively drawn to a spiritual truth outside the material world. Thus, in a
sense, Hugo's novel appears richer even than Goethe's *Faust,* which
lacks the monumental dimension. To clarify Hugo's intentions, I shall
trace his four threads—individual, political, monumental, and spiritual—one at a time, before showing how he weaves them together into
a transcendent vision.

The Romantic Plot

Woven through the lengthy digressions that characterize Hugo's
teacherly style, the main romantic adventure plot is unified by La
Esmeralda. When she was an infant, she was stolen by Gypsies from her
adoring mother, a prostitute. The infant Quasimodo—hunchbacked,
deaf, hideous, lacking one eye—was left in her place. Her mother travels
to Paris and abandons the changeling in the foundlings' box at the
entrance to the cathedral. Then she becomes a mendicant penitent in
the "Trou aux Rats," an unheated stone cell on the street. She hates all
Gypsies, La Esmeralda in particular, not recognizing her grown daughter in the young woman. Claude Frollo, the archdeacon, takes pity on

Quasimodo and adopts him. They learn to communicate through signs. He will become the bell ringer of the church. Its bass bell makes the only sound he can hear. Quasimodo's deformed presence within the cathedral heightens its glorious construction by contrast, according to the aesthetic—a combination of the sublime and the grotesque—that Hugo had defiantly advocated in the 1827 preface to his historical play *Cromwell*. The same contrast recurs in the juxtaposition of the alluring Gypsy dancer and the revolting foundling.[1]

With the four men drawn to La Esmeralda, the involuntary dramatic mover of the novel, Hugo illustrates a complete grid of possible reactions to her: frivolous but consciously benign (Gringoire), frivolous and destructive (Phœbus), earnest and destructive (Frollo), or earnest and benign (Quasimodo). The handsomer these men appear, the shallower are their feelings. Gaston Phœbus, captain of the King's Guard, feels a strong physical attraction to La Esmeralda but wants only to use her sexually before discarding her. The self-centered poet Pierre Gringoire, a historical figure, feels some affection for her but more for her pet goat Djali (after whom Emma Bovary's greyhound will be named). Claude Frollo longs for La Esmeralda with an intense sadomasochistic passion but is unaware of her as an independent person. And Quasimodo loves her with a pure, disinterested devotion that will endure after death.[2] Hugo places the novel under the sign of fatality—*ananké*—operating through religious dogma. Frollo's priestly celibacy drives him insane with lust.

Fatalism pervades the plot of which La Esmeralda will be the scapegoat, while her real pet goat, also accused of witchcraft, will go free. No matter what the characters do, they cannot escape their destiny. Each of the four men who is attracted to La Esmeralda makes an apparently free choice that helps weave a web of disaster around her. Hugo more than once emphasizes their specious freedom of choice by describing them literally deciding to turn in one of two possible directions.

After the failure of his mystery play, the penniless Gringoire chooses idly to follow La Esmeralda through the streets as he looks for a place to spend the night. Unknowingly, he wanders into the center of the Paris underworld, the Cour des Miracles. For trespassing there, he is condemned to hang. La Esmeralda charitably saves him by agreeing to "marry" him; he must also agree to become a *truand* (member of the underworld). Although La Esmeralda insists on a chaste relationship, from then until her death Gringoire's destiny is linked to hers. Later Gaston Phœbus decides to pursue her rather than attend to his fiancée, who has fainted when she realizes how strongly La Esmeralda and Phœbus are attracted to each other (7.1.272).[3] They arrange a rendezvous that will provoke Frollo's assault on Phœbus, for which La Esmeralda will be falsely accused, convicted, and eventually hung. Quasimodo carries her off to safety within the cathedral, on whose steps she has been forced to make public confession. But Gringoire makes the disastrous suggestion that the beggars and thieves of the Cour des Miracles organize an assault on Notre Dame to "rescue" her. Misunderstanding their intent, Quasimodo tries to drive off this people's army. The resulting tumult directs the king's attention to La Esmeralda and incites him to violate the sanctuary that the cathedral traditionally provided for all fugitives from justice. The disorder of the skirmish allows Gringoire to spirit La Esmeralda away unnoticed, but he ingenuously delivers her into Frollo's hands. When the three disembark on the bank of the Seine, Gringoire finally decides to save Djali the she-goat rather than the young woman, because the former is more affectionate toward him (11.1.477). La Esmeralda's own choices—to give the pilloried Quasimodo water, although he has just tried to kidnap her, and to refuse sex with Frollo, even to save her life (6.4.253–54, 11.1.480)—are respectively compassionate and courageous, but they cannot save her.

Phœbus, the handsome captain of the king's archers, is too narcissistic to see beyond himself and his needs. Gestures made on his own body illustrate this trait (as they do in the early scenes presenting Flaubert's Emma Bovary). Surrounded by his pretty fiancée and her friends, "while the pretty young women vied for his attention, he seemed preoccupied with using his suede gloves to polish the buckle of his sword belt" (7.1.261). When he leads La Esmeralda to a secret rendezvous, we first see him preening his mustache (7.8.311). When he finds himself alone with her, she admires his looks. He responds not by complimenting her in turn but by asking whether she has ever seen him in his splendid parade uniform. Hugo underscores his self-absorption by making him incapable even of learning La Esmeralda's name (7.8.313–14).

Because Gringoire lives for the moment, he, like the womanizer Phœbus, remains on the surface of things.[4] As Hugo makes clear, even pure aesthetic contemplation without a spiritual referent amounts to no more—and here Baudelaire might agree with him—than a sterile expansion of the self. Hugo later describes Gringoire lost in ecstatic contemplation of the sculpture on the outer wall of a chapel: "He was in one of those moments of supreme, exclusive, egotistical delight when the artist sees only art in the world, and sees the world in art" (10.1.404).

Hugo based this character on the historical Pierre Gringoire (c. 1475 –1538), who wrote both serious and comic plays, as well as propaganda for Louis XII. The real Gringoire would have been only seven years old when the action of *Notre-Dame de Paris* takes place, but he resembles his fictional counterpart in being a political reactionary, devoting his talents to supporting the existing regime. In the novel, he is not even paid for doing so, and being a supporter of divine-right monarchy turns him toward the past, blinding him to any original insights. (As such, the fictional Gringoire parodies Hugo's recent royalist self, and his poetic vocation as well, contrasted with his father's heroic career as a general under Napoleon.) He ends as a clown, earning his living on the street by balancing pyramids of chairs and other objects held with his teeth. But he lacks the stature of many later metaphoric artist-clowns in the work of Baudelaire, Apollinaire, Picasso, Michaux, and others: Gringoire is not an outcast, merely a parasite, and his art is not subversive. It has purely accidental, materialistic motivations, to which were later added a substantial portion of vanity (1.3.59). According to him, he tried every career when he turned 16 but found himself too cowardly to be a soldier, too skeptical to be a monk (besides, he couldn't hold his liquor), too weak to be a construction worker, and too illiterate to teach school. Concluding that he was good for nothing, Gringoire became a poet: "That's a line of work you can always take up when you're a tramp" (2.8.125 –26).[5] He lacks dignity and integrity. Begging for his life, he ludicrously grovels before both the king of the *truands* (brigands) in the Cour des Miracles and the king of France in the Bastille. Gringoire avoids any fight. In the end, by preferring Djali to his "wife," La Esmeralda, to whom he owes his life, he literally descends to the subhuman.

Claude Frollo is equally self-absorbed, although unlike the frivolous Phœbus or Gringoire, he is obsessed by La Esmeralda to the point of madness. During his long harangue in her cell, when he confesses his love and promises to rescue her if she will love him, he exclaims,

> Before I met you, young woman, I was happy . . .
> —And what about me! she sighed faintly.
> —Don't interrupt me. (8.4.342)

To nearly everything Frollo says, La Esmeralda, as blinded by passion as he, answers only with the name of Phœbus, the indifferent man she loves. In a series of ironic or pathetic coups de théâtre, she will be res-

cued in vain first by Phœbus, then by Quasimodo, next by Gringoire,
and finally by her mother, only to end in the grip of Frollo. When she
refuses him sex for the last time, he lets her be unjustly hanged. In one
way or another, the passionate characters—Frollo, her mother, Quasimodo—die with her, whereas the others, Gringoire and Phœbus, return
to their everyday lives, insensitive to the extraordinary drama in which
they were minor players.

The Political Drama

An initial guide to the novel's political meaning appears in the title,
Notre-Dame de Paris: 1482. Critics and popular culture alike nearly
always overlook the date (1482) that forms an integral part of the title.
When restored, the date contrasts with the first part of the title: an
apparently ageless monument confronts the instability of history.

This clash of timelessness and change strikingly reflects the evolution
of Hugo's political and religious convictions around 1831; it allowed
him to reconcile what he had been with what he would become.[6] Originally a virtual court poet, by 1828 he was becoming disaffected with the
monarchy. *Notre-Dame de Paris* allowed him to celebrate France's Catholic,
monarchical past while glorifying the people's revolution, anticipated
three and a half centuries earlier, and culminating in 1789 but still in
progress in Hugo's day. In 1831 the novel's ambivalent political spirit har-
monized fairly well with the early, liberal period (1830–1832) of the constitutional monarchy of Louis-Philippe (1830–1848). *Les Misérables*
(1862) would treat the military defeat of the Republican idealists who
fomented an insurrection from 5 to 6 June 1832.

The novel begins on Epiphany (6 January) in 1482 with the performance within the cathedral of Gringoire's *mystère*, an allegorical play celebrating the virtues of Marguerite de Flandre. The occasion reveals a
loss of a sense of the sacred. First, the Feast of the Epiphany (in French,
le jour des rois, or "day of the kings") should properly be consecrated to
what the three kings see—the Christ Child, the higher power they have
traveled far to worship. But the play makes kings themselves into the
spectacle: the Christ Child is forgotten. Second, the *mystère* genre itself
properly refers to a theatrical performance celebrating one of the mysteries of the Catholic faith, but Gringoire's play glorifies secular power.
The play has been commissioned to honor the Flemish ambassadors
come to Paris to negotiate the terms of Marguerite's marriage to the
French dauphin, heir to the throne (born in 1470, he ruled as Charles

VIII from 1483 to 1498). The situation is fraught with heavy ironies, based on the contrast between the conniving, unscrupulous Louis XI's family, national, and international plans for the future, and their eventual failure. He hopes to perpetuate his dynasty, crush the power of the nobility, and secure his northern border against the English. Relying on our knowledge of French history, Hugo spells out few of these ironies; the modern reader may need some reminders.[7]

At the time, the "royal domain" (the territory directly controlled by the king of France) was much smaller than it is now. The English had been driven out of France during the Hundred Years' War (1337–1456), but they still had great influence in Flanders and in the powerful independent Duchy of Burgundy, both on the northern frontier. When Louis XI's most formidable adversary, Charles le Téméraire of Burgundy (Charles the Bold or Rash), died in 1477, Louis could finally conquer the Duchy of Burgundy and annex it to the French crown. The projected marriage of the dauphin Charles at age 12 (in those days, politically inspired marriages were often arranged even during the future spouses' infancy) would bring Flanders, a territory just north of Burgundy, under French control. The French sphere of influence would be greatly expanded to the north, and Flanders, traditional ally of England for economic reasons, would be weakened. But Louis XI died in 1483, and the marriage of the dauphin to Marguerite de Flandre never took place. After a five-year regency blighted by civil war, Charles VIII lost Artois (the westernmost part of the Burgundian territories, along the English Channel) in 1493. The Spaniards seized the region and held it until 1659.

Louis XI had successfully curtailed the power of the nobility, so that they could not successfully rebel against the crown as the duke of Burgundy had done. Thus Louis secured national unity. But he was unaware of the slowly growing power of another class—the people (meaning petit bourgeois skilled workers and shopkeepers). That he was forced to negotiate with Flemish commoners regarding the terms of his son's marriage foreshadows the constitutional monarchies of the nineteenth century. When Louis XI died, the Estates General had to be convened— a representative, consultative assembly where the middle class sat in one chamber, and the nobility and clergy in two others. This meeting foreshadowed the gathering of the Estates General in 1789, which triggered the French Revolution when the deputies of the Third Estate refused to disband. Finally, Charles VIII was to have no male heirs; at his death, the monarchy passed to a collateral line sired by an enemy of his family.

The new king, Louis XII, had formerly been Duc d'Orléans and co-leader of the unsuccessful Guerre Folle (1485–1488), a civil war directed against the regency of Louis XI's daughter, Anne de France. The apparently digressive opening book of the novel juxtaposes three different realities: the virtual reality of an allegorical play to which no one pays attention; propaganda celebrating the established order by associating royalty with divinity; and Hugo's faithful reconstruction of a picturesque past. Gringoire's kitschy theatrical mixture of abstract virtues and Roman gods seeks to associate the present monarchy with the prestige of the Roman imperium and with the Roman pantheon. Second, historical reality forces the archbishop of Paris to mingle with middle-class burghers from Flanders while the public celebration of monarchy is interrupted and then taken over by the Feast of Fools run by the people and celebrating the deformed Quasimodo. As a further irony, the king's closest companions in the novel, his doctor and his barber, are themselves of lower social status than many in the Flemish embassy with whom the king must reluctantly negotiate.

Like *Les Misérables* 30 years later, *Notre-Dame de Paris* presents the political vision of the ultimate, inevitable triumph of democracy. Jacques Coppenole's prophecy that the Bastille will fall one day (10.5.462) thematizes historical progression. The rise of the people is most clearly anticipated in the novel by the steadily increasing prominence of a relatively minor figure: Clopin Trouillefou. When we first see him, he is a pitiable but brash beggar, disrupting the *mystère* with his plaintive appeals for alms (1.2.56). He acquires dignity when he is recognized and warmly greeted by Jacques Coppenole, one of the Flemish ambassadors; Trouillefou is revealed as an equal to that imposing working-class leader (1.4.66). Next Trouillefou appears in the Cour des Miracles as the king of the thieves (2.6.109), with the power of life and death over Gringoire. In preparation for the assault on the cathedral, Trouillefou assumes the role of a general, distributing arms and ordering his troops into battle (10.3.416–21). Finally, he achieves heroic stature as a symbol of Death the Grim Reaper and as the mightiest warrior among the ruffians storming Notre Dame:

> Among them you could see one who had a wide, gleaming scythe, and who for a long time lopped off the legs of the king's cavalry horses. He was fearsome. He was singing a nasal song; he tirelessly swept out with his scythe and then pulled it back. Every blow left a great circle of severed limbs around him. In that way he advanced into the thickest con-

centration of the cavalry, with calm deliberation, with the swaying head and the regular panting of a harvester wading into a field of wheat. It was Clopin Trouillefou. A shot from an arquebus [a primitive firearm] struck him down. (10.7.468)

The comparison to a harvester recalls the Homeric similes used to describe great warriors fighting in the *Iliad*. And through association with the Grim Reaper, Trouillefou foreshadows the end of the aristocracy and the monarchy. Hugo implies the link between the *truands'* expedition and 1789 when he recalls that three centuries before Louis XI, the Crusades were also a popular movement, and that "every great popular movement, whatever may be its cause and its goal, ultimately leaves a precipitate of freedom" (5.2.201).

The Spiritual Themes

Jacques Coppenole, the only political visionary in the novel, foresees the triumph of democracy. But none of the characters have a sense of the spiritual. Although Claude Frollo, a powerful portrayal of a self-deluded priest, knows more than the other characters, he cannot control them or even himself. Voyeurism, like eavesdropping a frequent motif in Hugo's novels as in his poetry and theater, dramatizes the futility of Frollo's "superior" knowledge. Hugo describes peeping as a basic human instinct—at least for Parisians: "We're already very curious when we see a wall behind which something is happening" (1.1.39). Voyeurism assumes two major forms in Hugo's work: the prurient sexual curiosity of the male observing the uncovered female body, and the eavesdropper learning of adversaries' plans. One would think that spying on another person should give the hidden observer an advantage, but neither form confers power on Hugo's voyeurs. Frollo's spying on La Esmeralda only tortures him with frustration and humiliates him with sexual jealousy. Through a hole in a wall, behind which he has paid Phœbus to let him hide, Frollo observes the captain undressing La Esmeralda. "Anyone who at that moment could have seen the face of the unfortunate man glued to the worm-eaten lathes would have thought he was seeing the face of a tiger in the depths of his cage, watching some jackal devour a gazelle" (7.8.316).

Later, when Frollo recalls the spectacle of the half-dressed Gypsy forced publicly to confess her sins before her execution, he is agonized to realize "how many foul glances had been satiated by that half-undone blouse; that beautiful young woman, that virgin lily, that chalice of modesty and delights that he could not have thought of kissing without trembling, had just been transformed into a sort of public drinking ladle, where the lowest commoners of Paris, thieves, beggars, and lackeys, had come to swill together a shameless, lewd, and depraved pleasure" (9.1.372–73). Pierre Gringoire (7.2.80) and Gaston Phœbus (8.6.357) can peep at a woman's body without self-consciousness or jealousy; but Frollo and Quasimodo (9.3.386), watching La Esmeralda from afar, are tortured because she disdains both of them (9.5.397). Frollo is secretly present at every moment of the trial of La Esmeralda that he has initiated, but her sufferings serve only to torment him more (8.4.343–47).

Frollo's blindness becomes obvious when he posits the duality of choice and fate. In his study, the priest meditates on Honorius d'Autun's book *De praedestinatione et libero arbitrio* (On Predestination and Free Will, 5.1.189). When we again see Frollo in his cell, a much-analyzed passage (7.5.298–99) describes a fly caught in a spider web as it seeks the light from a window. Alluding to La Esmeralda as both the fly caught in his plots to possess her against her will, and as the web that traps him in ungovernable lust, Frollo says:

> You were flying toward knowledge, light, the sun, all that concerned you
> was to reach the open air, the great light of eternal truth; but as you
> rushed toward the dazzling skylight that opens on the other world, the
> world of brightness, understanding and knowledge, blind fly, insane
> scholar, you didn't see the fine spider web that destiny hung between you
> and the light, you threw yourself wildly into it, wretched fool, and now
> you're struggling, with broken head and torn-off wings, in the iron
> antennae of fate![8]

The breathless sentence structure conveys his frantic desperation.

Confronting La Esmeralda in her cell as she awaits execution, Frollo admits that he had thought himself all-powerful, but that fate was stronger than he (8.4.345). After Quasimodo has rescued her, Frollo again blames fate for all that has happened to him: "Wild-eyed, he contemplated the twisting double track along which fate had driven their two destinies, until the point where it had pitilessly shattered them against each other. He thought of the madness of eternal vows, the emptiness of chastity, learning, religion, virtue, of the uselessness of God" (9.1.372). He overlooks Providence, the synthesis of destiny and will—"In Thy service is perfect freedom." Thus it is an undue simplification to say, as many critics do, that the spider-web pattern of the veins in a rose window suggests that the Catholic faith per se is a snare, like the spider web invisible to the fly. Rather, it is dogmas such as the celibacy of the clergy that are traps; Hugo will so identify them decades later when prefacing *The Toilers of the Sea*. The ardent faith that leads one to become a priest is not itself a trap.

The motif of a false light, of misleading appearances, is both thematized and dramatized in *Notre-Dame de Paris*. The Parisians miss the true light when they misread the Latin motto "TU, ORA" [You, pray] over the penitent's hole as the French near-homonym "Trou aux Rats" [rat hole] (6.2.227–28). Again, speaking of the decline of architecture, Hugo says that the Renaissance abandoned indigenous styles in favor of a pseudo-antiquity based on Greek and Roman models: "That's the decadence that we call 'renaissance.' That is the setting sun we mistake for a dawn" (5.2.206).

Frollo's supposedly superior knowledge is simply a form of blindness more elaborate than that of the other characters. As his idolatry of gold reveals, like them, he worships a false sun. "Gold is the sun; to make sun is to be God. That is the only science" (5.1.195).[9] The priest has devoted his life to learning the secrets of alchemy; so great is his fame that although alchemy is illegal, the head prosecutor Jacques Charmoulue and the king himself come to consult Frollo. He believes he can decipher all the secret alchemical messages carved in hieroglyphic form in the statues of Paris churches, particularly those revealing the legendary Nicholas Flamel's (1330–1418) art of making gold from lead. But Frollo never can make gold himself. All his learning is fruitless.[10]

Finally, La Esmeralda is doomed by a similar delusion. Gaston Phœbus's handsome face and his last name (meaning "sun") blind and deceive her because she cannot see past them to his amoral reality (8.6.365, 9.3.390, 11.1.492). Every time she calls desperately to him, either he is too far away to hear, or else he turns aside with irritation and indifference. Her final appeal to him betrays her hiding place in the "Trou aux Rats" to the departing king's soldiers, just when she might have been saved.

Numbers (especially measurements and sums of money), like proper names, create a sense of historical precision and realism, but characters who focus on money and possessions betray their lack of spiritual vision. As in Flaubert's novels or in Georges Perec's *Les Choses* (Things), the narrator's realism also functions as a form of higher sarcasm: it heaps things they want on the characters, while knowing those things to be worthless. The scene where Louis XI is micromanaging his country with the help of his barber as finance minister consists of the latter's reading a long list of expenses, to which the king responds with complaints or miserly reductions (10.5.440–50). The ironic chapter title "Retrait où dit ses heures Monsieur Louis de France" (The Retreat Where Monsieur Louis de France Recites His Breviary) refers to prayer; but instead the king's activities are pinching pennies and tormenting his wretched prisoner Cardinal Balue—suspended for 14 years in an iron cage—by pretending not to know he is there. Immediately after this scene of avarice and cruelty, Louis's barber and minister of finance, Olivier Le Daim, asks to be named to a vacant office to profit from its revenues. The king reminds his petitioner of the long list of lucrative sinecures he has already been granted (459–60). The proper names that designate these posts (the names of the forests, châteaux, and towns where they are situated) imply a sterile, corrupt accumulation of possessions by a man who—Hugo later reminds us—two years later would be hung. The motif of the courtier as parasite echoes *Hernani* the year before: already by 1482, Hugo suggests, the nobility at court has become morally bankrupt, concerned never with stewardship or development of the country and always with personal profit.

The Motif of the Monument

As greed is undiscriminating, so are the monuments of a materialistic society. The stylistic purity that Hugo dismisses as less interesting than the transitional style of Notre Dame becomes a positive value when the author digresses to condemn a modern building, the Stock Exchange, completed just five years before the publication of his novel. There, kitsch (a mixture of incongruous styles) betrays a lack of historical awareness and of history's hidden motor, Providence.

> As for the Palace of the Stock Exchange, Greek in its colonnade, Romanesque in the barrel-vaulting over the doors and windows, and Renaissance in its great flattened vault, it is indubitably a monument in the purest, most faithful style. . . . Let us add that if it is a rule that form should follow function so consistently that you can see at a glance what a building is used for, we couldn't marvel sufficiently at a monument that can be indiscriminately a royal palace, the chambers of a legislative assembly, a town hall, a high school, a dressage ring, an academy, a warehouse, a courthouse, a museum, a barracks, a sepulchre, a temple, a theater. Meanwhile, it's a stock exchange. (3.2.157)

In *Notre-Dame de Paris* relatively few structures figure as prominent scenes for events: the great hall of the Palais de Justice, the cathedral, the Bastille, and the gallows. The Palais de Justice initially is the site of the abortive theatrical performance of Gringoire's mystery play. Drowned out by the tumult in the audience, the play fails, dramatizing the incompatibility of the various social classes. This building returns in book 8 with a more somber illustration of social dysfunction through the trial, torture, and condemnation of the innocent Esmeralda. Superficially, the cathedral and the Bastille figure church and royal power respectively; the Palais de Justice is where these two powers converge.

La Esmeralda, their unfortunate focus, is considered guilty both socially and spiritually: she stands accused of murder (a civil crime) *and* sorcery (a heresy). She must confess her "sins" both in the Palais and in the church, where she is led with the hangman's noose around her neck to make an *amende honorable* (public confession of a crime, symbolically in the presence of God). The gallows illustrates how both material and spiritual power is exercised under Louis XI. Through the poignant death of an innocent, Hugo dramatizes his consistent opposition to capital punishment. More fundamentally, the Palais de Justice and the Bastille represent human power, ephemeral *sub specie æternitatis* (from the viewpoint of eternity). The Palais would burn to the ground in 1618. The Bastille would be razed shortly after its capture by the people on 14 July 1789. But the cathedral, representing providential power, would endure.

At first glance, Hugo's interpretations of architectural style appear contradictory: mixed modes impart rich meaning to the cathedral but void meaning in the Bourse (the stock exchange). The critical difference is that the cathedral reflects a natural accretion of history over time: the Bourse, constructed quickly, betrays an attempt to glorify financial power by concentrating references to as many great past monuments as possible.

Hugo manages to subvert divine-right monarchy and the established church even as he celebrates the cathedral that suggests their immutability. Transitions in architectural style imply that social transformations are possible—indeed, inevitable. Ultimate meaning inheres not in a single style (read: form of government), Hugo implies, but in the evolution from one style to the next. In his description of the composite architecture of the cathedral, transition becomes the ultimate meaning:

> Moreover, Notre-Dame de Paris is not what you could call a finished, definitive, classifiable monument. It's no longer a Romanesque church,

it's not yet a Gothic church. . . . The Saxon architect was completing the erection of the first pillars of the nave when the ogival arch brought back from the Crusades came to perch triumphantly on those broad Romanesque capitals that were supposed to bear only barrel vaults. . . . But these structures transitional between the Romanesque and the Gothic are just as valuable to study as are the pure types. They express a nuance of art that would be lost without them. . . . This central, generative church is a kind of chimera [a mythical monster made up from several different animals] among the old churches of Paris: it has the head of one, the limbs of a second, the hindquarters of a third—something of all of them. The greatest architectural productions are less individual than social creations; more the child of nations in labor than the ejaculation of men of genius . . . Every wave of time leaves its sedimentary deposit, every race deposits a layer on the monument, every individual brings a stone. Beavers work that way; so do bees; so do people. Babel, that great symbol of architecture, is a hive. (3.1.135–37)

Hugo underlines the social and political implications of the architecture of Notre Dame. The Gothic church, dominating the period from the Crusades to Louis XI and reflecting the middle-class, politically liberal, and capricious imagination, is grafted onto the earlier Romanesque church that dominated the period between the dying Roman Empire and William the Conqueror. The Romanesque style, symbol of divine-right monarchy and the theocratic state, is "hieroglyphic, immutable and sacerdotal." The Gothic style is "progressive, artistic, and popular" (135).[11]

Hugo is a capable, if overlooked, practitioner of bourgeois critique. He stresses the cosmic irony of a providential purpose that reduces human ambitions to nothing. Hugo enriches the ostensibly descriptive historical novel with a prophetic element. His digressions function like those in Herman Melville's *Moby Dick;* they allude to what narratologists call "events" (acts of God) rather than to "acts" (purposeful human actions). Superficially at odds with the plot, a tissue of human intentions, these digressions correspond to the light shining in the darkness that comprehends it not (John 1:5).

Coups de théâtre abound in this novel as they do in the plays. Here, however, they serve not merely to shock; instead, they suggest the intervention of an invisible Providence whose action the characters cannot predict or understand. La Esmeralda's disruptive appearance outside the Great Hall (1.6.78); her attempted kidnapping by Frollo and her rescue by Phœbus's archers (2.6.94); Quasimodo's rescue of her from the executioners (8.6.365 – 67); the coincidences that save her from Frollo's rape attempt and then save Frollo from Quasimodo (9.6.399 – 400); the coincidence that the recluse in "Le Trou aux Rats" discovers herself to be La Esmeralda's mother and changes instantly from fierce hatred to love toward her daughter (11.1.485): all these fail to save La Esmeralda and corroborate the impression that she must be doomed. Taken together, these many reversals of fortune sketch an ineluctable destiny.[12] In *Notre-Dame de Paris,* Hugo does not yet envision supererogation and redemption. The theme of a necessary, voluntary sacrifice will appear only later. The victimization of Hugo's heroes and heroines in the novels and plays of the 1820s and 1830s, as in much romantic literature, seems gratuitous. The message—perhaps inspired by the wife and best friend who betrayed Hugo (cf. Grossman 1986, 160)—is that life is unfair, and that we cannot know why.

In contrast, the implied author avoids hubris and positively transforms the *exegi monumentum* topos ("my work of art will be an enduring monument") in *Notre-Dame de Paris* through his loving preservation of the past. Rather than call his own work a monument as did the Roman poet Horace (*Odes* 3, 30), Hugo celebrates the cathedral, a monument built by others. He reminds us of what we are continually losing, by decisively altering the *ubi sunt* topos—a lament for vanished friends, beauty, and glory. Instead of asking where the past has gone, he says that a century or two ago, certain artistic and architectural treasures *could still be seen.* Thus he talks about a certain type of porch common 150 years ago (10.5.439), or Louis XI's bed that had been preserved until 200 years ago (440). Hugo's digressive evocations of Notre Dame and of all Paris in the fifteenth century (book 3) accomplish the same act of textual preservation on a larger scale. He makes us aware of the progressive losses of our heritage in the past, and the ever-present risk of more such losses in the future.

Hugo's Transcendent Vision

Hugo avoids the dangers of simplifying his vision by not inserting an author-surrogate into his novel, a masterful artist or prophet able to comprehend it all. There is no inspired prophet and no Wise Old Man in *Notre-Dame de Paris.* Claude Frollo, the most learned and studious of the characters, dissipates his energies first in his vain quest to make gold, to thus become superior to kings and equal to God (as he sees it), and then in a vain, lustful obsession with the Gypsy La Esmeralda. His helpless obsession with this social outcast humiliates his pride. Even the shrewdest character, Louis XI, depends superstitiously on his ineffectual, unscrupulous doctor. The king cannot see past the walls of the fortress he inhabits, the Bastille, to recognize the future rise of the people foreseen by the Flemish shoemaker Jacques Coppenole. The one artist figure with pretensions to creating something individual and enduring, Pierre Gringoire, is a pedantic clown. Hugo proves a "realistic" visionary here as again years later at the conclusion of *Dieu*. Ultimate spiritual awareness can be ours only in another life, which he does not try to depict: mere humans can intuit but not grasp a higher truth.[13]

Whereas his characters see only one source of light, Hugo can see many. His extraordinary visual imagination is both impressionistic—sensitive to changes of light—and cinematic, aware of varying angles of vision and shifting vantage points. When he evokes the changing light on the facade of Notre Dame, not only does he anticipate Claude Monet's famous series of paintings of the same subject, but he suggests the visionary's ability to see beyond the relativity of perceptions: "There's one time in particular when you have to go admire the portal of Notre Dame. That's the moment when the sun, already slanting toward the horizon, looks at the cathedral almost head-on. As its rays become increasingly horizontal, they slowly withdraw from the pavement of the public square in front of the church, and climb up the vertical facade where they make a thousand sculptures in full relief stand out against their shadow, while the great central rose window flames like a cyclops's eye lit by reflections from the forge" (7.1.259).[14]

Following this passage, Hugo executes the verbal equivalent of a zoom-in shot to approach the balcony where Gaston Phœbus, his fiancée, her mother, and her friends have gathered. The protracted traveling shot circling Paris from the top of the cathedral towers anticipates cinematic technique ("Paris à vol d'oiseau" [A Bird's-Eye View of Paris]) (3.2.143–54). The impressionistic viewpoint corresponds to a passive visionary experience; the cinematic viewpoint, to an active one. That Hugo can adopt either of these as he chooses suggests his mastery of his own visionary role.

Hugo's imagination ranges beyond France and Catholicism themselves. By insisting that the architecture of the most famous French cathedral is as much Islamic as Christian (the Crusades put Europeans into contact with Islam, and Moorish architecture inspired Christians with the idea of the broken arch), Hugo suggests a syncretistic view of ultimate truth.[15] No one religion provides a full understanding of Providence. The ultimate expression of such complexity appears in the long poem *Dieu*. There, 10 successive revelations by winged representatives of the various world religions lead only to the realization that absolute truth remains ever remote.

The image of the microcosm subtly conveys how the implied author's privileged vision extends beyond history. "To measure the big toe is to measure the giant" (3.1.132), he writes, echoing Voltaire's "Micromégas." Typical of the romantics, Hugo implies that apparently divergent views may reflect a single, central truth seen from different angles of vision. "The trunk of the tree is immovable, the foliage is wayward" (3.3.138).[16]

As La Esmeralda unifies the novel's plot, so Quasimodo unifies its themes. His full meaning includes spiritual and aesthetic as well as melodramatic dimensions that ensure the coherence of the work. He is the soul of the cathedral and is closest to the spiritual reality it represents. He frequents its highest reaches; his greatest delight is in ringing the bells, whose sound rises toward heaven in a traditional representation of prayer (compare Joris-Karl Huysmans's *Là-bas* [Down There]). Without Quasimodo today, Hugo says, Notre Dame seems incomplete and lifeless as an empty skull (3.3.177). Together, the bell ringer and the cathedral illustrate the union of the sublime and the grotesque that Hugo had first advocated as the supreme expression of art in "La Préface de *Cromwell*" (1827). That same union reappears at the conclusion, when Quasimodo's skeleton is found inextricably entangled with La Esmeralda's. Apparently, he has let himself starve to death in the arms of her corpse. In the spiritual order, the two are inseparable: when people try to pry the skeletons apart, his falls into dust (11.4.509). In other words, when Quasimodo leaves this world, his deformity disappears. In the dialectic of sin and sacrifice, the grotesque leads to a larger whole, a spiritualized *concordia discors* (a harmony of incompatible things): namely, the redemption that includes us all.

Chapter Three

The Leader of Romanticism: Triumph and Failure in the Theater

The Political Implications of Literary Genres

Odes reflect a static situation and praise the established order. Once Hugo started to question the legitimacy of divine-right monarchy, he needed to find another literary genre to express himself. Eventually he would explore four different ways to suggest possibilities for a new political order. The great visionary poetry of the 1830s and 1850s predicted the providential healing of injustice in a future world; the virulent satires of the early 1850s assailed dictatorship in the present, staging the poet as its adversary; historical dramas criticized political absolutism in the past, referring to the present only by implication, mediated by the voices of fictional characters other than the personified author; and the novel allowed Hugo to combine all three of these modes. He began with historical drama.

Initially, theater seemed a natural choice for a new direction. Plays thematize conflict. Moreover, the stage offered a public forum, and chances for rapid fame or notoriety. The success of Shakespearean revivals and adaptations such as Alfred de Vigny's *Othello* (1829), and of Alexandre Dumas *père*'s historical drama *Henri III et sa cour* (At the Court of Henri III, 1829), invited emulation. Whereas comedy limits conflict to a family or a small social group, tragedy often questions the entire political order. Yet it can do so indirectly. Once Hugo stops being a committed monarchist, he has to confront censorship. He must then choose between the evasive strategies of exoticism (focusing on another time or place) or religious meditation and prophecy (focusing on another world altogether). Otherwise he is obliged directly to address the moral problems raised by the inequities and iniquities of the French regimes of his time. He usually adopts a compromise: he examines the problems raised by royal power but situates his dramas in another time and place.

The shift of emphasis from celebrating to questioning the powers that be was overdetermined. Hugo's political opinions were moving toward a relative liberalism. Once he became the acknowledged leader of the French romantic movement in 1827 (displacing Charles Nodier, whose Salon de l'Arsenal was the romantics' central meeting place from 1824 to 1827), Hugo found himself heading an aesthetic struggle against the conservative literary values of neoclassicism. Contemporaries saw the political and the aesthetic struggles as intimately related.

Hugo's natural talents and his literary ambitions prevented him from creating a fully committed, didactic theater like that of Brecht, Wesker, or Sartre. First, Hugo's imagination is essentially lyrical: he creates unchanging, eternal, irrational character types in a fixed pattern of relationships. What counts most is the beautiful language they find to express their moods.[1] Second, his desire to be all-encompassing, and to rival Shakespeare, leads him to insert lively but distracting comic episodes within his plots (the seducer-king hiding in a linen chest in act 1 of *Hernani;* a roistering, likable, but dissolute nobleman stumbling into and disrupting a revenge plot in act 4 of *Ruy Blas*). In the famous "Préface de *Cromwell*" (1827), to illustrate his desired effect of mingling the sublime and the grotesque, Hugo invoked Ariel and Caliban from Shakespeare's *The Tempest*.[2]

Like Shakespeare, Hugo wrote many plays focused on the problem of a just revenge. How can a hero assert his independence, claim his rights, and oppose an unjust power without becoming guilty when he uses force to oppose force, crime to oppose crime? How can he define his identity while attacking a system in which his identity has been rooted?[3] The solution of benevolent intercession, explored provisionally in Hugo's moving novella *Le Dernier Jour d'un condamné à mort* (1829), opposing capital punishment, would be fully developed only much later during Hugo's political career and his exile.

Hugo explores the dilemmas of political power from various points of view: seventeenth-century England, sixteenth- and seventeenth-century Spain, medieval Germany, sixteenth- and seventeenth-century France. His Cromwell, a successful rebel, redeems himself by pardoning the royalist conspirators who had been plotting to assassinate him.[4] His king Don Carlos in *Hernani,* at first an unscrupulous would-be seducer, redeems himself after he is named emperor by pardoning the rebel conspirators against his throne. In *Les Burgraves*, the reigning emperor, Barberossa, is opposed by a league of princes led by his brother Job, who as the elder could claim to be the rightful ruler.

The motif of the suicide of Hugo's heroes such as Hernani, Ruy Blas, or Triboulet (in *Le Roi s'amuse*) suggests that revolt entails guilt. Only drastic self-punishment can assuage this oppressive feeling for the heroes. In later works, as in Charles Dickens's *A Tale of Two Cities,* the desire for self-punishment will be sublimated as sacrifice for the good of others.

Because their basic situations question the authority of a king or his prime minister while presenting a sympathetic portrayal of a rebel, Hugo's early mature plays could be read as coded messages of political opposition. Anne Ubersfeld interprets *Hernani* starkly as a parable of the Revolution, in which the king is replaced by a man of the people.[5] Of this interpretation Hugo's contemporaries had no doubt.[6] One reviewer wrote: "Let M. Hugo make no mistake about it, his plays will raise more opposition to his political than to his literary system: people have less of a grudge against him for not respecting Aristotle than for insulting kings; the battles swirling around his works, in the theater and in the newspapers, are embittered more by partisan politics than by literary dogma."[7] By 1827 Hugo was no longer a royalist or a Catholic. The title character of *Cromwell* (1827) is the Puritan leader who had his king executed. At the conclusion, Cromwell refuses the crown. *Marion Delorme* (1830), censored after one performance because it seemed disrespectful of the French monarchy, tells of a mysterious, whimsical man, Didier, condemned to death by Louis's prime minister Richelieu for having fought a duel; Didier is executed despite Marion's valiant efforts to save him. Blaming the sinister prime minister, however, salvages the possibility of at least exculpating the king.

Hernani

Hugo's best-known play, *Hernani* (1830), tells of the rivalry of three men for a young Spanish noblewoman, Doña Sol.[8] Her aged uncle Ruy Gómez, her guardian, wants to marry her; the king, Charles Quint (Carlos Quinto), the future ruler of the Holy Roman Empire, wants to seduce her; Hernani and she love each other, and she has resolved to elope with him although he is a banished bandit chief. Her name, "Miss Sun," hints at her unreality. As she says herself, "Je suis à vous. Pourquoi fais-je ainsi? Je l'ignore" [I'm yours. Why do I behave this way? I don't know].[9] Like Marion Delorme, or like the queen in *Ruy Blas,* Doña Sol exists mainly as a token of value: the heroine's love identifies the worthiest man. For that man to be an outlaw, and to have that outlaw sharing scenes with a king, was shocking to the conservative audiences of 1830.

None of the three rival male characters knows everything or dominates events. Each surprises one of the others on occasion. In act 1, just
before Hernani arrives to arrange an elopement with Doña Sol, the king
in disguise intervenes to try to seduce her. Before he finds her, he hears
Hernani coming and hides. The presence of another man in Doña Sol's
quarters at night makes the king assume that she is promiscuous. When
Hernani appears, the king emerges from hiding and cynically offers to
share Doña Sol with Hernani, who indignantly challenges him to a duel.
The two men are about to fight when Ruy Gómez appears. The king
reveals his identity and lies that he has come to see Ruy Gómez on official business; he claims Hernani is one of his followers, thereby allowing
him to go free.

The second act reverses the situation of the first: the king comes early
to the midnight rendezvous that he has overheard the lovers make. He
signals Doña Sol to come outside, where he has minions and a carriage
waiting to kidnap her. Hernani appears in time to thwart the abduction.
The king's men are surrounded by a ring of Hernani's bandits, but the
king now refuses to duel with Hernani because he has learned that Hernani is an outlaw chief, thus apparently of an inferior class. Hernani
could have the king assassinated but instead allows him to escape.

In act 3, the marriage of the unwilling Doña Sol to Ruy Gómez is
about to take place. Disguised as a pilgrim, Hernani unmasks himself
and denounces Doña Sol in a jealous rage. Despairing, he tells Ruy
Gómez there is a bounty on his head and invites him or his servants to
turn him over to justice. Meanwhile the king has gathered troops to
pursue Hernani and his band. When the king suddenly arrives, Ruy
Gómez insists on honoring the laws of hospitality by hiding Hernani.
Alone for a moment with her love, Doña Sol vindicates herself by showing him the dagger she has taken from the king. With it she intends to
commit suicide before the marriage is consummated. Ruy Gómez orders
Hernani to hide, and then admits to the king that the bandit leader is in
his house, but refuses to reveal his hiding place. Ruy Gómez stands firm
even when the king threatens to take his life and then instead takes
Doña Sol hostage. Hernani feels that he owes his life to Ruy Gómez and
gives the old man his horn as a pledge (in French, *cor,* "horn," is a
homonym for *corps,* "body"). Hernani swears by his father's memory to
forfeit his life to Ruy Gómez whenever the latter asks, provided that
Hernani can first avenge himself on Carlos.

In act 4, Hernani and Ruy Gómez have joined a conspiracy against
the unjust king. They meet at Aix-la-Chapelle, where electors will

decide who will be the next ruler of the Holy Roman Empire. Don Carlos, who craves that honor, has also come there. He awaits the results in the caverns where Charlemagne's mausoleum lies (the elections actually occurred at Frankfurt-am-Main, but Hugo wants to create more coincidences). Charlemagne symbolizes imperial grandeur and dignity at their best. Hearing the conspirators coming to plot his assassination, Don Carlos hides inside Charlemagne's memorial. There, through some mystical transference of merit, meditating on his great predecessor transforms Don Carlos into a worthy ruler. He hears that Hernani draws the short straw, meaning that he will strike the first blow. Hernani insists on keeping that privilege, although Ruy Gómez offers Hernani's life in exchange for it. Then three cannon blasts announce the choice of emperor. It is Don Carlos. He emerges to confront the conspirators, who are promptly surrounded by a ring of Carlos's soldiers (the situation of act 2 reversed). But discovering that Hernani is outlawed because his father had been wronged by Carlos's father, and having acquired an unwonted magnanimity, the new emperor pardons everyone, restores Hernani's titles, and gives him Doña Sol's hand in marriage.

In act 5, the lovers exult in the imminent consummation of their love after the marriage ceremony. Ruy Gómez returns, sounding Hernani's horn as a sign that it is time to die. When he refuses to respond to the lovers' pleas, Doña Sol seizes the poison Ruy Gómez has brought for Hernani and drinks half of it. The two lovers die in each other's arms, leaving the jealous old man alone to kill himself in despair. One recognizes the influence of Shakespeare in the stage littered with bodies as the curtain falls, but Hernani carries self-defeating behavior to an extreme that makes even Hamlet appear resolute. Not infrequently, romantic literature seems an ill-sublimated tantrum, during which the heroes often forget to "use their words."[10]

During the rehearsals for *Hernani,* Hugo often had to be away from home, struggling with the actors who were disconcerted by the colloquial language, the violent passions, and the deaths shown onstage.[11] He had difficulty dealing with the illustrious leading lady, Mlle Mars, who was offended by Hugo's lack of deference. She occasionally replaced what she considered extravagant language with readings of her own; in her words, Doña Sol's "vous êtes mon lion superbe et généreux" became "vous êtes mon seigneur" [you are my splendid, magnanimous lion/lord].

Hernani was intended as the first flagrantly public demonstration of the new romantic literature. It aimed to replace the melancholy, vapid elegance of the first generation of romantics, and to open the doors of the literary world to Hugo's younger friends. Performances of the play were the founding public event of high romanticism. Using the dozens of free tickets he had demanded, Hugo packed the audience of *Hernani* with strategically placed rows of "Jeunes-France," the hippies of the day. They vehemently applauded at critical moments. With jeers and insults, they tried to intimidate and silence the indignant older generation of classicists in the audience. The latter, in turn, vociferously condemned every violation of good taste. Whistling and catcalls nearly every 10 lines made substantial sections of the play inaudible.

We are fortunate to have a copy of the play annotated by Hugo during a performance; we can see what the conservatives found objectionable.[12] The word "bandit" provoked laughter throughout the first three acts, probably because the spectators thought that the dignity of serious theater should have prevented the mixing of social classes that allowed an outlaw to interact with nobility and royalty on the stage. Booing from the conservative members of the audience greeted the unaccustomed use of familiar expressions ("il fait les doux yeux; à la bonne heure" [He's making eyes at her; sure thing]); references to commonplace realities (old age, the time of day, being cold); particularly extravagant expressions ("j'accueillerais Satan, si Dieu me l'envoyait" [I would host Satan, if God had sent him]); and elaborate metaphors ("Dans l'ombre, tout au fond de l'abîme, —les hommes. / Les hommes!—c'est-à dire une foule, une mer, / Un grand bruit; pleurs et cris; parfois un rire amer" [In the shadowy depths, humanity. / Humanity! That is, a crowd, a sea, / An uproar; shouts and weeping; bitter laughs]). The restrained, solemn, elevated tone deemed appropriate for classical tragedy seemed marred both by Hugo's sometimes commonplace language and by his excesses of lyricism. These violations of decorum called attention to the present-day author at the expense of the historical drama. The promiscuity of tragic and comic moods in the play seemed to suggest a democratic, revolutionary mingling of aristocrats and commoners. The conclusion, where the dying lovers pretended to lie down together on their marriage bed, provoked jeers for being too overtly sexual.

Unlike the contemporary reviewers with the text in hand, the audience was insensitive to metrical violations. They seldom noticed the enjambments (the device of breaking a closely linked group of words over two lines) that disrupted Hugo's classical alexandrine (12-syllable) rhyming couplets. Nevertheless, when pointed out, such prosodic disturbances could, like Hugo's other extravagances, seem to challenge the established order.

The leading characters themselves are clearly confused about how formal their relationships should be. Hugo often shifts between the formal second-person pronoun *vous* and the intimate *tu* to enrich character depiction and to reflect the violent mood swings of love.[13] Hernani and Doña Sol use *vous* to each other during their first conversation (1.3), although they are planning to elope the next night. The exchange of the formal *vous* continues between them on the next midnight in act 2, scene 4, after Hernani has rescued Doña Sol from the king, who has come in disguise to kidnap her. But Hernani switches to *tu* when he refuses to let her follow him because the king has condemned him to death. Hernani returns to *vous* in his next reply, considering their separation to be inevitable. Doña Sol uses *tu* for the first time to plead to be allowed to follow him. Hernani responds with *tu*. She angrily returns to *vous* momentarily when Hernani insists on fleeing alone. When he agrees to stay with her she returns to *tu,* which both use until a general alarm directed against Hernani and his band separates them.

A similar instability of pronoun reference reappears in act 3, scene 4. Owing to her maidenly modesty, Doña Sol persists in using a non-reciprocal *vous* to respond to Hernani's *tu* except for one exclamation. It occurs after Hernani says that love would be a supreme blessing if one could die of too much love. Doña Sol responds: "Je t'aime! / Monseigneur! Je vous aime et je suis toute à vous" [I love you (familiar). / Sir! I love you (formal) and I am wholly yours] (vv. 1030–31). The non-reciprocal *tu* and *vous* between Hernani and Doña Sol persists even after their wedding ceremony, when they are left alone together. Modest, she resists his eager attempts to lead her off to bed. To reassure her, Hernani twice reverts to *vous* (vv. 1941, 1943). She then twice alternates between *vous* and *tu* (four times in all by the end of the scene), as if experimenting with intimacy.

After Ruy Gómez sounds Hernani's horn in act 5 to remind the hero of his pledge to surrender his life, both lovers return to *vous* when the hero insists on reverting from his ducal name (which entitles him to marry Doña Sol) to his bandit's name. Under the pressure of Doña Sol's anxious pleading to know what has suddenly troubled Hernani, both revert to *tu* for the remainder of the scene. In the final scene, Hernani once and Doña Sol thrice address the other with *vous* when she sees Ruy Gómez and realizes her husband has been hiding something from her. They return to *tu* during their mutual suicide until they die in each other's arms at the end. Their frequent pronoun shifting suggests a total abandonment to the other, alternating with fears that the other may not have made an equally strong commitment. Such romantic theater dramatizes and glorifies the stresses of a morbidly dependent relationship in which life without the other seems impossible.

The romantic playwright often has trouble integrating the self-destructive, evanescent heroes (Hernani famously says "je suis une force qui va" [I am a fleeting force; 2.4.992]) into a plausible historical narrative.[14] Such confusion gains structural significance in the *dilemme,* the crucial scene where the hero, alone, debates with himself whether to yield to love or to preserve his honor. The romantic *dilemme* differs from neoclassic models (e.g., from Corneille) by consisting only in effusions of feeling rather than in reasoning. It concludes not with an act of resolve but with a passive acquiescence to fate. When the king Don Carlos leaves after his attempt to seduce Doña Sol, Hernani says:

> Un instant
> Entre aimer et haïr je suis resté flottant,
> Mon cœur pour elle et toi n'était point assez large,
> J'oubliais en l'aimant ta haine qui me charge,
> Mais puisque tu le veux, puisque c'est toi qui viens
> Me faire souvenir, c'est bon, je me souviens!
>
> (1.4.385–90)

> [For a moment
> I remained drifting between love and hate,
> My heart lacked room to hold both her and you,
> My love made me forget my heavy rage,
> But since you wish it so, crossing my path
> To make me remember you, then I do!]

Throughout the play, Hernani suffers a progressive loss of autonomy. In act 1, he leads a large troop of bandits. This troop is diverted from its mission—avenging Hernani for the unjust execution of his father by the present king's father—to serving the cause of Hernani's love; the king's forces then wipe them out. Act 3 makes Hernani voluntarily subject to the will of Ruy Gómez. Act 4 leaves him subject first to chance, then to the plans of the league of conspirators opposing the king (Hernani is now merely their follower); in act 5, honor no longer permits him to live. The energies of Hugo's anti-monarchical revolt seem gradually drained by the activity of the very character who embodies them. According to George Moskos, Hernani's death stages "the apotheosis of the male protagonist through his re-inscription into the very system *against which* he has been defined as a romantic hero."[15]

Ruy Gómez's despairing remark at the end underlines the characters' lack of control: "La fatalité s'accomplit" [fate is consummated] (v. 2149); and Doña Sol's last word supersedes Hernani's when she briefly survives him to make the final pronouncement on their love. The king himself cannot decide his fate, despite his strength of will. Yearning to be elected ruler of the Holy Roman Empire, he must await the decision of others. He lacks sufficient votes to be elected until the other main aspirant to such rule, Frederick of Saxony, withdraws. After being elected, the king must immediately worry about circumstances beyond his control— notably, Luther's reformation. The latter event suggests that no sooner has the Holy Roman Empire been won than its unity will start to be undermined. Finally, all three men depend on the choice among them made by Doña Sol, who refuses to be intimidated or ordered about.

Even the unfair advantage gained by spying confers only temporary superiority on the villains of *Hernani* and *Ruy Blas*. Because Don Carlos overhears Doña Sol and Hernani arranging a rendezvous at midnight the next day, he can come a bit early and try to carry Doña Sol off. But she resists him effectively until Hernani arrives with a stronger band than the king's. At the conclusion, to be worthy of empire, Don Carlos must renounce his attempt to seduce Doña Sol. And although he hears the conspirators plotting against him, he nevertheless feels obligated to pardon them to display a magnanimity suitable to an emperor. Similarly, Don Salluste eavesdrops on Ruy Blas and learns of his passion for his queen; Don Salluste can therefore effectively use Ruy Blas as a cat's-paw, but Ruy Blas will ultimately kill him anyway. Don Salluste's plans come to naught. Eavesdropping gives both villains only a temporary advantage, because those they overhear have more integrity than they.

In an anagogic perspective, one concerned with the characters' ultimate spiritual destiny, the disjunction between the sentimental and the political in *Hernani* becomes much less important. Act 1 focuses on the idealistic mutual passion of Hernani and Doña Sol. Act 2 centers on cynical, libertine love—the king's attempt at a kidnapping. Act 3 foregrounds the legitimate but jealous love of an old man, who can preserve the seriousness of his role only by concealing its pathos. Act 4 shows Don Carlos sublimating his lust for Doña Sol with the aid of his lust for empire. And act 5 glorifies a romantic love stronger than death. In each of the four latter acts, the predominant form of love expressed becomes nobler and more imposing than the last, until we return to the point of departure. (*Notre-Dame de Paris,* published the following year, has a similar ascensional structure.) The progressive purification of love feelings will be transformed in Hugo's later visionary work into the progressive purification of the soul: through successive reincarnations, life by life, God's creatures ascend the rungs of the Great Chain of Being.

Hernani enjoyed great popular success. The run of 49 performances, excellent in those days, ended only because the leading actor had to leave for a prior engagement elsewhere. Seven theatrical parodies promptly appeared, replacing the ancient Spanish nobility with the contemporary Parisian bourgeois, and changing the main setting from a palace to a public inn. The parodies eliminate the threefold exoticism of time, place, and social status.[16] Most of the critics, however, roundly condemned the play for being already too ordinary—for its vulgarity, absurdity, and incoherence—easy targets if one does not read it as lyric, rather than mimetic, theater. But the publicity, both good and bad, raised Hugo to the uncontested leadership of French romanticism.

The preface to *Hernani* had adopted a militant pose, defining romanticism as "liberalism in literature" (*Hernani,* 27). Hugo urged that all clear-sighted, logical minds work toward the twofold goal of freedom in art and in society. It seems strange that with such a goal, Hugo should write a play glorifying the most imposing moment of the Spanish monarchy; he explains that *Hernani* lays the first stone of an edifice already fully formed in the author's mind. This structure must be completed, Hugo claims, before the meaning of *Hernani* can be accurately judged. He compares himself to the architect of Bourges, who placed an almost Moorish door on a Gothic building. The implication is that as Islam is to Christianity, so the monarchy glorified in *Hernani* is to the inevitable triumph of the people in the entire structure. One must pass through the first to reach the second. Thus the *exegi monumentum* topos acquires a third meaning: not only that of conventional pride in one's artistic achievements that memorialize the past, but also a social role for the romantic movement, where prophecy guides the French people toward democracy.

Ruy Blas

By the time he composed the preface to *Ruy Blas* (1838), Hugo had achieved an even broader overview that explicitly synthesizes the separate domains of history, theater, and audience. He begins with a characteristic tripartite division. There are three essential kinds of drama, Hugo claims: the crass, inferior form of melodrama to amuse the public; tragedy, which analyzes the passions, in order to move women [sic]; and comedy, which analyzes humanity, to instruct the thinkers. All generalities have exceptions, he quickly adds, so as not completely to disparage either women or the people. Le drame (ideal romantic theater), he claims, will combine comedy with tragedy by depicting the clash of personalities (the purview of comedy) and passions (the purview of tragedy) with the great laws of Providence. According to Hugo, Shakespeare illustrates such a synthesis: "Corneille and Molière would exist separate and apart if Shakespeare did not stand between them, giving Corneille his left hand and Molière his right. Thus the contrasting electric charges of comedy and tragedy meet, and the spark that spurts from them is drama." Hugo then explains the meaning of Ruy Blas: once monarchy decays, corrupt and opportunistic nobles remain at court, whereas the nobler part of the nobility retires to its estates in the country. Don Salluste and his cousin Don César represent these two tendencies for Hugo; but when one contemplates them, Hugo adds, "one sees something great, dark and unknown stirring in the shadows. It is the people. The people, to whom the future but not the present belongs" (Ruy Blas, 24–29).

Typical of the synthesis of relativism and absolutism in the romantic Weltanschauung, Hugo explains that this summary does not exhaust the meanings of the play: "One can look at an idea, as at a mountain, from several different points of view." Meanings, he adds, are like a thousand branches springing from one trunk. He concludes with another move characteristic of romantic thought. By reminding us that Charles Quint was born in 1500, whereas Charles II died in 1700 and Napoleon assumed the greatness of Louis XIV's dominion in 1800, Hugo invokes century anniversaries as signs of kairos: a hidden order that underlies human affairs and reflects a single, predominant law. In Hernani the sun of the royal house of Austria rises, and in Ruy Blas it sets. A new dawn will bring a new order (Ruy Blas, 30–32).

As Hernani depicted the emergence of Spanish grandeur, so Ruy Blas depicts the moment of disastrous Spanish decline under Charles II, the last of the Hapsburg rulers. The preface, and act 3, where Ruy Blas apostrophizes Charles V, makes the connection clear. It is a man of the people who must recall to the nobility their obligations to their country. The courtiers remain parasites as they had been in Hernani; but there, their profits were granted disdainfully by the future emperor, who had grander projects in view. The courtiers' activities did not detract from his triumphant representation of his country on the world stage. In *Ruy Blas,* the king has abdicated responsibility. He never appears, he spends his time hunting, and the corrupt courtiers have been running the country for their personal benefit. Even when the king listened to them from hiding, the queen reveals, he did nothing to intervene.

Hugo displays a greater mastery of the theater in 1838 than in 1830. He insisted that the actors first encounter the text through hearing him read it aloud, to avoid any erroneous preconceptions on their part. Hugo himself designed the sets and costumes. He attended rehearsals and checked the blocking (the positioning of the actors on the stage). His stage directions become more elaborate (Ubersfeld, 334; this feature also reflects Hugo's move from a classical aesthetic, where the conventions of performance are taken for granted, to an individualistic romantic aesthetic where the author establishes the norms). The characters have become more believable. In *Hernani,* the title character's motivations were inconsistent: he forgot his plans for revenge when he pursued his love; he did not identify himself to the king as a duke when the king refused to fight him in a duel; he sacrificed his followers to his love; losing faith in his love, he denounced himself suicidally and then put his life in the hands of his greatest rival. The king begins as a base seducer (the nature of his love for Doña Sol never is made clear but seems lustful and cynical at best) and dramatic mover. But after granting Hernani both amnesty and Doña Sol, the king literally steps outside the plot in act 4 to pursue his imperial ambitions on another stage. It is the pitiable, foolish Ruy Gómez who becomes the dramatic mover in act 5. He unwittingly ensures the death of the woman he loves in a gesture that anticipates Claude Frollo's "personne ne l'aura" [then *nobody* will have her] of *Notre-Dame de Paris.*

In *Ruy Blas,* the sinister Don Salluste is the dramatic mover from beginning to end. His motive throughout is revenge. Relishing his considerable political power under the reign of a weak, indifferent king, Don Salluste is furious at having been expelled from court at the queen's order. He has refused to marry one of her ladies-in-waiting whom he had seduced and made pregnant. In revenge, he will try to have the queen in turn expelled from court for adultery.

First he attempts bribery to enlist in the scheme his good-hearted cousin Don César, a ruined nobleman who lives on petty larceny. When César refuses, Salluste has him arrested secretly. Before departing to exile, Salluste orders Ruy Blas, his well-educated but common-born valet, to pose as Don César, to please the queen and make her love him. He will wait till they arrange a compromising rendezvous, and then expose them.[17] Although an honorable man, Ruy Blas secretly loves the queen; he unwisely agrees to play a role. Salluste's speech to his episodic mentor Gudiel, who appears only in the first scene and has only two one-line replies, and his soliloquy later are both more plausible sources of information than the speeches made to other characters at the beginning of *Hernani*. Those speeches tell the others things only the audience needs to know, and tell them twice for good measure.

Act 2 shows us the queen, bored, terribly neglected by her husband, and oppressed by the rigorous court etiquette. When she meets Ruy Blas in disguise, she senses that he is the man who wrote her an anonymous love letter and has been sending her flowers every day. Returning his feelings, she saves him from a duel with a jealous old man also in love with her. Thanks to her support, Ruy Blas quickly becomes influential at court. In act 3, he chastises the corrupt ministers who have been stealing from the royal treasury and from the people. The queen overhears and admires him; once they are alone, she declares her love. But soon afterward, his master, Don Salluste, returns in disguise to humiliate Ruy Blas and to remind him that he can be exposed at any moment.

Don César, who has escaped from confinement, returns in act 4 to stumble into one of Salluste's secret lairs. This act is filled with ribald, colloquial language and provides comic relief. It seems at first that César will foil Salluste's plot, but his cousin again manages to have him arrested on a false pretext.

The queen answers an urgent appeal from Ruy Blas, one that Don Salluste had deviously made his valet write out earlier. She is lured to Salluste's secret house at midnight. The presumption of adultery, and forced exile with or without a mere valet, seems certain. The title character can defeat Salluste only by admitting that he is not a gentleman, and by acting accordingly to kill his unarmed master. After doing so, the queen can flee back home undetected, but Ruy Blas commits suicide to expiate the crime of his love that has sullied the queen with his social inferiority. Only as he dies of poison does she forgive him, and they end in each other's arms as Ruy Blas dies.

The metaphorical mine shaft that Don Salluste digs under the queen is more believable than the secret closets and stairways of *Hernani*. And in a clever reversal, the queen who eavesdrops on Ruy Blas from a hidden compartment is herself caught by her subterfuge: she becomes so impressed by his dignity and integrity that her feelings become a trap.

The scene where Ruy Blas explains to his old friend Don César (Don Salluste's cousin) his reasons for working as Salluste's valet—he loves the queen and wants to be at the court so that he can be close to her—seems natural as theater goes. This scene, moreover, moves the plot: although Don César has refused to court the queen, Salluste overhears Ruy Blas's avowal and realizes that he can substitute his valet for his cousin to achieve an even more effective revenge.

As act 4, only an apparent digression, reveals, Don Salluste is aided by an invincible ally, fate, a force that gives Hugo's theater a coherence greater than that of any other French romantic drama. Everything Don César does to thwart Don Salluste's plot to humiliate the queen either has no serious effects or helps the plot work better. Loyalty and innocence become the vehicles of cosmic irony (Gaudon 1985, 100–101).

What seems most implausible is the weakness and acquiescence of the title character. Ruy Blas agrees to assume a false identity to make the queen fall in love with him, and he never questions why Salluste would order him to do this, nor why Salluste makes him sign an admission that he is only a valet. No matter how blindly passionate his love, one would expect him to be less imprudent. Nor does Ruy Blas seem aware that Salluste has been banished from court, nor comment on his departure—he forgets him altogether. His love (unlike that of the bored queen—"La Reine s'ennuie" [The Queen Is Bored] was the play's original title, echoing "Le Roi s'amuse") has irrational origins and can be consummated only in and through death. Death similarly replaces consummation in *Hernani*. In both plays, social obstacles to love may vanish, but human hatred remains as a second layer of fatality.

Hugo rejects the happy endings of melodrama. In his tragedies, the good die. I would agree with Jean Gaudon that "tragedy, when it leads to the annihilation of whatever, throughout the play, seemed to voice opposition, amounts to a return to the established order. Thus the historical play with political implications loses its meaning to acquire another: resignation. There is, it seems to me, the deep contradiction at the heart of Hugo's theater" (Gaudon 1985, 106). But it would be a mistake to identify these weak and self-destructive "heroes" with their vibrantly healthy, productive, self-actualizing creator.

Critical Reception of Hugo's Theater

Hernani was a great financial success. In exchange for the book rights, the publisher Mame offered 5,000 Francs (enough to live on for two years) on the spot. *Ruy Blas* was less of a financial and critical success,

but it represented a social triumph: it was written at the urging of the
duc d'Orléans, a liberal second in line for the throne, whose new wife,
Hélène de Mecklembourg, adored and memorized Hugo's poetry (Maurois, 275 –77). Hugo was frequently invited to court and showered with
honors: officer of the Légion d'Honneur (1837), member of the
Académie Française (1841), and Pair de France (1845; a member of the
upper chamber of government, analogous to the British House of Lords).

His very success as a playwright, leading to social prominence,
appeared to drain Hugo of the intensity he needed to create. The 1840s
were rather unproductive for him. He would need the stimulus of exile
(1851–1870) to spur him again to create ambitious works. The political
confusion of the French nation, torn between democracy and authoritar-
ianism, was provisionally resolved by the paradoxical situation of
Napoleon III, an elected emperor. Hugo could not accept this outcome
and went into exile.

From that point on, he shifts from theater to satire—outright denunciation of the bad ruler—and replaces the earthly ruler with the good
heavenly ruler who always forgives. Hugo's entire cosmology is based on
the assumption of a divinely ordained mechanism of universal redemption (the Pelagian heresy). The renegade's acceptance of divine grace,
like Satan's in *La Fin de Satan*, accelerates but does not determine atonement, since grace is prescient and relentless. Hugo's later works focus
less on conflict between characters than on revelation by the author. The
characters acquire an increasingly allegorical function. The author's
guidance aims to hasten our own redemption through our acceptance of
the divine order.

The strikingly different interpretations to which Hugo's theater lends
itself today show its great richness. Affron insists that it is essentially
musical, occurring outside time in a static eternity of emotional effusions,
and that of romantic theater, today only opera survives (7). Raser claims
that it is essentially visual, that staging must be called on when words fail
(397). Thomasseau finds Hugo's theater basically written, observing that
letters or notes are read in 20 of the 27 scenes of *Hernani;* at least one
scene per act consists entirely in reading such texts. Much dictation is
staged as well, and one finds 73 different words concerning paper, writing, or reading, in more than 200 instances.[18] Perhaps the best way to
understand such a wide divergence of opinion is to realize that the broad
net of Hugo's genius, cast into the swirling sea of rapid and profound historical change, brings many things to the surface at once.

Chapter Four
The Birth of a Visionary Poet

The Turn from Political to Religious Poetry

Poetic odes celebrate the existing order of things. In early-nineteenth-century France, to write odes meant to support the divine-right monarchy. Hugo's political shift toward liberalism was foreshadowed when he abandoned the traditional ode to write the picturesque *Ballades* of 1828. Some were actually composed as early as 1823. More directly, by opposing capital punishment, a godlike prerogative of the divine right of kings, Hugo's *Le Dernier Jour d'un condamné à mort* (The Last Day on Death Row, 1829) in effect suggested limiting royal power. Also in 1829, Hugo moved from French subjects to the spectacular exoticism of the Arab world, treated with extraordinary metric virtuosity in the *Orientales*.[1] Finally, he gradually elaborated the mixture of intimate, visionary, and prophetic poetry that would dominate his production till the end of his career.

One stylistic habit dates nearly all romantic poets, making their verse at times seem tedious or quaint. As if the poet's complete control of the lyrical world (like any author's control of any text) did not suffice, Hugo, like Wordsworth, Keats, and Shelley, frequently resorts to rhetorical questions. These create the impression of a pseudo-dialogue while actually usurping an extra turn in the conversation—one both asks and answers one's own question.

Compared to the lyrics of his great contemporaries, however, on close examination Hugo's poetry suggests a communion with nature that is both more open-ended and more precise. It makes the natural world seem alive, as if meaning were emanating from that world in vague, faint voices that only the poet could intuit and decipher. It is less stagy than the poetry of English romanticism, where we are continually reminded that meanings have been imposed by the poet.[2] For example, William Blake, like Hugo, believes in a sentient world; but to describe it, Blake adopts a hammering, aphoristic style:

47

A dog starv'd at his Master's Gate
Predicts the ruin of the State.
A Horse misus'd upon the Road
Calls to Heaven for Human blood.[3]

Wordsworth often retreats into nature, but there he remains aware of the city he has left. Nature serves him as a frame for contemplating another human being; or he evokes a companion; or he dominates his communion with nature by addressing speeches (apostrophes) to it, and not allowing it to answer. Keats writes in a stiffly conventional pastoral mode that seems neoclassic today—more like André Chénier than like Hugo. Shelley is closer in spirit to Hugo, but his nature is inhabited by conventional spirits from classical mythology. Intensely self-conscious, Shelley continually turns back upon himself, to "the Poet" and his thoughts and his words. To understand Shelley's solipsistic (self-imprisoned, self-referential) vision, consider these three examples from the 144 lines of "Mont Blanc":

> Thou art the path of that unresting sound—
> Dizzy Ravine! and when I gaze on thee
> I seem as in a trance sublime and strange
> To muse on my own separate fantasy
> . . . .
> Thou hast a voice, great Mountain, to repeal
> Large codes of fraud and woe; not understood
> By all, but which the wise, and great, and good
> [notably, the poets]
> Interpret, or make felt, or deeply feel.
> . . . .
> . . . The secret Strength of things
> Which governs thought, and to the infinite dome
> Of Heaven is as a law, inhabits thee!
> And what were thou, and earth, and stars, and sea,
> If to the human mind's imaginings
> Silence and solitude were vacancy?
>   (vv. 34–37, 80–84, 138–44; Noyes, 977–78)

Like dancers who watch their feet—Blake excepted—English romantic poets seem distracted from their visions by their fixation on practicing their trade. Intellectuals all, they produce far more quotable lines than does Hugo, but they fall short of his fluid merging of mind and world, which one can see in many of the texts cited hereafter.

Hugo's turn from political to religious poetry is announced clearly in *Les Feuilles d'automne* (Autumn Leaves), in a poem dated to coincide with the July 1830 revolution that installed a constitutional monarchy:

> Que t'importe, mon cœur, ces naissances des rois.
> Ces victoires, qui font éclater à la fois
>   Cloches et canons en volées,
> Et louer le Seigneur en pompeux appareil,
> Et la nuit, dans le ciel des villes en éveil,
>   Monter des gerbes étoilées?[4]

> [What do you care, my heart, about those births of kings.
> Those military victories we celebrate
>   With pealing bells and cannonades,
> Praising our [worldly] Master with a pompous show,
> And by shooting over the wakeful towns,
>   Starry clusters of fireworks?]

The poems of the 1830s reverse the ode's traditional order, in which inspiration from a spiritual being (usually the Muse figure) is followed by a report of the resulting vision. Hugo's growing democratic sensibilities inhibit him from continuing to present himself as an intellectual or spiritual aristocrat—one who can summon inspiration at will (as does Goethe in *Faust*) at the beginning of his poems. Instead, an imaginative encounter with the physical world leads him and the reader together toward the visionary insight suggested at the conclusion of the poems.

Hugo's new visionary mode already appears in the last poems to be composed for *Les Orientales*.[5] "Novembre" introduces a sentimental, realistic note: accompanied by his muse, Hugo turns explicitly away from Oriental spectacle toward memories of childhood. If (imaginary) travel (to a fictive Middle East) disperses the self, memory in "Novembre" recenters it, opening it to an inward, spiritual vision. "Extase," Hugo's "first poem where intimate communion with nature ends by inspiring a message of general import," according to Elizabeth Barineau, reflects this shift.[6] On a cloudless, starry night beside the sea, the poet's eyes see deeper than the material world. For Hugo, visionary "seeing" often leads to hearing voices from the beyond. Here the woods and mountains seem to question (what they ask about is not specified) the waves and the fiery stars, which bow and answer "C'est le Seigneur, le Seigneur Dieu!" [It is the Lord, the Lord God!] (*OP* 1, 680). The topos (traditional subject) from Psalm 19 (see also Psalm 148), "cœli enarrant gloriam Dei" [the Heavens are telling the glory of God], often recurs in Hugo's later verse. The prophetic poet's stance between two abysses, the heavens and the deeps of the sea, will also become typical. A good Latinist, Hugo knew that *altus* means both "high" (the heavens) and "deep" (the sea): this latent syllepsis reflects his vision of organic unity. All Creation, high or low, reflects the Creator, and evolves back toward Him.

Hugo's poetry of the 1830s—*Les Feuilles d'automne* (1831), *Les Chants du Crépuscule* (Songs of Dawn/Dusk, 1835), *Les Voix intérieures* (Inner Voices, 1837), and *Les Rayons et les Ombres* (Sunbeams and Shadows, 1840)—represents his greatest lyric achievement before the *Contemplations*. Critics tend to exaggerate the novelty of the poems of the exile period (1851–1870), and the importance of Delphine de Girardin's seances (1853–1855) as inspirations for Hugo's mystical visions. Most of the cosmic motifs of his later work appear during the 1830s: the poet persona is already a visionary who can discern the voices of nature, of heaven, and of the human souls lingering in nature after death. What Hugo adds to his cosmic system during the 1850s, in *Les Contemplations, La Fin de Satan,* and *Dieu* (Contemplations, The End of Satan, God), is a narrative framework: sin, punitive reincarnation, passive expiation of one's sins, the correspondence of cosmic with historical events to reveal the operation of Providence, and universal redemption at the end of time. The 1850s enriched his eschatology (his theory of how Creation would end) with doctrines from the Pelagian heresy and from the Cabala, but much of his religious inspiration derives from sources he had known well since his youth—in particular, Dante and the Bible.

Les Feuilles d'automne

The core of Hugo's vision in the 1830s consists of discovering affinities between the microcosm, or human scale, and the macrocosm, or universal scale. This motif so prominent in the *Contemplations* (e.g., in "Magnitudo parvi") already appears clearly in *Les Feuilles d'automne*, associated with the primitive neo-Platonic dualism inherited from Lamartine.[7] Thus Hugo calls God the "foyer du vrai jour qui ne luit point aux yeux" [the hearth of the true light unseen by mortal eyes] in "Dictée en présence du glacier du Rhône" (Dictated before the Rhone Glacier) (*OP* 1, 731). Both ideas appear together in this poem—the illusoriness of the material world, and the macrocosm: "Mon esprit, de la terre oubliant le prestige, / . . . / . . . contemple de près ces splendeurs sidérales, / Dont la nuit sème au loin ses sombres cathédrales" [Forgetting the illusions of the earth / My spirit contemplates from close at hand / . . . / Those stelliferous splendors which the night / Strews afar through its dark cathedral vaults] (732). The apparent absurdity of the contrast of "close" and "afar" distinguishes material from spiritual distance. Such deliberate illogic is akin to Hugo's use of antithesis and oxymoron (a condensed antithesis, as in this poem the phrase "terrestre océan," the "terrestrial ocean" of human society).

"Ce qu'on entend sur la montagne" (What One Can Hear on the Mountain) (*Les Feuilles d'automne*, 5) exemplifies Hugo's visionary poetry. It contains three levels of spiritual awareness: the reader is not yet attuned to the supernatural order; the poet persona (the "lyric self," meaning the poet personified within the poem) encounters spiritual realities but cannot yet make sense of them; the implied author (not personified, but inferred from the text as a whole) suggests an explanation for the vision. That this poem, like so many others after the virtuosic *Orientales* of 1829, is written in alexandrine rhyming couplets suggests a narrative progression toward some goal rather than a sentimental, ornamental conception of poetry. Couplets are like steps forward. Hugo begins by addressing the reader with a series of five rhetorical questions. They create suspense. And by saying "you," he attracts our attention and involves us in the experience of the poem.

Hugo, a capable draftsman, has often been praised for his precise descriptions, but as we have observed in *Notre-Dame de Paris*, what we can see often is misleading. His hearing is acute as well; it proves more reliable than sight in allowing him to penetrate beneath the surface of appearances. By linking words, sound echoes (rhyme, alliteration, and assonance) can suggest meanings extending beyond single material objects. Hugo's skillful use of rhyme in "Ce qu'on entend sur la montagne" (*OP* 1, 726–28) illustrates how profoundly he associates his auditory sensitivity with his worldview.

Have you sometimes climbed a mountain and listened? he asks. Elevation and isolation prepare us, like Moses on Sinai, for enlightenment. Rhyme changes along with meaning. *Rimes suffisantes* (having two identical final sounds) are the "unmarked choice," the expected in French verse. In "Ce qu'on entend sur la montagne," the first block of verses (1–12) is written entirely in couplets in *rimes riches* (having at least three identical final sounds). Such rhymes can reinforce suggestions of certitude, security, stability and harmony already implied by the text. The opposite marked choice, *rimes pauvres* (having only one identical final sound), can reinforce suggestions of change, uncertainty, threat, and absence. Here the *rimes riches* describe a majestic landscape of mountains next to the sea: first, as seen by anyone; second, as thought and heard by the poet. Between the two landscapes, the poet interjects a couplet in *rimes suffisantes* to mark a transition from the general to the particular, and from the screen of material appearances to the spiritual reality that lies beneath them. The letters corresponding to the rhymes are shown in boldface type: "Et là, penché sur l'onde et sur l'immensit**é**, / Calme et silencieux, avez-vous écout**é**?" [Leaning over waves and immensity, / Calm and silent, have you listened to them?]. "Pencher sur" has both a literal and a figurative meaning: to bend over something, and to turn one's attention to an idea.

In the second block of verses (13–28), as Hugo listens to the symphony of ocean sounds, *rime riche* appears only in verses 15–16 and 27–28, to help describe a totalizing experience of harmony: "Le monde, enveloppé dans cette symph**onie**, / Comme il vogue dans l'air, vogu**ait** dans l'harm**onie**" [The world, enveloped in that symphony, / As it sails in air, sailed in harmony]. The third and fourth blocks of verses (29–42) use only *rimes suffisantes* to describe a second, discordant chorus of voices, emanating from the suffering earth. The fifth block (43–54) uses *rimes riches* in the first three couplets to describe the harmonious song of the ocean celebrating the beauty of creation. It shifts into *rimes suffisantes* as the poet listens to individual waves, and finally, the supreme vision, owing to its transient, uncertain quality here, is reported only in *rimes pauvres:* "Et moi je croyais voir, vers le couchant en f**eu**, / Sous sa crinière d'or passer la main de Di**eu**" [And I thought I saw, toward the west in flame, / God's hand passing beneath its golden mane].

Surprisingly, at first, given the content, Hugo changes to *rimes riches* again for the first eight verses of the sixth block (55–62), describing the jarring medley of human plaints. Such harmony may hint at an eventual answer to the problem of evil (why does God allow the innocent to suf-

fer?) posed at the conclusion of the poem: suffering contributes to expiation and prepares an eventual reunion with God. Except for Hugo's final
questioning, the remainder of the poem is almost entirely in *rimes suffisantes*. In the final block of verses, he asks, "Quel peut être après tout le
but de tout ceci" [And what might the purpose of all this be?]. Note the
extraordinary accumulation of hard consonants, 9 in 12 syllables. The
sounds are hard because life seems hard.

To characterize what he hears, Hugo evokes uniqueness and inexpressibility: "[E]t jamais voix pareille / Ne sortit d'une bouche et n'émut
une oreille. / . . . / C'était une musique ineffable et profonde" [Never did
such a voice / Emerge from a mouth to affect an ear. / . . . / It was deep,
undescribable music] (11–12, 19). It swelled like a symphony, Hugo
continues, to bathe the earth in a sea of harmony. As the poet tunes in to
these sounds, he makes out two separate choruses. One, the voice of
nature, rises from each wave of the sea, praising the beauty of Creation.
The second chorus, the voice of humanity, rises from the earth: it
laments, complains, insults, curses, blasphemes, and finally rejects God.

Hugo again addresses his personified reader as "Brother!" before
introducing his conclusion, another rhetorical question. He wonders
what is the purpose of existence and of the soul, whether it is better to be
conscious or merely to exist, "Et pourquoi le Seigneur, qui seul lit à son
livre, / Mêle éternellement dans un fatal hymen / Le chant de la nature au
cri du genre humain?" [And why God, whose book He alone can read /
Forever mingles in fateful embrace / Nature's song with the cries of
humankind?]. The implied answer appears only during a second reading,
in the last word of the second block of verses, "l'harmonie." Why does
God eternally link the harmony of nature to the suffering of humanity?
"Ce qu'on entend sur la montagne" clearly raises the same doubts about
Providence that we shall find again years later in the poem "A Villequier"
of the *Contemplations,* to say nothing of the novel *Les Misérables*.

That questioning is cast in what one could call super-rich rhymes,
each having four identical final sounds. The exceptionally extensive
sound harmony is reinforced by the recurrence of two sounds, the *n* and
the *i*, in all four lines:

> Frère! de ces deux voix étranges, inouïes,
> Sans cesse renaissant, sans cesse évanouies,
> Qu'écoute l'Éternel durant l'éternité,
> L'une disait: NATURE! et l'autre: HUMANITÉ!

[Brother! of those two strange voices, unheard [by humans],
Forever reborn, then fading away,
That God listens to through eternity,
One said: NATURE! the next: HUMANITY!]

"Inouïe," like the expression "pencher sur" discussed earlier, is a syllepsis
linking the abstract and the concrete: figuratively the word means
"unprecedented," and literally (a meaning no longer in everyday language) "unheard." Taken literally, "unheard" is an absurdity, since both
God and the poet hear these voices. Taken figuratively, "unheard" means
that if we humans learn to hear both voices together, we will become
able to understand the meaning of human suffering in the general context of a divine redemptive plan.

Because the poet returns to share his unprecedented experience, the
poem as a whole, like all Hugo's visionary poetry, corresponds to the
archetype of Withdrawal, Enlightenment, and Return. The three parts
of the poem, separated by two short groups of verses, describe the poet's
encountering, distinguishing, and meditating on the two blended voices
of humanity and of nature. This is the first of his major visionary com-
positions based on synesthesia (the combination of two or more sense
impressions in a single perception), a device that will soon generate the
vast ode in praise of Palestrina, "Que la musique date du seizième siècle," in *Les Rayons et les ombres*.[8] Through synesthesia, Hugo, like Baudelaire after him, intuits a cosmic harmony ordinarily concealed from our
limited human faculties.

In a synthesis analogous to that of the sublime and the grotesque recommended in *La Préface de Cromwell* (1827) and exemplified in *Notre-
Dame de Paris,* joy and suffering must combine to create a general harmony that includes human freedom. In "Ce qu'on entend sur la
montagne" nature sees God and rejoices; humanity cannot see God and
suffers. The doctrine of punitive reincarnation will often reverse this pattern in the *Contemplations* (see, for example, the poem "Pleurs dans la
nuit" [Tears in the Night]). There humans, who cannot see God, suffer
less than the beasts, plants, and even minerals, who do see God. These
lesser beings grieve at being unable to do anything to approach Him,
other than passively to endure a long cycle of rebirths.

"Ce qu'on entend sur la montagne" is dated 27 July 1829 and was
probably first composed in September 1828 (*OC* 1, 1329), when all was
going well for Hugo. He was happy in his personal life, intensely productive, and the acknowledged leader of romanticism in France. It does

not appear, despite what critics and Hugo himself have said, that set-backs and stress inspired his visionary poetry.

"Dictée en présence du glacier du Rhône" (Dictated at the Rhone Glacier) (*OC* 1, 731–32) is the visionary masterpiece of the *Feuilles d'automne*. There the romantic vision of correspondences between the microcosm and the macrocosm appears in frequent anthropomorphism and in frequent similes (introduced in French by "ainsi," "comme," or "tel"). A mountain is "old" (using an adjective, "vieille," ordinarily reserved for people), a "giant" and "colossus" with feet, a gleaming white forehead (the glacier), and a serene face. The nine stanzas of the poem also introduce at least five similes: here these are not decorative but organic, emphasizing the bonds between the poet's thought and natural phenomena.

Hugo compares his poetic inspiration, struck by the idea of God, to the dew that ascends into the sky to form a cloud when struck by a ray of sun. It wanders through the changing light of the sky, shunning the cities. Eventually an envious wind breaks the cloud on a lofty mountain, where it freezes into a glacier, only to melt into a torrent and rush back to earth to enter a new cycle.[9] The initial influence of God, "Mystérieux soleil dont l'âme est embrassée" [Mysterious sun that sets the soul on fire], recalls the transformation of the apostles at Pentecost. The poet's androgynous soul transcends sexuality; by turns it wears a veil and a warrior's helmet. More overtly represented as a liminal phenomenon in space, in time, and in the hierarchy of created beings, the mountaintop glacier stands at the frontier between earth and sky; at night its white forehead seems an eternal dawn; and even the chamois, the eagle, and the tempest, kings of nature, fear it, "Tant il est avant dans les cieux" [So lofty is it in the skies].

Violations of logical and prosodic structure mimic the unpredictably rapid changes the poet sees. Shining on the snow, the sun "changes the glacier to a crater." Two violent, successive transformations condense into one: the sun changes ice into water, and the running water hollows out a gorge on the mountainside. As the lofty glacier seems to contemplate the night skies, Hugo's mind also contemplates them "Jusqu'à ce qu'un rayon de Dieu // [stanza break] Le frappe de nouveau" [Until a ray from God // Strikes it again]. Here we have not merely an enjambment (a close-knit grammatical unit continuing past the end of a line of verse) but a "super-enjambment" carried over from one stanza to the next. Such unusual versification implies that whatever aesthetic order the poet can impose (suggested by the customary limits, for sentences, of the stanza) is overmastered by the will of God.

Near the end of the collection *Les Feuilles d'automne,* "Pan" (no. 38, 803–5) becomes more overtly self-conscious. It rejects a trivializing conception of poetry, instead sending all true poets forth throughout the world to pursue a sacred mission, like the apostles after Pentecost.

Si l'on vous dit que l'art et que la poésie
C'est un flux éternel de banale ambroisie,
Que c'est le bruit, la foule, attachés à vos pas,
Ou d'un salon doré l'oisive fantaisie,
Ou la rime en fuyant par la rime saisie,
    Oh! ne le croyez pas!

O poètes sacrés, échevelés, sublimes,
Allez, et répandez vos âmes sur les cimes,
Sur les sommets de neige en butte aux aquilons,
. . . .

Car, ô poètes saints! l'art est le son sublime,
Simple, divers, profond, mystérieux, intime,
Fugitif comme l'eau qu'un rien fait dévier,
Redit par un écho dans toute créature,
Que sous vos doigts puissants exhale la nature,
    Cet immense clavier!

[If people tell you that poetic art
Is an unending flow of cheap perfume,
That it is fame, and the crowd at your feet,
The idle fancy of gilded salons,
Or fleeing rhyme pursued and seized by rhyme,
Do not believe them!

O sacred poets, wild-haired, sublime,
Go forth and spread your souls on mountain crests,
On snowy peaks lashed by the wild north wind,
. . . .

> For, blessed poets! art is the sound sublime,
> Simple, varied, mysterious and deep,
> Fleeting as water that a trifle turns,
> Answered by echoes within every being,
> That nature exhales beneath your strong hands,
> Nature, vast keyboard!]

Hugo, like Lamartine, characterizes his poetry as sound to exert an immediate, physical effect on the reader.

The hammering anaphoras (line-initial repetitions) of "Allez . . . sur les . . . partout où" [Go . . . over the (mountains, deserts, forests, lakes), everywhere that (there is life)]" reinforce the rhetorical links between the poet and nature while emphasizing his authority over his fellow poets. The world is a living temple to God; the visionary experience of "Dicté en présence du glacier de Rome" has been generalized for those worthy to find it.[10] In "Pan," the poet becomes the interpreter as well as the recipient of messages from a panpsychic nature, of "le mot mystérieux que chaque voix bégaie" [the mysterious word that each voice stammers]. He invites other poets to join him in mingling their souls with creation. In an inversion of the poet-as-Aeolian-harp topos (like grass stretched tight between tree branches and making melodious sounds in every wind), here nature becomes a keyboard passively responding to the poet's strong fingers.

Les Chants du crépuscule

Les Chants du crépuscule (1835) chooses an untranslatable sylleptic title (Songs of Dawn/Dusk) to convey Hugo's personal, political, and religious uncertainties, which reflected those of his age. As in the poem "Spes" (Hope) of the Contemplations, a distant gleam may mean either that a spiritual night is falling or that a new and better age will soon dawn. In 1835, France, still a monarchy, seemed to waver toward a republic or toward socialism. Hugo likewise was wavering in both his political and personal life. He could no longer accept the Catholic faith and was seeking another outlet for his profound religious sensibility.[11]

Hugo's wife, Adèle, had fallen in love with his former best friend, the literary critic Sainte-Beuve. Her relationship with Hugo would never again be more than a platonic friendship centered on their mutual interest in the children. In 1833, the despairing Hugo had himself begun a lifelong affair with the actress Juliette Drouet. Their relationship went through two years of uncertainty before she agreed to abandon her wealthy "protectors" and her mediocre career in the theater to devote herself totally to Hugo. Always living nearby, she was kept under virtual house arrest for many years by her jealous paramour.

The preface to *Les Chants du Crépuscule* aligns Hugo neither with those who affirm nor with those who deny, but with those who hope. The initial poem, "Prélude," develops the motif of uncertainty: "C'est peut-être le soir qu'on prend pour une aurore!" [Perhaps we have mistaken dusk for dawn!]. There the versification in quatrains with crossed rhymes *(abab)* reinforces the impression of vacillation between opposing extremes. Sadly but calmly, the poet's verses echo what the waiting world sings, stammers, or says.

At such an unsettled moment in his life, it was natural for Hugo temporarily to regress to the familiar formula of the ode. That genre dominates the first half of *Les Chants du Crépuscule*. The major topic for an ode often is emulation of one's forebears. In the first poem after the "Prélude," "Dicté après juillet 1830" (Dictated after [the revolution of] July 1830), the poet exhorts his compatriots: "Soyez fiers; vous avez fait autant que vos pères" [Be proud; your fathers did no more than you]. Such an address reflects the general assumptions of the traditional ode: virtue is transferable; example can inspire. Implicitly, within such a worldview, the ideal identity is knowable and can be approached by successive approximation.

Les Chants du Crépuscule (1835) shows progress toward the unorthodox panpsychic religion of the *Contemplations*. Here clarification is needed. Pantheism means that the world is God's body, that all Creation is God. Panpsychism means, instead, that one can find a spark of soul in everything, a spark that in turn dimly reflects the spiritual essence of God.[12] One can see Hugo's evolution by recalling "Dicté en présence du glacier du Rhône." There the personified entities from nature were either grandiose objects such as the mighty mountain or conventionally "noble" animals—the chamois, the eagle—who do not speak. Only the torrent formed by the melting ice makes a sound; the ray of sun that strikes it is tacitly compared to the animating force of the poet's imagination. "Prélude," in contrast, is filled with nearly inaudible, inchoate prosopopoeias (ventriloquized discourse) from conventional poetic sources. Is the earth saying "hail" or "farewell"? Trees, birds, humans, and the ocean murmur with either joy or pain. Beyond these, however, one finds hints of a possible soul even in human artifacts: Hugo alludes to what the plowshare says to the furrow and what the wheel says to the pavement (813, v. 28). To complete his religious system, the poet need only claim (as he does later) that the development of such embryonic souls will fulfill a divine redemptive purpose.

Les Rayons et les ombres

Les Rayons et les ombres (1837) associates a humble visionary creature (representative of all subhuman beings in Hugo's later poetry) and a divine vision. In "La Vache" (The Cow) (no. 15, *OP* 1, 969–70), a nurturant cow dreams of her god. She transcends a simple polarity of good and evil, innocence and violence: she and her setting are described so as to make her symbolism all-inclusive. She is compared to both a doe and a leopard. Her hide combines the colors white and russet (ice and fire); both a sedentary oldster and noisy children appear in her barnyard. The visionary climax equates her with universal nature. Here animism (attributing life to inanimate objects) and personification (attributing human consciousness and will to subhuman beings) blur the categories of human and nonhuman, sentient and inanimate. See the phrase "children sootier than old walls" or the term "bonne" [kindly] applied to the cow. The commonplace title and subject of this poem have a democratizing effect. In those days, not all French people had seen treasures and palaces, mountains and oceans, but they had all seen cows. Imposing, conventionally romantic landscapes are no longer necessary to glamorize the poet's vision. The poet, unlike Moses on Sinai, is no longer a being set apart: God can be found everywhere. Dignity inheres in the vision, not necessarily in the visionary or in the site of the vision. In both theme and subject, Hugo's rural landscape with figures revives the celebration of the cosmic order of *concordia discors* (the harmony created by disparate elements) in seventeenth- and eighteenth-century descriptive poetry.[13]

"Passé" (The Past) (no. 16, 970–71) in the same collection echoes Gérard de Nerval's nostalgia for the Renaissance and the seventeenth century. The poet adopts a royal persona (touring the palace of Versailles with Juliette Drouet, he compares the two of them to Louis XIV and one of his royal mistresses). Historical accuracy does not matter: in one moment of fictional time, Hugo mingles names and details from the sixteenth, seventeenth, and eighteenth centuries. On the secular plane, he performs the equivalent of God's redemptive acts. His conclusion "Ô temps évanouis! ô splendeurs éclipsées! / Ô soleils descendus derrière l'horizon!" [O vanished ages! O faded splendor! / O suns that beneath the horizon set!] (971) verbally retrieves what had disappeared.

At the moment when the past becomes most vividly present to the poet's feelings, at the moment when historical memories embedded in his preconsciousness reemerge to present awareness, the artful arrangement of the words mimics and reinforces the impression of an inner, deeper layer of reality. A complex tangle of chiasmus evokes the past that has revived within the experience of the present. *Chiasmus* means an arrangement of elements—similar parts of speech, or identical words, or both—in a nesting pattern, thus: *abba*. Here the *b*s within the frame of the *a*s suggest recovered memories (the past) within the frame of the poem (the present). We shall have to number the 14 elements of the seven chiasmuses to keep them straight (see note 14 for details): my arrangement of the lines here tries to suggest some of the layering.

Dans cet antre, où la mousse a recouvert la dalle,
Venait, les yeux baissés et le sein palpitant,
Ou la belle (1) Caussade ou la jeune (2) Candale,
Qui, d'un (3) royal (4) amant (4) conquête (3) féodale,
(5) En entrant disait (6) Sire, et (6) Louis (5) en sortant.

(7) Alors comme aujourd'hui,
    (8) pour (2) Candale ou (1) Caussade,
    La nuée au (9) ciel (10) bleu mêlait son (10) blond (9) duvet,
    (11) Un doux (12) rayon dorait (12) le toit
        (11) grave et maussade,
    Les vitres flamboyaient sur toute la façade,
    Le soleil souriait, la nature rêvait!

(7) Alors comme aujourd'hui,
    (8) deux cœurs unis, deux âmes,
    Erraient sous ce feuillage où tant d'amour a lui;
        (13) Il (14) nommait sa duchesse un ange entre les femmes,
        Et l'œil plein de rayons et l'œil rempli de flammes
        (13) S'éblouissaient (14) l'un l'autre,
    (7) alors comme aujourd'hui![14]

                                                                    (971)

[In this cave, where moss has covered the floor,
Came with eyes lowered and with trembling breast
The beautiful Caussade or young Candale,
Who, feudal conquest of a lover-king,
Going in, said "Sire," "Louis" coming out.

Then as today, for Candale or Caussade,
With skies of blue the clouds mixed their blond down,
A gentle ray gilded the solemn roof,
The windows flamed all along the facade,
The sun was smiling and all nature dreamed!

Then as now two united hearts, two souls,
Wandered these woods where so much love has shone;
An angel among women he called her,
And their eyes burning with radiant flames
They dazzled each other, then as today.]

The first stanza describes the seventeenth-century lovers Louis XIV and his mistresses (fictitious names) disappearing into a grotto and reemerging. The grotto contains the lovers as the chiasmuses contain the words they frame. Penetrating the grotto also symbolizes sexual intercourse.

Chiasmus in the next two stanzas suggests how the past is both repeated by, and retained within, the present. Simultaneously they mark progress from an outer to an inner reality: from the light of the sun and the social glory of the "Sun King" to the interior light of love. Used to describe the clouds, the metaphor "duvet," the delicate, pale down on a blond person's skin, prepares the transition from the natural to the human. The three stanzas could be said to form a super-chiasmus, nesting nature and culture alike within a framework of human subjectivity:

(A) the human: *yeux, sein, amant* (eyes, breast, lover)
(B) the natural: *nuée, ciel, rayon* (cloud, sky, ray)
(C) the cultural: *toit, vitres, façade* (roof, window panes, facade)
(B) the natural: *soleil, nature* (sun, nature)
(A) the human: *cœurs, âmes, femmes, œil* (hearts, souls, women, eye; this schema has been simplified.)

"Oceano Nox" (Night over the Ocean) (1116–17) in the same collection reveals Hugo's further progress toward the idea of reincarnation. The poet laments the death of seafarers drowned in storms and whose fate must remain unknown. Those who remained at home wonder whether the travelers have become settlers in a more fertile land, or kings on some island. After a time, only their widows remember the departed and "Parlent encor de vous en remuant la cendre / De leur foyer et de leur cœur!" [Still speak of you while they stir up the ash / Of their hearths and their hearts!]

The striking image of "the ash of hearths and hearts" illustrates a device called in French *hypallage* (a form of catachresis, which is itself a form of metonymy). It applies two modifiers to the same word (ash), one modifier ordinarily referring to a concrete object, and the other to a feeling or to an abstraction ("hearts" here means "love feelings"). A famous example is Hugo's "vêtu de probité candide et de lin blanc" [clothed in artless candor and white linen] in "Booz endormi" (v. 14) in *La Légende des siècles*. Literary conservatives who reviewed the *Odes* had strongly criticized Hugo for using this device; he rebutted them by showing that it was commonplace both in classical Latin literature and in the Bible. For him as for the authors of the biblical books, *hypallage* reflects the belief that the material order—Creation—indirectly reveals the spiritual order and the Creator.

Throughout "Oceano Nox," everything associated with the drowned sailors steadily becomes more insubstantial. They will have no gravestone, no memorial. They are present first as dead bodies, next as dreams, then as names, and finally only as the unintelligible murmur of the waves. (The rich rhymes in which stanza 6 is entirely written, however, anticipate the affective resonances of memory at the very moment when the sailor's former friends stop thinking of them and return to their daily tasks.) In contrast, the material decor evoked becomes progressively more detailed and concrete, especially in stanza 7. The sea acquires a vital energy that overshadows and crowds out the energy of human life.

The sailors' disappearance from living memory is a second death.[15] But the poem concludes with a startling intuition of a world-soul that preserves the identities of human individuals elsewhere forgotten. More than once, in other texts, Hugo celebrated the multitude of hidden harmonies in nature, invisible threads that transform the world-all into a seamless net of being.[16] Here he says:

Où sont-ils, les marins sombrés dans les nuits noires?
Ô flots, que vous avez de lugubres histoires!
. . . .
Vous vous les racontez en montant les marées,
Et c'est ce qui vous fait ces voix désespérées
Que vous avez le soir quand vous venez vers nous!

[Where are these sailors sunk in the dark nights?
O waves, what dismal stories you can tell!
. . . .
You exchange them while breaking on the shore;
That's what gives you those voices of despair
That you have when you come toward us at dusk!]

Hugo suggests a mystic horror at the prospect of being engulfed by the world-soul. Taking another step, in the visionary poetry of the 1850s, he will move from the idea of the waves' voices telling the sad stories of the drowned to the idea that guilty spirits in a second life have been embodied in the waves and in other destructive things. These spirits suffer from witnessing the harm that their physical nature forces them to inflict, and which they are powerless to prevent.

Hugo's New Threefold Vision

Hugo's middle-period poetry refines the conventional ode's moral segregation of sheep and goats by adopting a three-fold vision. Instead of simply discriminating between darkness and light, good and evil, he undertakes a mission of mediation and reconciliation, which provide his third term. His new habit of tripartite thinking, already evident in "La Préface de *Cromwell*" (1827), *Notre-Dame de Paris* (1831), and the preface to *Les Voix intérieures,* does not become associated with a hierarchy of body, mind, and soul (the Swedenborgian triad) until the "Prélude" of the *Chants du Crépuscule.* Here the poet as mind mediates between soul and body. In the "Prélude," the nearest approach to the anti-selves of the conventional ode is the uncertain poets and priests who seek revelation and a new role. Hugo's poet persona of the middle period seeks to penetrate and reveal a mystery instead of distributing praise and blame.

The symbolists attempt to create an autonomous world of words; the romantics, to understand the world we have. By itself, the pun of the title *Les Feuilles d'automne* (Autumn leaves/sheets of paper) suggests an organic connection between poetry and nature. The romantics' emphasis on content over form explains and justifies characteristics that would otherwise make us consider romantic poetry relatively unoriginal and dilute. As an insensitive virtuoso pianist can be "finger proud," sacrificing nuances of interpretation for speed, symbolist and modernist poets can be "metaphor proud," condensing isolated inspirations and arbitrarily assembling them to the point of incoherence. What the romantic poets sacrifice in local density, they often recuperate through the supersegmental richness of their visionary systems, which are at once autotelic (an end in themselves) and allotelic (serving a higher purpose), lyric and prophetic.

Chapter Five

Liberal and Exile: The Political Career

Hugo's Royalist Origins

Like many a prominent politician today, Hugo began his political career as a draft dodger. Graham Robb notes that Hugo used his poetry prizes at the famous Jeux Floraux of Toulouse "to negotiate a legal precedent [that] granted him special dispensation from military service."[1] To be fair, he was opposed to violence. Although the son of a prominent revolutionary general, Hugo from his earliest works was revolted by the death penalty, by deportation to tropical hellholes (tantamount to a slow execution), and by the murder of hostages and prisoners of war. *Han d'Islande* expresses more disgust at the royal executioner than at the cannibalistic title character who drinks his victims' blood from his son's skull.

Several critics have claimed that when the five-year-old Hugo traveled to join his father in Italy, and when the nine-year-old Hugo went to join his father in Spain, the severed heads and the hanged and mutilated bodies he saw horrified him and inspired his lifelong opposition to the death penalty. I would agree. But *Victor Hugo raconté par un témoin de sa vie,* the "as-told-to" biography he dictated to his wife, traces that opposition to the public executions that he witnessed between 1820 and 1825. Perhaps for the record he wished to suppress or repress his father's role in killing freedom fighters in both Spain and Italy.

The issue of capital punishment was much discussed throughout the 1820s. The famous historians Jules Michelet and François Guizot wrote against the death penalty in 1820 and 1822 respectively.[2] Essay contests on the subject of capital punishment were widely publicized. American and British convicts' journals from death row appeared in leading journals; and in 1828, the memoirs of François Vidocq, a criminal turned chief of police, created a sensation with accounts of prison life, the underworld, and thieves' cant (slang). The portrayals of Balzac's Vautrin in several novels and of Hugo's Potron-Minette gang in *Les Misérables* owed much to Vidocq. Hugo explicitly joined the abolitionists in the 1832 preface to *Le Dernier Jour d'un condamné à mort* (1829), which had previously been mainly poignant and picturesque. "For the first time, Victor Hugo was no longer satisfied with being a story teller or a poet; he expressed the first stirrings of the vocation of a social reformer."[3]

Sympathy for the poor also characterized Hugo almost from the first, but his liberalism in politics was a late vocation. The first open break with the monarchy came in August 1829. Always opposed to censorship, Hugo became a hero to the romantics by refusing to accept a royal *pension* increase of 4,000 francs and a post on the Council of State in return for withdrawing his play *Un duel sous Richelieu* (later known as *Marion Delorme*) from production. Every newspaper printed his letter of refusal (see Robb, 144–57). By 1830 he was no longer a royalist or a Catholic, but he cheerfully accepted the honors lavished on him by three successive royalist governments between 1822 and 1845. He believed monarchy and democracy to be compatible—as the English parliamentary model demonstrated. His direct experience of the insurrection of 1832, described in *Les Misérables,* was accidental: he was trapped in a recess between buildings when he wandered into a firefight between rioters and government troops on 5 June 1832. In late December of that year, he refused to draw his *pension* any longer. He would no longer depend on the monarchy for money—only for honors (Robb, 173 and 178).

After election to the Académie Française in 1841, Hugo became eligible for appointment to the peerage. No sooner had he become a peer in 1845 than he embarrassed the monarchy: a police agent led by the aggrieved husband caught him having adulterous sex in a love nest. As a peer, Hugo was immune to prosecution on such charges, however; and once released, he promptly redeemed himself politically by speaking in defense of the institutions of the throne and the hereditary peerage. As late as February 1848, he risked his life to advocate that Helena von Mecklemburg-Schwerin, the widow of the duc d'Orléans (legitimate pretender to the throne) be named as regent with the possibility of later becoming queen. She loved Hugo's poetry and knew some by heart (Robb, 214–16). Today we might call Hugo a "Teflon" politician: his middle-of-the-road positions, and his popularity with the people, allowed him to shift allegiances easily: he remained a peer throughout the monarchy and then was elected to the Assemblée Constituante (Constitutional Convention) when the Second Republic began in 1848 (cf. Robb, 263).

Hugo insisted that poverty could be eliminated and denied that hard labor was needed to curb the appetites and angers of the people. He recommended paternalistic intervention as enlightened self-interest by the ruling classes, to prevent uprisings by the oppressed. He had blamed prisons for creating criminals, in *Claude Gueux* (1834). But only in a first draft version of *Les Misérables* ("The Underclass"), in 1847, did he begin to implicate society as a whole in causing poverty and blue-collar crime.

After the birth of the Second Republic, he was elected to the new French congress as a representative from Paris (4 June 1848). Given 75 professional soldiers from the Republican Guard, Hugo actually oversaw assaults on the rebellious monarchist-worker coalition barricades from 24 to 26 June. "The new Republic had defended itself like a tyranny," and martial law continued till 4 November, when the constitution was proclaimed (Robb, 273–276). Hugo had been responsible for a number of deaths.

But he played a courageous role as the voice of the liberal conscience of France from 1849 to 1870, including 19 years in exile to protest Louis-Napoléon's coup d'état that turned the republic into a new empire. Hugo's repeated refusal of amnesty was prescient and principled during those years—not stubborn and foolish as some imply. He could not have accepted amnesty without promising to uphold the empire; to accept amnesty at all would have meant giving the usurper's regime legitimacy.

On the other hand, one must admit that Hugo played a major role as "a useful idiot" in making the empire possible. Already in 1847 he had asked Parliament to end the Bonaparte family's exile, to prevent their becoming the heroes of seditious movements (Robb, 281). He stood better with several of Bonaparte's relatives than Louis-Napoléon did himself; Hugo provided valuable contacts and unequaled eloquence when the future emperor returned to Paris. The ephemeral newspaper *L'Événement,* founded by Hugo's two sons and two friends, had vigorously supported Louis-Napoléon for president. One supplement to that paper simply printed his name 100 times (Robb, 282–83).

Hugo Moves to the Left

By May 1849, the assembly of deputies was sharply divided between the extreme Right and the extreme Left. Perched uncomfortably in the middle, Hugo tried to maintain a conciliatory position, preserving order and forestalling Socialism by delivering limited reforms (Robb, 282). He delivered many important speeches between 1848 and 1851. He continued to oppose the death penalty (15 September 1848; see also 5 April 1850). As a writer, he considered himself a representative of publishers and writers: therefore he steadfastly opposed censorship of the theater and of the press (20 September 1848; 9 July 1850). He advocated universal (manhood) suffrage as a way of preventing revolutions (5 April 1850) but also defended compromise bills to limit such suffrage (21 May 1850). He could imagine a day when women would vote.

Aside from his opposition to legalized murder, his main cause during this period was the separation of church and state in public education. I have no objection to religious instruction, he declared; indeed, I recommend it, but only if it takes place inside the church (15 January 1850).[4] He initially supported the Falloux Law in 1849, however, and changed the published versions of his speech to conceal the record of his right-wing views from posterity.[5] From 1850 until 1905, the Loi Falloux gave the Catholic Church—in particular, the militant "clerical party" of the Jesuits—effective authority over French primary and secondary education. Only the uproar created by the Dreyfus Case (1894–1906) would lead to creating public schools that were secular in fact, not just in name. In July 1851, Hugo at last became a bona fide Republican by delivering a famous speech opposing the French Republic's drift toward empire.

Guy Rosa has compiled a definitive analysis of Hugo's voting record during the Second Republic (1848–1851). From June 1848 to June 1850, Hugo's positions change little, but the assembly as a whole moves steadily to the Right. As a result, siding with the Left only 25 percent of the time in August 1849, Hugo is voting with them 80 percent of the time by January 1850. From then on his political orientation does not significantly change.

During this period, Hugo consistently supports the suppression of civil unrest but staunchly defends individual liberties such as the right to free association, an expansion of the jury system, and the freedom of the press. Today we would call his positions those of a typical bourgeois: pro-rights but also pro-capitalist. Economically conservative, Hugo votes to reextend the legal workday from 10 to 11 hours; he also opposes graduated taxes. Starting in 1849, however, he expresses his ambivalence and discomfort with his right-center group by frequent absences from roll call—in effect, by abstentions. And by June 1850, his dismay at severe restrictions on voting rights forces him to acknowledge himself a member of the opposition to the government. His signature on a

Democratic-Socialist manifesto in August 1851 finally allies him formally with a group whose policies he had been supporting for a year, the petit bourgeoisie (artisans, small shopkeepers, and farmers who own the means of production), at a time when the upper bourgeoisie (investors and the plutocracy) were abandoning the republic. Hugo himself prepared a selection of his political speeches during the summer of 1851: his notes for a preface declare that "for a long time, I thought the Republic was only a political vehicle. . . . I didn't realize that it partook of that essential, absolute truth of which all principles are composed. The Republic is a principle. The Republic is a right. The Republic is the very embodiment of progress."[6]

Most prophetic among Hugo's speeches during this period were his proposals for a United States of Europe. In the European Enlightenment of the eighteenth century, William Penn and Immanuel Kant had already advanced this idea. And in the mid-1820s, at the Pan-American Conference in Panama, Simon Bolivar had advocated a "holy alliance of nations" in Latin America. Hugo at first merely imagined an alliance of France and Germany to ward off Russia and England on either side of the continent.[7] His preface to the play Les Burgraves (1843) also anticipates a united Europe (OC 6, 574).

Like Bolivar, Hugo found a live international forum when he chaired the Paris Peace Conference on 21 August 1849. "A day will come," he announced, "when war between Paris and London will seem as absurd as it would seem today between Rouen and Amiens. A day will come when you, nations of the continent, without losing your distinctive qualities and your glorious individuality, will form the European fellowship" (OC 7, 220; several ellipses not shown). Haranguing his rebel troops on the barricade in 1832, the idealized hero Enjolras of Les Misérables (1862) echoes Hugo's profession of faith in European unity.[8]

That Hugo was egocentric leaves no doubt. But a revisionist condemnation of his politics as patronizing and outmoded is one-sided; it scants his historical importance as a politician. True, his speeches as a representative of the Second Republic (1848–1851) are reactive. He does not initiate specific legislation to ensure a more equitable distribution of wealth. Instead, he appeals to benevolence, charity, and enlightened self-interest. But he opposed fundamental abuses of human rights. His opposition to the death penalty, deportation, censorship, limitation of suffrage to the wealthy, and church control of education was essential in shaping opinion at the time. Initially he did support the Loi Falloux in June 1849. (All printed versions change "I support it" to "I reserve the right to reexamine it.") But on 19 October 1849, he denounced government brutality; *L'Événement* turned against Louis-Napoléon on 25 October, and Hugo knowingly sacrificed proffered ambassadorships to Italy and Spain—perhaps the chance of a cabinet ministry as well—through his growing opposition to the government (Robb, 285–86). He often failed to win majority support, but his appeal to conscience provided a model that would later help guide the Third Republic. By avoiding excessive topicality, he gave his moral protests lasting general import.

His opposition hardened when Louis-Napoléon had himself legally elected emperor, by a 10 to 1 margin, on 2 December 1851. Because of their protests, Hugo's two sons were arrested and thrown in jail. A warrant was issued for Hugo's arrest; police came to his house in his absence. He fled to Belgium and then to the islands of Jersey (from which he was later expelled) and Guernsey in the English Channel.

In exile, Hugo became an active satirist in both prose and poetry. First he published the polemical tract *Napoléon le petit* during his initial rush of indignation. The tract appeared in print in Brussels two days after Hugo's arrival in Jersey, on 5 August 1852. It was smuggled into France bound inside prayer book covers, buried in bales of hay, sewn inside the linings of women's clothing, and sealed inside plaster busts of Napoleon III. It was carried across the channel in balloons. Forty thousand copies were circulating by the end of 1852, read widely in secret meetings in France and copied by hand. Extraordinary police security and border searches failed to stop the flow (Robb, 318–23).

Les Châtiments

Then Hugo returned to his strongest genre, poetry, to castigate Napoleon III at leisure. The result was *Les Châtiments* (Chastisements, 1853). His major model was the Roman satirist Juvenal (ca. 60–140 C.E.), who had denounced the vices of imperial Rome. Hugo repeatedly referred to him and dedicated one poem of the *Châtiments* to him as well.[9] But he also creates his own repertory of satiric devices. To avoid lulling the reader into the passive contemplation of a lush spectacle, Hugo becomes unwontedly sober in his use of color, synesthesia (the combination of more than one sense in a single impression), and metaphor. Like Berthold Brecht in his epic theater, Hugo wants to alienate his readers from the sociopolitical order he depicts so that they will be more inclined to judge its tyranny and to engage in an intellectual and political struggle. The usual relationship one finds between the ode poet and society has been reversed. No longer an official supporter of what is most commendable in the social order, one who denounces and ritually expels the scapegoat, the poet himself becomes the exile, the anti-self of the society that has expelled him. Sarcastic antiphrasis (saying the opposite of what you mean) for a time preserves the illusion of the reversal of values, until near the end of many poems the author reveals himself as an avenging prophet.

Hugo finds in Napoleon III's Second Empire a total perversion of values. "Le mal prend tout à coup la figure du bien" [Evil suddenly wears the face of good] ("À Juvenal," OP 2, 6.13.170). "One of the things that will most painfully astonish the people of the future is that . . . laws were made to protect what all human laws, in agreement with all divine laws, have in all ages called crimes," he says in his preface (5).

The frame poems "Nox" and "Lux" (Night and Light) use Latin titles to recall not only the language of Juvenal but also the language of the Bible and the Catholic Mass as Hugo knew them before Vatican II. Those titles contrast darkness-ignorance-evil with light-knowledge-goodness according to Hugo's familiar antithetical symbolism. But within that framework, his thought develops differently than in the earlier and later visionary odes. He uses antiphrasis continually to say that what is bad is good. The title of each of the first six books of poems sarcastically praises the accomplishments of the empire: "La Société est sauvée; L'Ordre est rétabli; La Famille est restaurée; La Religion est glorifiée; L'Autorité est sacrée; La Stabilité est assurée" [Society is saved; Order is reestablished; The Family is restored; Religion is glorified; Authority is sacred; Stability is assured]. Only in the title of the last book does a broad pun give away the game: "Les Sauveurs se sauveront" [The Saviors will save themselves/run away]. In many poems, he apparently encourages evil and complaisantly reports its triumph before introducing a brusque refutation of it at the end.

The liminal "Nox," for example, starts by urging on the furtive usurper-prince. The poet offers him an army that is only waiting for a highwayman so that they can make an emperor of him. Napoleon III speaks in the third of the nine books, vaingloriously calling himself superior to his uncle. Not until book 6 does Hugo directly insult him. And only in the last book does Hugo summon his own muse:

Toi qu'aimait Juvénal, gonflé de lave ardente,
Toi dont la clarté luit dans l'œil fixe de Dante,
Muse Indignation! viens, dressons maintenant,
Dressons sur cet empire heureux et rayonnant,
Et sur cette victoire au tonnerre échappée,
Assez de piloris pour faire une épopée!

                                                        (18)

[You whom the volcanic Juvenal loved,
You whose brightness beams from Dante's fixed glare,
Muse Indignation! come, let us erect,
Erect on that empire's prosperity,
On that victory that escaped God's wrath,
Pillories enough for an epic poem!]

This conclusion reduplicates the structure of the entire poem: evil's triumph followed by verbal condemnation. To name the "Muse Indignation" with a *métaphore maxima,* a juxtaposition of noun with noun foreign to normal French syntax, associates her syntactically with the transcendent inspiration she represents connotatively: her name escapes the trite structures of language just as her meaning transcends the widespread but deluded social acceptance of Napoleon's regime.

"À l'obéissance passive" (In praise of passive obedience) shapes an entire poem with antiphrasis: Hugo ironically praises the undesirable quality of blind respect for authority.[10] Corrupt leaders have so perverted the French soldiers that

Le meurtre est pour eux la victoire;
Leur œil, par l'ivresse endormi,
Prend le déshonneur pour la gloire
Et les Français pour l'ennemi.
                                                        (59)

[Murder for them is victory;
Stupefied in a drunken sleep,
They mistake dishonor for fame
And see the French as enemies.]

Napoleon III invites his generals to execute the coup d'état that brings him to absolute power by driving out legally elected representatives of democratic government. When he says that he will pay well, they accept; Vidocq (a famous criminal turned police chief), Hugo comments, would have refused. A similar movement of thought, placing the emperor lower than the lowest, occurs in "L'Égout de Rome" (The Sewers of Rome) (7.4). The poet shows us the sewers, lists the foulest forms of decay to be found there, and finds the most disgusting debris in a heap of decomposed refuse that once might have been the carcass of a dog—or of an emperor. Hell itself, Hugo speculates elsewhere (3.6, "À l'autre Président" [To the Other President, 54]), might be too proud to admit the imperial scoundrels.

Hugo dramatizes antiphrasis by allowing the villains of the *Châtiments* to speak for themselves as he had done earlier in "La Bande noire" (The Vandals) of the *Odes,* his famous condemnation of those who despoil historical monuments. The Jesuit anti-selves of "Ad majorem dei gloriam" (To the greater glory of God) (1.7), grotesque caricatures, vaunt their power and influence for the first 64 lines before the Lord retorts in the last two:

> "Nous régnerons. La tourbe obéit comme l'onde.
> Nous serons tout-puissants, nous régirons le monde;
> Nous posséderons tout: force, gloire, et bonheur;
> Et nous ne craindrons rien, n'ayant ni foi ni règles . . . —"
> —Quand vous habiteriez la montagne des aigles,
> Je vous arracherais de là, dit le Seigneur!

> ["We will reign. The turf obeys like the waves.
> All-powerful, we shall direct the world;
> We shall possess all: strength, happiness, fame;
> And we fear nothing, lacking faith or law . . . —"
> —Were you to live with eagles on the mount,
> I would snatch you from there, answers the Lord!]

In "Paroles d'un conservateur à propos d'un perturbateur" (A Conservative's Words Concerning an Agitator) (7.11), the Pharisaic temple scribe complains throughout the poem about a rabble-rouser. Only in the last half line is that person revealed as Jesus.

Hugo sees the Second Empire regressing to a medieval divine-right monarchy and ultramontane religious order (one subservient to the pope). Hugo's darkness is priestly and feudal. His light is capitalist democracy. For the time being, he cannot see the people as the mainspring of progress because they voted overwhelmingly for the empire. Therefore progress must depend on providential grace, which permits scientific progress somehow destined to make the world impossible for tyrants. In terms of intellectual content, Hugo's moral opposition to Napoleon III ultimately amounts to little more than a thunderous acceptance of a fait accompli, the revolution of 1789. Hugo urges a paternalistic benevolence that will induce the rich to share with the people the profits of technological advance.

In short, the battle that *Les Châtiments* stages against the empire does not really occur in an historical theater: it consists in the false claims of Hugo's political adversaries being drowned out by overwhelming messages from the supernatural order. Like sentinels, the poet's words sound the alarm against oppression:

> Le banni, debout sur la grève
>
> . . . .
>
> Parlera dans l'ombre tout haut;
>
> Et ses paroles qui menacent,
> Ses paroles, dont l'éclair luit,
> Seront comme des mains qui passent
> Tenant des glaives dans la nuit.
>
> . . . .
>
> Elles crieront: honte aux infâmes,
> Aux oppresseurs, aux meurtriers!
> Elles appelleront les âmes
> Comme on appelle des guerriers!
>
> . . . .
>
> Et si ceux qui vivent s'endorment,
> Ceux qui sont morts s'éveilleront.
>   (1.1.19–20)

Banished, standing upon the strand

. . . .

He shall speak aloud in the shade;

And his words that are threatening,
His words, in which the lightening shines,
Shall be like many hands that pass
Holding aloft swords in the night.

. . . .

They cry: Shame to the infamous,
To oppressors, to murderers!
They shall call forth the sleeping souls
As one might summon warriors!

. . . .

And if the living fall asleep,
Then those who are dead shall awake.]

Later, his words are transformed to a brand marking the criminal
Napoleon III on the shoulder with the stigma of historical disgrace
("L'Homme a ri" [The Man Laughed], 3.2.67). "L'Expiation" (Expiation) ends with two words of flame, "DIX-HUIT BRUMAIRE" (9 November
1799, the day that Napoleon took the decisive steps that allowed him
the next day to dissolve the revolutionary directorate and found a con-
sulship, a triumvirate that led to his dictatorship), inscribed by a supernatural hand as at Belshazzar's feast, and burning before the captive
soul of Napoleon I in the darkness. The meaning is that the first
emperor's high-handed actions set a precedent for the present coup
d'état and caused the ignominious decline of France that followed. Elsewhere, Hugo imagines God himself marking Napoleon III with a word
of definitive condemnation: "[T]on sceptre est de l'argile. / Dieu, qui t'a
mis au coche, écrit sur toi: fragile" [Your scepter is of clay. / Putting you
in the kiln, God writes on you: "Fragile"] (untitled, 3.12.87). Replacing
a false vision with a true one, these surprise endings create the shock of
satire. Hugo makes his words come alive with supernatural power, so

that they serve as effective performatives: writing them makes something happen. Like a prophet, he gives himself the power to judge and condemn.[11]

The subtlety of both Hugo's earlier and later political writing has often been underestimated. True, in the heat of political battle he reverts to a bipolar distinction between good and evil. But he saves *Les Châtiments* from becoming mere invective by deploying the archetype of Inversion—here, in the form that what seemed good, proves bad. The device of Inversion recalls Christ's Beatitudes and the prophetic voices of the Bible.

Does Hugo achieve effective satire? The distinguished, articulate critics Jean-Marie Gleize and Guy Rosa have disparaged *Les Châtiments* as lacking historical relevance, either because the collection is so self-centered, or because it is politically naive and condescending.

> The personal-historical "I" is affirmed only to be obliterated or transcended by an abstract-ideal "I." . . . [Hugo] completes the transformation of his self into an historical role embodying resistance to despotism. . . . Several signs show that the text of the *Châtiments* indeed is often self-referential: the number of poems that speak only about the poet; the location of Book IV that [situates the origins of the poet's historical role as opposition leader] at the center of the book; the structure of the collection that leads it to conclude with the "I" of "Ultima Verba" [the last word]; and, finally, many poems that, wherever they begin, end by presenting the figure or the gesture of the avenging poet so that, like that of the book, their trajectory imitates the trajectory of their creation [others' crimes provoking the poet's denunciation].[12]

The Marxist Pierre Barbéris complains that Hugo accepts capitalism and bourgeois democracy without question. Hugo would see Napoleon III not as the watchdog of capitalism but as a regression to the Middle Ages. Because the people voted for the empire by an overwhelming margin, Hugo considers them not yet enlightened. God and thinkers must make the revolution, which the people will then *signify*, without having participated. In a more humane society, the proletariat will be reconciled with its natural masters. Grace, not economic forces, is the motor of history as Hugo sees it. Therefore he can envision only a moral opposition to evil, Barbéris concludes.[13] But Hugo's novel *Les Misérables* and his political career after exile give the lie to Barbéris's interpretation.

The Late Novels: *Les Travailleurs de la mer*

Hugo himself once claimed that 20 years of good, free, mandatory education would be the last word, and raise the dawn. Having become a utopian socialist like M. Madeleine in *Les Misérables,* Hugo thinks that salaries will increase naturally as do profits, and that the dynamism of capital expansion will eventually resolve the problems of working conditions and urban poverty. You will have recognized the contemporary right-wing "trickle-down theory" of economics. In 1862, however, a true proletariat had not yet formed. Labor union movements grew influential only 20 years later. Hugo still thinks that guidance and enlightenment must descend on the people from "above," from the intelligentsia.

Because these works do not deal immediately with the contemporary political struggle between republic and empire, I have reserved the next two chapters to treat Hugo's prophetic verse epics *Dieu, La Légende des siècles,* and *La Fin de Satan,* mainly written during the latter 1850s, and the great novel *Les Misérables* (1862) that followed. I speculate that Hugo's increasing loneliness as his family spent more and more time in France, and his suppressed desire to accept amnesty, led to his breaking off the composition of *La Fin de Satan,* never completed, to concentrate on *Les Misérables.* As Hugo himself said, the latter work allows him to make a nostalgic, imaginary return to Paris, depicting the city as it was during his early years there. The last two major works of the exile period, the novels *Les Travailleurs de la mer* (*The Toilers of the Sea,* 1866) and *L'Homme qui rit* (*The Man Who Laughs,* 1869), unduly neglected by most critics, have been richly analyzed by Grant (1969) and by Brombert (1984) in terms of symbolic and mythic structure. Lacking space to do these novels justice, we can nevertheless suggest how they indirectly reveal the intersection of the personal and the political in Hugo.

Les Travailleurs de la mer is a novel of renunciation. In it Hugo turns his attention from Paris, the site of a longed-for return, to the channel island of Guernsey, where he actually lives. The substantial opening section, an essay on the channel islands, expresses gratitude to the land that has sheltered him in exile, by lovingly describing its landscape, flora, people, and customs. The whole is a great regional novel, which, if we did Hugo justice, ought to rank with classics such as Jean Giono's *Colline* (1929; on the Basses-Alpes), Marie-Thérèse Humbert's *Un fils d'orage* (1992; on the Camargue), Louis Pergaud's *De Goupil à Margot*

(1910; on the Doubs), Henri Pourrat's *Vent de mars* (1941; on the Auvergne), and many a Québecois or Francophone Caribbean work. A lyrical style like Hugo's is particularly suited to such a celebration of place.

On this rich tapestry, Hugo weaves two converging stories, one of crime and one of love. The enterprising Lethierry has established the first steamboat service in the region. His scrupulously honest captain, Sieur Clubin, has long awaited the occasion to profit from his mask of virtue. When a considerable fortune has been stolen from Lethierry, Clubin tracks down the thief and recovers the money at gunpoint, carefully returning the small change that is not due after calculating principle and a reasonable rate of interest. He then tricks his alcoholic helmsman into getting drunk, arranges a wreck on a reef near Guernsey, and plans to feign drowning. After hiding among the rocks, Clubin will swim to shore unobserved, wearing his money belt, and arrange a secret passage overseas. But a huge octopus seizes and drowns him, leaving his carcass to attract the crabs on which it itself feeds.

Meanwhile, the reclusive fisherman Gilliat has fallen in love with Lethierry's pretty, superficial daughter Déruchette, after seeing her playfully write his name in the snow. Once the steamboat, *La Durande,* is wrecked, Lethierry promises his daughter in marriage to any man who can salvage the engine. Only Gilliat takes up this challenge, without telling anyone. He spends weeks in heroic struggle on the isolated reef, working with primitive, improvised tools, starving, and withstanding a fierce storm as well as an assault by the octopus.[14] Robb has called this novel "a metaphor for the nineteenth century—technical progress, creative genius and hard work overcoming the immanent evil of the material world" (414).

After defeating the octopus, Gilliat discovers Clubin's body with the money belt. He returns both the engine and the money to Lethierry, who insists on making Gilliat his new captain, and on marrying him to his daughter right away. She, however, has fallen in love with a handsome young minister new to the island. (Gilliat had earlier saved the minister from drowning; the man was looking at the ocean from a natural stone armchair, not realizing that if he stayed on it, he would be trapped and submerged by the rising tide). She has said nothing of her feelings to her father, but Gilliat perceives them. He selflessly arranges their secret marriage and elopement; he even provides the young woman with the trousseau his mother had given him for his own bride. Blinded by intense egotistical happiness, the young couple accepts these selfless gifts without understanding what is happening, and they depart. Then Gilliat sits in the stone armchair and, as the tide rises, watches the couple's ferry sail away until he drowns.

This story seems to sublimate Hugo's political and personal feelings at the same time. Renouncing his own happiness, from afar he longingly, benevolently watches over both a wife (see his many affectionate letters to her) and a country too shallow to be able to appreciate his extraordinary devotion. Hugo's legendary promiscuity throughout his later life should not obscure the material reality of his marriage. Like Gilliat laboring to salvage the steam engine, Hugo worked hard to provide a comfortable life for his family. The Hugos remained together although Adèle had refused to have sex with Victor for decades, whereas his own father and mother, likewise mutually unfaithful, had been legally separated. Victor thus proved more loyal than his father. Gilliat's looking across the ocean at the conclusion may well reflect the situation of the historical author's contemplating the distant shores of France, and the departing wife and children who were ever more frequently abandoning him to go back there.

The Late Novels: *L'Homme qui rit*

Gilliat's suicide reveals what psychoanalysts would call a "melancholic" attitude: turning anger at the other against the self. The hero of *L'Homme qui rit* (1869) likewise allows himself to be swallowed up by the water (a clear suggestion of the effects of voluntary exile on an sea island). Here, however, the emotional problems posed by renunciation of the homeland have been sublimated more thoroughly. The setting is seventeenth-century England, farther from France in both time and space than *Les Travailleurs de la mer* had been.

To avenge himself on an exiled duke, the king of England orders the man's son to be kidnapped and sold to *comprachicos* (in Spanish, "purchasers of children"—apparently an invention of Hugo's), who skillfully mutilate children in order to display them at fairs. Little Gwynplaine's mouth is slit from ear to ear, leaving him with a ghastly permanent grin. Pursued by the police, the gypsylike *comprachicos* flee England by ship, leaving the child alone in the snow to die. He survives; rescues the blind infant Déa, whose mother has just perished in the winter wilderness; and finds his way to the wagon where the traveling performer Ursus ("bear" in Latin) lives. With his pet wolf Homo ("man" in Latin), this eccentric hermit lives by performing strange allegorical dramas as he journeys from town to town. He trains Gwynplaine and Déa as actors.

Perversely tempted by his deformity and by the social degradation involved in having sex with a mountebank, the sadistic virgin duchess Josiane tries to seduce Gwynplaine until suddenly she learns that the piquant appeal of social difference has disappeared. His true identity is finally recognized. A bottle containing the confession of the *comprachicos,* who wanted to make peace with God before being drowned in a storm, has found its way to shore and attracted the attention of the authorities. Gwynplaine is restored to his rightful rank as duke. He gives an impassioned speech in the House of Lords, but because of his appearance and his message, his appeals for justice for the people provoke only laughter. (Hugo's many futile appeals to the conservative French peerage, speeches often drowned out by hostile shouts, ground this scene in his personal experience.) Gwynplaine returns to Déa to find her dying in a cabin of a boat that Ursus plans to take to leave the country. After an exalted farewell, as if following a celestial apparition, Gwynplaine steps off the bow of the ship to drown and be reunited with Déa in the afterlife. This conclusion, an idealized reunion of chaste lovers, replaces frustrating realities with wish-fulfilling fantasies. It may well have been inspired in part by Théophile Gautier's novella *Spirite* (1866).

John Porter Houston has taxed *L'Homme qui rit* with being outlandish and incoherent: but it is supposed to be so.[15] Because of his beautiful, ornate language and his bombast, many critics read Hugo in dead earnest, not realizing that he is often playful. This novel exemplifies romantic irony (defensively mocking the illusions that one cherishes, as do Byron, Heine, and Musset). In part intended as a parodic medley, *L'Homme qui rit* deliberately invents grotesque names for many characters. Like the surgical mutilation of Gwynplaine as opposed to the natural deformity of Quasimodo, those names present the grotesque with a wink; they are self-conscious. At the opposite pole, idealization is likewise parodied by exaggeration. "Déa" is a playful feminization of the Latin *Deus,* "god." Several scenes, such as Ursus's interrogation by the ecclesiastical authorities on suspicion of heresy (one recalls a similar ludicrous scene in *Notre-Dame de Paris* when the deaf Quasimodo is tried by a deaf judge), are broadly comical. And by way of a memorial, Hugo slyly but affectionately digs an elbow in the literary ribs of a late friend (deceased 1863) who always *did* take himself too seriously—Alfred de Vigny. The *comprachicos'* bottle with its elaborate message and its improbable discovery by the right persons mocks Vigny's idealistic poem in *Les Destinées* (Destinies), "La Bouteille à la mer" (The Bottle Cast into the Sea: "On it God lays His hand, to guide it to its port"). Ursus's rolling hut evokes the shepherd's wagon in Vigny's "La Maison du Berger" (The Shepherd's Hut). Both in her real role as idealized companion and in her theatrical role of spirit, Déa recalls Vigny's fictive Eva, as well as the otherworldliness of Vigny's climacteric poem in *Les Destinées;* "L'Esprit pur" (The Pure Spirit). The romantic ironist longs and laughs in the same breath. Hugo, in the 19th year of an exile that seemed to have no end, realizes here, as his ironic title suggests, that one way to solve a problem is to make fun of it.

The Years of Transition: 1870–1875

Meanwhile, although in exile, Hugo did not neglect his international political role. He protested the execution of the abolitionist John Brown in the United States in 1859 and accurately predicted the American Civil War. Hugo thus became a national hero in Haiti, the first black republic to emerge from slavery (in 1804; see Robb, 371). He has been credited with having the death penalty removed from the constitutions of Geneva, Portugal, and the Republic of Colombia. In Mexico, then occupied by France, French army positions were bombarded with leaflets of quotations from *Napoléon le petit* (Robb, 401–3).

Hugo's politics in the 1870s, after he returned from exile, deserve more attention than they have received. Like the romantic poet Lamartine, who had led the provisional government for three months during the 1848 revolution, Hugo now had a brief starring role in *la grande histoire* (major historical events). That two poets could exercise such authority in politics represents a sharp contrast with the United States, where intellectuals and creative writers have far less prestige.

Hugo now considered himself *le fonctionnaire de Dieu* (God's civil servant), above political parties. He came back to a country at war, rashly declared against Prussia in the summer of 1870. As soon as Emperor Napoleon III had been captured at Sedan (2 September), a republic was declared in Paris (4 September), but the war continued. Hugo's appeals to both the Prussians and the French for peace, since both had now defeated "a common enemy" (Napoleon III), went unheeded. Paris was besieged until the French surrender on 28 January 1871; the inhabitants, Hugo included, survived by eating rats, dogs, and zoo animals. But he was enormously popular during this national crisis: his picture was sold everywhere in the streets; there were plans to rename the

Boulevard Haussmann after him. With the end of censorship, the first French edition of the anti-imperial *Châtiments* finally could appear, in October 1870. Twenty-two thousand copies, extraordinary for a book of poetry, had been sold by mid-December, when his Paris printer ran out of ink.

In February, receiving more votes than anyone but Louis Blanc (a socialist historian and workers' rights advocate), Hugo was elected deputy from Paris to the Constituant Assembly (appointed to negotiate an armistice and to draft a constitution for the Third Republic). This body met in Bordeaux. It contained 400 royalists divided among various pretenders to the throne, and 200 disciplined Republicans. Hugo served for only a month (8 February to 8 March) and then resigned in protest. By the end, only he, Blanc, and Edgar Quinet (another exile of conscience during the empire, who shared Hugo's anticlerical views) were advocating continued resistance to Prussia. By a vote of 540 to 130, the Assembly accepted Adolphe Thiers's policy of appeasement. The Treaty of Frankfurt of 10 May 1871 stipulated that France would pay a heavy indemnity and cede the province of Alsace and much of Lorraine (rich in coal) to Prussia.

Hugo returned to Paris, where his son Charles promptly died. The funeral occurred on 18 March, the same day the revolutionary Paris Commune began. It was more a patriotic than a Communist movement, although it defended the rights of workers. The Communards did not want to surrender to Prussia. Thiers's army attacked the city. Similar movements in other French cities quickly collapsed. Deploring the violence on both sides, Hugo took the opportunity to go to Belgium to settle his son's estate, and he remained there. Meanwhile both sides committed atrocities. The Communards executed three Versaillais (Thiers's forces) for every Fédéré (Communard) who was killed; they also executed many clerics, including the archbishop of Paris. When General MacMahon's troops forced their way into Paris on 21 May, a week of bloody reprisals followed; more people were summarily executed than during the entire Reign of Terror; children and pregnant women went before the firing squads. In an open letter to *L'Indépendence belge* of 27 May, Hugo offered asylum to any refugee from the Commune. But the Catholics had recently come to power in Belgium; the refugees were no longer accepted. That evening a mob (including the son of the minister of the interior) stoned Hugo's house for two hours without police intervention. Hugo was soon expelled from the country and went to Luxembourg.

He returned to Paris to fight for amnesty and for the abolition of the death penalty but failed to be elected to the Legislative Assembly in 1872. Some detractors considered him "the quasi-official candidate of the Commune" (*Le Français*, 4 January 1872). For a year, he withdrew to Guernsey, the Channel island where he had spent his exile. His efforts to win amnesty for the Communards would fail until 1880. But after this agitated period of the Second Empire and the Commune, now freed from the necessity of opposing a totalitarian regime, he finally had the leisure to consolidate his attitude toward France's historical past and to look to the future.

The Late Novels: *Quatrevingt-treize*

His first enterprise of this kind—and the last great work he completed—was the novel *Quatrevingt-treize* (1874) treating the Terror, and the royalist counter-rebellion against the Revolution, in the Vendée (Brittany, Anjou, Poitou, 1793–1795). The peasants of Western France on both sides of the Loire had resisted the suppression of freedom of religion by the Revolution. Throughout France, 20,000 souls were executed during the Terror; the revolutionary *colonnes infernales* sent to suppress the Vendée uprising burned villages in vain. Always strongly opposed to capital punishment, Hugo nevertheless came to believe that the Terror could be justified by recalling the 15 centuries of feudal oppression that it brought to an end.[16] As the hero Gauvain would say, "Beneath a scaffolding of barbarism a temple of civilization is being constructed," (368). He absolves the present moment "because it's a tempest. A tempest always knows what it is doing. For every oak blasted by lightning, how many forests are cleansed! Civilization was sick with plague; this hurricane frees it. The storm perhaps is not sufficiently selective. Could it do otherwise? Its task of sweeping clean is so arduous! Faced with the horror of the miasma, I can understand the fury of the blast" (371–72).

To explain the peasants' support of the king during the Vendée, Hugo's thesis seems to be that they resisted the Revolution out of blind loyalty, a habit created by 1,500 years of subservience. Powerful satire worthy of Voltaire expounds this view near the beginning of *Quatrevingt-treize:* a company of Parisian soldiers discovers a dazed refugee woman with three children in the woods. Her husband has been killed and her home burned. She has no surviving relatives, nowhere to go. When interrogated about her family to make sure that she is not a spy, she answers:

—My family was farmers. My father was ill and couldn't work because he had been beaten by the orders of the master, his master, our master, and that was a kindness, because my father had poached a rabbit, an act for which one was condemned to death; but the master had pardoned him and said: Just give him a hundred blows with a staff and my father was crippled.

—Go on.

—My grand-father was a Protestant. Our priest had him sent to the galleys. I was just a little girl.

—Go on.

—My husband's father sold salt without paying the royal tax. The king had him hung.

—And what does your husband do?

—Just now, he was fighting.

—For whom?

—For the king.

—And then [after the king was guillotined]?

—Why, for his master, of course.

—And then [after your master fled the country]?

—Why, for the priest, of course. (30–31)

Hugo underlines the irony with an astonished reaction by a soldier, a bald summary of the above, just one page later.

The Glory Years: 1876–1885

In 1876 Hugo returned to government when he was elected Sénateur de Paris. "Cohabitation," so much discussed as a striking novelty in France under President Mitterrand (1981–1995) and afterward, existed in Hugo's day too. The Republicans had a substantial majority in the Chamber of Deputies (analogous to the U.S. House of Representatives); the Monarchists had a slim majority in the Senate. This time, Hugo appealed to enlightened self-interest in opposing deportation and advocating amnesty for former Communards. The skilled workers thus lost, he argued, were essential to maintain France's economic base.

Hugo had one of his finest hours in May 1877, when Marshall MacMahon (the hero/villain of the suppression of the Commune) attempted to dissolve the government and was close to becoming a dictator. Hugo led the opposition. The Senate endorsed dissolution by 20 votes, but Hugo directed the fight to organize a coalition of the Left, and its success in the reelections was such that MacMahon hesitated to attempt a coup d'état. He was to flee in disgrace two years later. Meanwhile, on 1 October, Hugo reworked the unpublished manuscript of *L'Histoire d'un Crime*, the analysis of Louis-Napoléon's coup in 1851, warning the French not to let history repeat itself. In three weeks, 120,000 copies were sold. Hugo's book played a major role in saving the republic.

At last, in the protracted debate during which Hugo's final political speech was given (3 July 1880; see also 28 February 1879), amnesty for former Communards was approved. For the rest of his life, Hugo was revered as the living embodiment of the republic and its liberties. In 1881, 600,000 Parisians paraded beneath his window on the Avenue d'Eylau (a section of which was later to be named after Hugo) to celebrate the beginning of his 80th year. When he died in 1885, the government attempted to limit the size of the crowds by scheduling the funeral procession on a Monday, and routing it through the most conservative right-wing neighborhoods. Nevertheless, more than a million joined the triumphal procession from the Arc de Triomphe to the Panthéon. (Some say two million, more than the entire population of the city.) Emergency legislation reconsecrated the Panthéon as a tomb for great men, for the first time in a century. There Hugo's body was laid among the French leaders honored "by a grateful country," and there you can find his memorial today.

Chapter Six
Grief Work: *Les Contemplations*

Hugo's Personal Religion

Like Baudelaire's *Les Fleurs du Mal* (1857, 1861), the other great verse collection of nineteenth-century French literature, Hugo's *Les Contemplations* (1856) is a spiritual autobiography. Changing the dates of composition freely to create a symmetrical structure, Hugo divided the collection into two parts: "Autrefois" (Formerly), dated 1830 to 1843, and "Aujourd'hui" (Today), dated 1843 to 1856. He makes his daughter's accidental death by drowning in 1843 the pivotal event, suggesting that losing her shifted his attention from this life to the next.

In reality, Hugo's poetry had revealed visionary tendencies as early as 1828. What redirected his career in 1843 was less Léopoldine's death than his political ambitions. He came to want above all to become a Peer of France (a position analogous to membership in the British House of Lords), to emulate Chateaubriand as a public servant as well as a writer. From the time of Hugo's appointment in 1845 until his exile, he participated actively in government. Only afterward did he have leisure to reflect on his loss.

From 1853 to 1855, the spiritualist seances organized at Guernsey by his guest Delphine de Girardin (formerly Delphine Gay, a noteworthy poet) helped deepen his religious vision. The visiting spirits communicated by tapping on a small three-legged table set on a larger table around which the participants had gathered. Each letter of the alphabet was represented by a fixed number of taps. The seances were recorded for two years. Those spirits who came to speak included the souls of both dead and living persons—a cringing Napoleon III, Shakespeare, and Jesus Christ revealed the secrets of human destiny and of Providence. Hugo magnanimously corrected Shakespeare's versification for him. Skeptics say the entire household was so saturated with Hugolian poetry and ideas that unconsciously or not, they could readily produce Hugolian pronouncements even when the master himself was not attending a seance. His son Charles proved the best medium; Hugo himself was ineffectual in that role. But the authenticity of the messages is beside the point. As psychotherapy can benefit people by stimulating them to think creatively about their problems between sessions, so the seances encouraged Hugo to ponder our relationships with the spirit world: thus his system of beliefs developed.

His basic cosmology was "l'échelle des Êtres" (the Great Chain of Being; a notion that gave rise to P. T. Barnum's "missing link"), perfected by the mystical pagan thinker Plotinus in the early Christian era. Plotinus combined Plato's conception of God with Aristotle's notion of privation. Plato believed that a perfect God, free from "envy," allows all conceivable forms of being to exist. Aristotle believed that all existents were arranged in a hierarchy according to degrees of "privation." The more attributes they had, the higher they ranked. (This system theoretically leaves no place for an active supernatural principle of evil such as Satan.) To the static Great Chain of Being cosmology, Hugo added two dynamic elements inspired by the Cabala, the Jewish mystery religion of the Middle Ages. Because any being who could see God would be overwhelmed by His goodness and incapable of not doing His will, God ensured human free will and moral independence through an "occultation." He withdrew the fullness of His glory from the world of our senses. The stars are the masks of God; they will fall at the end of time.

Hugo embellished the notion of occultation with a belief in punitive reincarnation. He extended this idea beyond animals and plants: he believed that natural objects such as stones, and even artifacts such as nails could contain suffering, previously human souls. Unlike humans, all nonhumans, including angels, animals, plants, minerals, and artifacts, could see God, Hugo claimed. But all subhumans had to suffer passively in the purgatory of their ontological distance from God. At times, these lesser beings suffered further from the pain they were obliged to inflict involuntarily, owing to their very nature. The ravening wolf and the torturer's whip hate the evil that they do. Gradually and fitfully, however, all existents will reascend toward God, one day to be reintegrated into the divine essence from which they emanated at the moment of creation. The prophetic poet's mission is to preach the hope, prayer, and meritorious action that will hasten universal redemption.[1]

After Louis-Napoléon's coup d'état of 1851, the brief imprisonment of Hugo's sons, the arrest warrant directed at him, and his flight into exile, he must have thought that history had started going backward. To preserve the idea of a God who was the source of goodness, Hugo had to sacrifice the coherence of his cosmology by imagining a quasi-Manichaean

opposition in which Satan both caused and represented social ills. As the
Sibyl explains in *La Fin de Satan,* the Demon flutters restlessly back and
forth in his underground prison:

> A chaque mouvement de ses lourds ailerons,
> Pendant qu'il plane, il sort du monstre des fumées;
> Elles montent sur terre, et ce sont des armées;
> . . . .
> Ce sont des lois, des mœurs, et des religions.[2]

> [With each movement of his heavy pinions,
> While he hovers, smoke spurts forth from the Beast;
> It rises to earth, and forms armies there;
> . . . .
> It forms laws, customs, religious beliefs.]

But Hugo will reserve the Satan figure for the conclusion of *Les Contemplations* and for the third part of his visionary trilogy *Dieu, La Légende des
siècles,* and *La Fin de Satan.* First, as a political dissident in exile, he must
try to make sense of his own life.

To help us understand what it means to be a visionary poet or
prophet, Hugo frequently revives the topos (literary commonplace) of
the *liber mundi.* Creation is a book where God has inscribed His purpose for those who know how to read. The title "Nomen, Numen,
Lumen," for instance (The Name, The Spiritual Power, The Light)
(6.25), placed in *Les Contemplations* just before the supreme revelation
of "Ce que dit la Bouche d'ombre" (What the Mouth of Darkness
Says), depicts God naming himself to the just-created universe. He
calls out his name, "JEHOVAH!"; the seven letters form the seven stars
of the Big Dipper. In the physical world, they point to the True North
or *axis mundi* (the hub of the universe), and in the spiritual order, to
the Creator.

The Poet's Role

The poet being an apostle, Hugo's mission is to decipher Creation and
share with humankind what he has learned. This essential theme
appears from the beginning of *Les Contemplations.* Similarly to the first

section of Baudelaire's *Fleurs du Mal*, the first seven poems define the poet's role. In the introductory poem, Hugo contemplates a speedy ship sailing by, suspended between the abyss of the sky and the abyss of the sea. A mysterious voice encourages him:

> Poëte, tu fais bien! poëte au triste front,
>   Tu rêves près des ondes,
> Et tu tires des mers bien des choses qui sont
>   Sous les vagues profondes!

> La mer, c'est le Seigneur, que, misère ou bonheur,
>   Tout destin montre et nomme;
> Le vent, c'est le Seigneur; l'astre, c'est le Seigneur;
>   Le navire, c'est l'homme.—[3]

> [—Poet, you're doing well! With your sad brow,
>   You dream next to the waves,
> And from the seas you draw forth many things
>   Beneath the churning deep!

> The sea, that is the Lord, whom, pain or joy,
>   Every existence names;
> The wind is the Lord; the star is the Lord;
>   The ship, humanity.]

"À ma fille" (to my daughter), the first poem of the collection proper, shares the knowledge of Providence with her. She receives fatherly advice shortly before her marriage: "Dieu nous éclaire, à chacun de nos pas, / Sur ce qu'il est et sur ce que nous sommes" [God enlightens us, at our every step, / Concerning who He is and what we are] (OP 2, 488). The second poem, the untitled "Le poëte s'en va dans les champs" (The poet goes forth into the fields), shows the flowers flirtatiously greeting him; then the imposing trees respectfully bow like lawyers before a judge (489). (By using the Arabic words "ulémas" and "muphti" for these personages, Hugo suggests a vision that transcends the revelations of Christianity.) He communes with all nature; his forehead, transfigured like that of Moses descending from Mount Sinai, glows with spiri-

tual illumination. Note the two instances above of the archaic spelling
"poëte" instead of "poète." Like Alfred de Vigny, who also insisted on
the older spelling, Hugo uses it to associate the poet with a venerable
tradition beginning with the inspired authors of the Bible and of ancient
Greece.

Poems of Youth and Joy

"Autrefois," the first of the two main divisions of *Les Contemplations*, is
subdivided into the three books "Aurore," "L'Âme en fleur," and "Les
Luttes et les rêves" (Dawn; The Blossoming Soul; Struggles and
Dreams). These three titles reflect the dawning of a child's consciousness,
the joys of young love, and Hugo's early literary career as leader of the
upstart romantic movement. The first and second books of the *Contemplations* are filled with charming poems celebrating love and the beauties
of nature: "Lise," "Vere Novo" (At the return of spring), "La Coccinelle"
(The Ladybug), "Vieille Chanson du jeune temps" (An old song from
when the earth was young), and "Premier Mai" (The First of May). They
owe much to the pastoral tradition in classical Greek and Roman
poetry—to Theocritus and Anacreon, Horace and Vergil. Critics seldom
pay these poems much attention, but they are rich in meaning despite
their apparent simplicity. Consider the untitled second poem of book 2:

> Mes vers fuiraient, doux et frêles,
> Vers votre jardin si beau,
> Si mes vers avaient des ailes,
> Des ailes comme l'oiseau.
>
> Ils voleraient, étincelles,
> Vers votre foyer qui rit,
> Si mes vers avaient des ailes,
> Des ailes comme l'esprit.
>
> Près de vous, purs et fidèles,
> Ils accourraient nuit et jour
> Si mes vers avaient des ailes,
> Des ailes comme l'amour.
>
> (537)

[My delicate poems would flee
Toward your garden, so lovely,
If only my poems had wings,
If they had wings like the birds.

They would fly like fleeting sparks,
Hovering round your cheerful hearth,
If only my poems had wings,
If they had wings like the mind.

Close to you, faithful and pure,
They would hasten night and day,
If only my poems had wings,
If they had the wings of love.]

The last two lines of each stanza form a refrain with only one word changed each time. Such simplicity and so much repetition suggests naïveté and innocence. (In the event, this poem probably was dedicated to Mme Biard, a married woman with whom Hugo had a five-year affair while deceiving his devoted mistress, Juliette Drouet.) The heptasyllabic (seven-syllable) lines conform to the fleeting movement that dominates the poem. They do not divide into the two even parts that might suggest a walking pace; they cannot plod. Flight may also be suggested by the dense accumulation of *vs* shaped like birds on the wing. Like Charles Nodier before him and Stéphane Mallarmé after him, Hugo saw hieroglyphic meanings in letter shapes. The verse anticipates by decades the airy imparisyllabic virtuosity of the impressionist poet Verlaine, who owes much to Hugo. The crossed rhyme (*abab*) effectively mimics a conflict between the poet's wish to be near the loved woman (expressed by the first two lines of each stanza, in the conditional tense) and the frustrating reality of their separation. In conformity to the traditional literary portrait, first the loved woman's physical attributes—her beauty—and then her cheerful personality are suggested. Hugo makes the implied description of her stand out by placing the key words at the ends of the lines: he says "jardin si beau" instead of the ordinary "beau jardin" ("beau" in French is one of few adjectives that ordinarily fall before its noun), and "foyer qui rit" instead of the cliché "riant foyer." "Riant" is a common adjective to describe an agreeable landscape; changing it into a relative clause makes the hearth seem to come alive.

Being the source of warmth and light, "foyer" has strong emotional connotations in French; "foyers" can refer to how many homes or families
there are in a village; the "foyer" is something you risk your life to defend.
A seductive speech, the poem moves steadily toward greater intimacy: first outside the house, then inside, then near the woman
addressed. More subtly, the time of day suggested in each stanza has the
same effect: first day, then evening, then night. Courtship leads to
spending the night with her. As if the poet were gaining confidence,
after the "rime pauvre" of the first stanza ("beau" and "oiseau" share
only one pronounced sound) he uses "rimes suffisantes" (sharing two
pronounced sounds) for the rest of the poem. Given an appropriate context, fuller rhymes suggest greater stability and assurance. The last
word makes an indirect avowal of love and offers a surprising, delicate
compliment: each stanza associates the flying poems with some detail
appropriate to their surroundings. It is natural for a garden to be filled
with birds; it is natural for sparks to fly up from a hearth; and it is natural for anyone near the woman in question to be in love with her. A
winged love, moreover, suggests Cupid, the attendant of Venus, the
goddess of love. By implication, the loved woman is compared to the
goddess.

Hugo's Mystical Vision in Books 1–3

After depicting his childhood and youth, Hugo begins to reintroduce
visionary subjects in the third book of *Les Contemplations*. The first poem
of book 3, "Écrit sur un exemplaire de *La Divina Commedia*" (Written on
a copy of Dante's *Divine Comedy*), outlines Hugo's dynamic view of the
Great Chain of Being as a continuous hierarchy of existents. One
ascends it involuntarily, step by step, drawn by God's grace. One
evening Hugo has a vision: he sees a man passing, wearing a great cloak
like that of a Roman consul. Like the winged messengers of revelation in
Dieu, the man seems a dark spot against the brightness of the sky. He
fixes Hugo with a bright, deep, fierce gaze:

> Et me dit:—J'ai d'abord été, dans les vieux âges,
> Une haute montagne emplissant l'horizon;
> Puis, âme encore aveugle et brisant ma prison,
> Je montai d'un degré dans l'échelle des êtres,

Je fus un chêne, et j'eus des autels et des prêtres,
Et je jetai des bruits étranges dans les airs;
Puis je fus un lion rêvant dans les déserts,
Parlant à la nuit sombre avec sa voix grondante;
Maintenant, je suis homme, et je m'appelle Dante.

(568)

[And said: At first I was, in ancient times,
A high mountain that filled the horizon;
Then, a blind soul, I broke from my prison,
And rose one step on the Great Chain of Being,
I was a sacred oak, worshipped by priests,
And who cast strange noises into the air;
Next, a lion dreaming in the desert,
Speaking to the night with its booming voice;
Now I am a man; Dante is my name.]

Although Hugo usually dramatizes expiatory reincarnation as the principle that elevates us on the Great Chain of Being, here sin is not at issue.[4] Dante began life as an imposing mountain. Then Providence drew him upward toward God. Dante's earlier forms reveal that he was predestined to greatness. Throughout his successive existences, he became ever more articulate. Now he is one of the rare prophets who can see and reveal God.[5]

The third book of *Les Contemplations,* "Les Luttes et les rêves," introduces extensive social critique. For example, "Melancholia," the second poem, denounces absentee fathers, the poverty that fosters prostitution and child labor, cruelty to animals, a legal system that punishes the poor and exonerates the rich, the venality of lawyers, the unequal distribution of wealth, and capital punishment. Written in 1854 but backdated to 1834, "Réponse à un acte d'accusation" (Reply to an Indictment) (1.7.494–500) links Hugo's literary and political careers. This poem makes a particularly aggressive, exaggerated claim that Hugo accelerated or even produced social change by changing how poetry was written. He begins with a sarcastic confession (lines 1–29): he is indeed the satanic figure he has been accused of being, the anti-hero creating darkness instead of light: "J'ai foulé le bon goût et l'ancien vers françois [*sic;*

the archaic spelling mocks conventional prosody] / Sous mes pieds, et, hideux, j'ai dit à l'ombre: Sois! / Et l'ombre fut" [I've trampled good taste and classic French verse / Beneath my feet; ordered darkness to be / And there was night] (494, vv. 3–5). Jarring enjambment (vv. 3–4, 7–8) strengthens the shock effect. Hugo ends this section with deliberately trite, familiar language: "I have ruined the old A B C D; / Let's chat." The second section (495, vv. 29–59) describes his childhood education at a time when classical aesthetics ruled. There Hugo initiates the extended metaphor that continues until the end of the poem: to segregate words into the distinct categories of "noble" or elevated style, "popular" or humble style, and slang resembles the iniquitous discrimination among social classes—nobility, commoner, and convicted criminal— that determined each person's rights before the Revolution. From this point on Hugo begins deploying his characteristic *métaphores maximas* at the stress points of this invidious, forced discrimination: "[L]e bagne lexique (v. 52), mot sénateur, mot roturier (v. 67), le substantif manant, le verbe paria (v. 128), la lettre aristocrate, la lanterne esprit (v. 159), la balance hémistiche (v. 181), la cage césure (v. 188)" [the lexicon prison, senator word, commoner word, peasant noun, pariah verb, aristocrat letter, mind-lantern, hemistich scales, caesura cage]. These uses of one noun to modify another, a violation of classical French syntax, suggest two identities blending into a new, revelatory identity. The lantern alludes to the commonplace revolutionary call—sometimes acted out— to hang nobles from the streetlights, and the caesura is the major rhythmic pause after the sixth syllable of 12-syllable alexandrine verse. The long third part beginning "Alors, brigand, je vins" (vv. 60–155; the *OP* 2 text is not divided after verse 59, but the *mot charnière* [hinge word] "alors" shows that it should have been) stresses Hugo's accomplishments in liberating verse structure and lexicon: "Who sets the word free also frees the thought" (v. 153). In the fourth part (vv. 156–89), he again confesses his "transgressions," but even more proudly than before. And in the final section (vv. 190–233), he sings a hymn to universal liberty in expression and in politics. Revolution is now identified as "holy progress" (v. 211), for God wishes the degraded crowd to be exalted (vv. 230–32).

Many poems, particularly in the latter three books, evoke a universal context of human suffering, ignorance, and death. Pervasive darkness symbolizes this condition; the material light is absent. At the conclusion, a spiritual light appears: it synthesizes material light and darkness (good and evil from the limited human point of view) by representing a providential order of things for which evil is necessary. For any beings lesser than God to exist, Hugo believes, they must be imperfect. Otherwise they would immediately be reabsorbed into God's essence. Once it begins to act independently, imperfection inevitably produces more imperfection and therefore falls progressively further from God through a series of degrading metempsychoses.

Hugo claims that humans, unlike other created beings, have free will but enjoy such freedom only because they cannot directly see God. If they could, they would be too overwhelmed to disobey. Charity and prayer can nevertheless guide us toward atonement with the supreme being. This reconciliation, accompanied by a direct vision of the deity who is mind, love, and light, can be consummated only after our death. God, ungraspable by frail human thought, is from our point of view both immanent and transcendent. We can dimly sense the immanent God as a spark of soul or spirituality in all created beings. The visionary poet can hear their voices. Hugo creates an inversion of the pathetic fallacy: no longer does nature respond to and reflect human longings; instead, the poet translates the faint, inarticulate longing of nature. *Bégayer* (stammer) is a key word for the motif of redemption in Hugo's verse; he translates what nature can only imperfectly express.

Hugo uses many devices to suggest an overarching spiritual presence invisible to, although sometimes sensed by, humans. To express the immanence of the spiritual, he—like other romantics—uses animism (describing inanimate objects in ways that suggest they are alive), hyperbole (exaggeration), positive comparisons of inequality (saying that something is more than something else), totalizing noun phrases beginning "tous/toutes les" (all of the . . .), anaphora (the repetition of the same word or phrase at the beginning of more than two successive lines of poetry, suggesting a hidden unity), and chiasmus (the *abba* arrangement of parts that can imply a secret core of a more profound meaning). More than the other romantics, Hugo makes language strain to reach beyond what it can ordinarily express. He uses unusual plurals of abstract nouns ("les immensités," the vastnesses); oxymorons (condensed antitheses or contradictions in terms); and the *métaphore maxima* (the juxtaposition of noun and noun as in "monde châtiment" [punishment world]). As in the writings of other romantics, in Hugo's verse, anniversaries and chronological regularities suggest a hidden order.

From the beginning of the collection, Hugo dramatizes the idea of a spiritual meaning indwelling in nature by frequently using prosopopoeia, a speech by a nonhuman entity or by a person absent or dead. In the untitled fourth poem, for example, "Le firmament est plein de la vaste clarté" (The firmament is filled with the vast light), he says:

L'hosanna des forêts, des fleuves et des plaines,
S'élève gravement vers Dieu, père du jour;
Et toutes les blancheurs sont des strophes d'amour;
Le cygne dit: lumière! et le lys dit: clémence!

(490–91)

[The hymn of praise from forests, fields and streams
Rises gravely toward God, father of day [of the light];
The whitenesses are all stanzas of love;
The swan says: light!; the lily: clemency!]

In such poems, "says" primarily means "provides us an intuition of." More so perhaps than for any other romantic poet except Novalis, Hugo's world is an intuitive world. One does not sketch or reason: one communes.

Hugo soon extends his vision throughout the solar system. Planets are to the sun as humans are to angels. But the angels who inhabit the stars can also sin and fall. The moons and planets too are suffering worlds; the farther a moon or planet lies from the sun, the more intense its punishment. These "specter worlds" beseech Christ and the apostles to come to help redeem them (3.12, "Explication" [Explanation], vv. 26, 29).

"Explication" suggests how to interpret the suffering cosmos as a whole. "La Chouette" (3.13, The Screech Owl) suggests how to interpret its details. The pretext is the spectacle of the owl, "larve d'ombre" (v. 2), nailed to a door. "Larve" (Latin *larva*) refers to the ancient Roman legend of the restless souls of people who died violently and now roam the night. But the main etymological meaning of *larva* is "mask." As the stars are the bright masks of God in Hugo's quasi-cabalistic system, the owl is a "mask of darkness": its apparently sinister appearance conceals God's redemptive purpose. Hugo explains his panpsychism. One finds a soul everywhere in nature.

La nature . . .
. . . .
Toujours en dialogue avec l'esprit de l'homme,
Lui donne à déchiffrer les animaux, qui sont
Ses signes, alphabet formidable et profond;

(590–92)

[Nature, . . .

. . . .

In constant dialogue with human minds,
Gives us the beasts to decipher: they are
Its signs, an awe-inspiring alphabet.]

Nature, Hugo claims, speaks in two languages. One is elevated and
splendid, the Word conveyed by elephants, lions, eagles, horses. The
other is the vague stammering patois of bats, toads, owls, pigs. Contemplating the owl's skeleton hanging from three nails, Hugo tries to "spell
out" and understand what it is telling us. Implicitly, the allusion to
Christ's crucifixion immediately suggests redemptive suffering. As
Hugo translates the message, he switches from the noble alexandrine
"Word" to an octosyllabic "patois" of the deformed owl. Without naming Christ, the owl describes His hanging corpse. He who did good is
suffering, the owl explains, as am I who did evil. During His life, His
soul flew everywhere like an owl, with glowing eyes hunting down evil
in the shadows. But humans did not understand: they crucified their
benefactor, and "Railla cette chouette immense / De la lumière et de
l'amour!" [Derided that enormous owl / Consisting of light and of love!]
(592). All the winds of night, however, could not extinguish Christ's
halo. The owl concludes by pitying blind, stupid humanity that indiffer-
ently persecutes good and evil alike.

Hugo urges us to recognize kindred spirits in even the most repellent
creatures. In an untitled poem (3.27), he says:

J'aime l'araignée et j'aime l'ortie,
    Parce qu'on les hait;
Et que rien n'exauce et que tout châtie
    Leur morne souhait;

. . . .

Pour peu qu'on leur jette un œil moins superbe,
    Tout bas, loin du jour,
La mauvaise bête et la mauvaise herbe
    Murmurent: amour!

                                        (611–12)

[I love the spider and the thistle,
  Since people hate them;
And since nothing grants, all punishes
  Their dejected wish;

. . . .

If only one casts an eye less proud,
  Faintly, far from light,
The foul vermin and the noxious weed
  Murmur to us: love!]

The crossed rhymes *(abab)* and halting rhythms (10 alternating with 5 syllables in the French) imitate the painful ungainliness of these outcast beings. But as part of Creation, such beings reflect the divine love that brought us all to life. They also aspire to expiate their sins and rejoin God. In context, the "rimes pauvres" ("poor rhymes" with the identity of only one pronounced sound) of the short lines in the first and third quatrains suggest an alienated world. The anaphora of "parce que" (because), eight times plus two partial repetitions (of "que" alone) in the first 16 lines frames the repellent spectacle of spider and thistle with an implied continuity of providential purpose. In the fifth through the eighth stanzas, Hugo addresses the passersby directly. He asks for their pity for disgraced creatures. We should be merciful, not crushing them but instead listening to their aspirations, which should also be our own.

"Magnitudo parvi" (The Greatness of Little Things) (3.30.614–38) closes the first half of the collection with a magnificent long poem. It has the greatest metrical variety of any poem in the *Contemplations*. The beginning and concluding sections mix alexandrines and hexasyllables (six-syllable lines) into heterometric *sixains* (six-line stanzas): at first with a couplet followed by a final quatrain in *rimes embrassées (aabccb);* at the end that quatrain becomes *bcbc*. A second section alternates blocks of octosyllables and alexandrines; the next sections before the end are entirely in octosyllables. Such variety suggests the diversity of Creation itself.

The poem begins at sunset. Characteristically for romanticism, a change of light announces a change of vision; the spiritual order will become apparent. The poet is isolated, but not entirely alone. He holds his silent daughter by the hand.[6] The earth resembles a boat sinking beneath the advancing shadow. Thus Hugo implies a compound comparison of vastness: a ship is in proportion to the sea as the earth is in proportion to the cosmos. Things lose their color and shape. Emotionally, "On sentait à la fois la tristesse descendre / Et monter la douleur" [At the same time you felt sadness descend / And rise, suffering] (615). But the chiasmus "tristesse / descendre / monter / douleur" locates human grief and pain in the outer, superficial layer. Falling and rising, the eternal movement of creation and redemption, occupy the inner, fundamental layer. At the same moment, clouds "rampent" (creep) along the peninsulas while shadows creep up the hill sides (stanzas 4 and 7). A key word in Hugo's verse, "ramper" suggests the earthbound, the thwarting of transcendence even for what normally could rise.

In the sixth stanza (615), the poet's daughter asks him what two distant twin lights are. Hugo answers that one is a star, the other a shepherd's fire. These two fires represent the macrocosm (the cosmos) and the microcosm (the human scale) respectively. These two worlds are linked by the indwelling spark of soul present in all created things and thus providing an intimation of the existence of God. In an enormous sentence stretching for 34 lines, the poet evokes the immeasurable journey his daughter and he could undertake together if they had wings (616–17). Entering the awesome shadows that surround God (this imaginary journey reappears in a more assertive, heroic mode in "Ibo," 6.2), their flesh would melt like wax (an allusion to the flight of Icarus). Nothing would remain but a dazzled gaze beneath hair standing straight on end from awe.

The following stanza suggests an experience outside time; it has no main verbs. The collection's title is embedded in the first line of this stanza: "Ô contemplation splendide!" [O splendid contemplation] (617). The title functions here as a metonymy (the spectacle is referred to with a word that denotes the act of looking at it) that implies the visionary has fused with the vision. Next an accumulation of *métaphore maxima* ("Monde rêve! idéal réel! . . . / Mot nouveau du noir livre ciel!" [Dream world! Real ideal! . . . / New word in the dark heaven book!]) shows we have departed from the physical world, where matter and spirit seem distinct. In the heavens, the poet and his daughter would see "des fourmillements de sphères vagabondes" [swarmings of wandering spheres]. "Fourmillements," a characteristic neologistic plural of an abstract noun (a device later favored by Rimbaud), again takes us beyond human reason. After a torrent of nearly continuous exclamation points, the animate and the inanimate blend: "Ce qu'on prend pour un mont est une hydre; ces arbres / Sont des bêtes; ces rocs hurlent avec fureur; / Le feu chante; le sang coule aux veines des marbres" [What seems a mount is a hydra; those trees / Are animals; rocks bellow with fury; / Fire sings; blood flows through veins in marble blocks] (618). They encounter alien humans from other worlds, who find them monstrous; do those beings also seek the truth? Being swirls like a hurricane around its radiant center; one day, the stars will fall like snow. Rimbaud's visionary poems such as "Barbare" or "Le Bâteau ivre" were directly inspired by such passages in Hugo.

The grandiose vision continues for 10 more stanzas. At its culmination, the masks of God—suns, and false gods—fall.

> [The priests of many religions]
> Ont crié: Jupiter! Allah! Vishnou! Mithra!
> Un jour, dans les lieux bas, sur les hauteurs suprêmes,
> Tous ces masques hagards s'effaceront d'eux-mêmes;
> Alors la face immense et calme apparaîtra!
>
> (621)

> [Cried: Jupiter! Allah! Vishnou! Mithra!
> One day, in low places and sublime heights,
> All those haggard masks will fade by themselves;
> Then the enormous, calm face will appear!]

Hugo then returns to earth to describe the microcosm of the human heart, the false knowledge that deludes us, and the resemblances between the shepherd and the ancient prophets, both alone with nature and contemplating the night sky. Starting with the sentence "Lui, ce pâtre, en sa thébaïde" (Shepherd deep in solitude), this lonely, humble shepherd's insight gathers depth throughout a monstrous sentence lasting for 24 quatrains (96 lines) until it concludes: "Il voit l'astre unique; il voit Dieu!" [He sees the only star: sees God!] (632). Hugo then describes the shepherd's contemplative state at length. Yet he is not dissociated from his fellow beings: perhaps his fire will save a struggling ship on the high seas by guiding it to port. Hugo situates this vision, like so many others in his poetry, on a promontory extending into the ocean. The landscape symbolizes the mind venturing into the metaphysical void.

In the short final section, Hugo explains the moral to his daughter (637–38). The shepherd's fire and the star communicate. The fire laments the suffering and evil of this world; the star answers "Certitude!" God unites these two flames from above and below, transforming them into "the two wings of prayer." This phrase anticipates the ascensional movement of the remainder of *Les Contemplations*.

Grief Work

"Aujourd'hui" (Today), the second part of the collection, is subdivided into the books "Pauca meæ," "En marche," and "Au bord de l'infini" (My little girl, En route, At the edge of the infinite). Léopoldine's premature death was even more of a loss than the death of one child: her new husband also drowned trying to save her, and she was pregnant with Hugo's first grandchild. The poet suggests that this tragedy turned him toward meditations that finally led to a definitive revelation of God's purpose from the mysterious "Bouche d'ombre" (Mouth of shadow). All Creation, including Satan, would be redeemed at the end of time.

The fourth book, "Pauca meae" ("My little girl," a tag taken from Vergil's 10th bucolic poem), concentrates on what today would be called "grief work."[7] A series of three poems toward the end of "Pauca meae" illustrates how Hugo realistically dramatizes the successive phases of grieving. These are the untitled "Demain, dès l'aube," "À Villequier," and "Mors" (Tomorrow, at the break of day, At Villequier, and Death) (4.14, 15, and 16). The first of these (657–58), dated the day before the fourth anniversary of Léopoldine's death, consists of only three alexandrine quatrains. The absence of a title suggests spontaneity. During the anticipated journey to his daughter's tomb, the poet will be absorbed in thoughts of her. His surroundings will mean nothing. The viewpoint of the lyric self, of the traveler, is shallower than that of the implied author. The descriptive details of the setting sun and of fishing ships' sails disappearing below the horizon as they return to port suggest the universal message that physical death is a false disappearance. The spirit survives, and it will return. But the lyric self can think only of his personal loss. Hugo knows Léopoldine is waiting; when he arrives, he will lay on her gravestone a bouquet of evergreen holly and flowering heather, symbols of immortality.

"À Villequier" (658–62: the site of Léopoldine's death) shows the poet a bit later, emerging from the apathy caused by his crushing loss to question God, to ask why the death of an beloved, innocent person was necessary. Crossed rhymes *(abab)* reinforce Hugo's depiction of his inner

conflict between submission and revolt against God's will. This opposition is further emphasized by alternating stanzas that correspond to the
poet's unstable moods: alexandrine quatrains are followed by heterometric (mixed-verse) stanzas alternating alexandrines with hexasyllables
(six-syllable lines). At first, the speaker seems submissive:

> Je dis que le tombeau qui sur les morts se ferme
> Ouvre le firmament;
> Et que ce qu'ici-bas nous prenons pour le terme
> Est le commencement.
>
> (659)

> [I say that the tomb closing on the dead
> Opens heaven's door;
> And what on earth we assume is the end
> Is the beginning.]

But he cannot sustain his resignation: he accuses God of being indifferent to the children's deaths that make their parents despair. First he
humbly asks permission to grieve; then he becomes so absorbed in his
grief that he forgets to justify a providential purpose. In the previous
poem, he had been stunned; now he has revived sufficiently to lament
and complain.[8]

The following poem, "Mors" (Death) (4.16.663), uses a title in
Latin—the language of the Catholic Church and of the Bible as Hugo
knew it from the Vulgate—to suggest a religious meaning for his
daughter's death that transcends personal concerns. Despite his grief, he
now can generalize and write allegory for the rest of us. Crossed rhyme
has been replaced by alexandrine rhyming couplets, suggesting a cumu-
lative movement and the gradual realization of a purpose. First the poet
has a vision of the skeleton Death as a sinister harvester with a great
scythe. This vision provides the pretext of the poem: here it is given, not
sought. The gleaming blade provides the only light amid a universal
darkness.[9] "Et les triomphateurs sous les arcs triomphaux / Tombaient;
elle [Death] changeait en désert Babylone, / Le trône en échafaud et
l'échafaud en trône" [And beneath arches of triumph victors / Fell;
Death made a wasteland of Babylon, / Changed throne to gallows and
gallows to throne]. The energetic enjambment "Tombaient" emphasizes
the abrupt fall of empires. The chiasmus "throne/gallows/gallows/ throne"

works two ways. From a materialistic perspective, the inner layer, shameful death, is the ultimate reality; triumphs are an illusion. But from the spiritual perspective, the allusion to the Crucifixion in the second pair of words (gallows to throne) evokes the higher knowledge that Christ's shameful death prepared His reign in heaven.

In the second part, lines 10–18, weeping mothers serve as surrogates for the poet; they assume the helpless mourning that Hugo can now surpass. The peoples of the earth flee frantically into the shadows. But in the final couplet, a universal twilight of terror and death suddenly yields to a deeper response to death, a response that not frightened humanity but only the visionary poet can make. As the harvester Death slashes down human lives with her great scythe,

> Les peuples éperdus semblaient sous la faulx sombre
> Un troupeau frissonant qui dans l'ombre s'enfuit;
> Tout était sous ses pieds deuil, épouvante et nuit.
> Derrière elle, le front baigné de douces flammes,
> Un ange souriant portait la gerbe d'âmes.
>
> (vv. 16–20)

> [Beneath the dark scythe, nations of the earth
> Seemed a trembling flock fleeing in the night;
> Beneath Death's feet lay terror and despair.
> Behind her, forehead bathed in gentle flames,
> A smiling angel bore the sheath of souls.]

Hugo has regained the hope of an afterlife.

The ending of "Ô gouffre!" (O abyss!), depicting doubt and darkness, reinforces Hugo's optimism: "Et par moments, perdus dans les nuits insondables, / Nous voyons s'éclairer de lueurs formidables / La vitre de l'éternité" [And at moments, lost in an endless night, / We see illumined with imposing gleams / The window of eternity] (6.14.762–63). Again, the poem "Spes" (Hope, 6.21.778–79), a microcosm of the collection, ends with the visionary's declaration that sets things right. From his elevated place atop a hill, this *songeur* (thinker/dreamer) sees a faint glow on the horizon. The rest of humanity scoffs at the idea that a dawn could be coming. But the visionary replies: "Cette blancheur est plus que toute cette nuit" [That pale light is more than all this night].

The Great Prophetic Odes

Except for "Magnitudo parvi," the greatest visionary odes of the *Contemplations* appear in the sixth and final book, "Au bord de l'infini" (At the edge of infinity), half as long as the other five books combined. All but 2 of the 26 poems here were written after the exile, but many were inspired by the biblical verse paraphrases that Hugo wrote in 1846. In the first poem, "Le Pont" (The Bridge, 721), Hugo stands at the edge of an abyss. He glimpses God far on the other side. Despairing of ever crossing, the poet is about to weep with grief and fear when a phantom appears, offering to build a bridge. The phantom then identifies itself as Prayer.

Reflecting the violent mood swings characteristic of grieving, the second poem, "Ibo" (I will go, 722–25), trumpets Promethean assurance and audacity. In energetic crossed-rhyme quatrains where octosyllables and four-syllable lines alternate, he says at one moment that he has wings like a bird because the spirit of God bears him aloft. Two stanzas later, he confusingly claims that humanity should imitate Prometheus and Adam, stealing God's fire from heaven or eating the forbidden fruit of knowledge. One can somewhat reconcile these contradictory statements by saying that Hugo thinks that as *l'homme devoir* (the duty man) he should accept the frightening mission of being God's prophet. At heaven's gates, he will confront the guardian storms, "Et si vous aboyez, tonnerres, / Je rugirai" [If you bark at me, thunder, / I shall roar]. Compared to the hounds of heaven's natural forces, the poet is a lion. Thus the former acquire connotations of inferiority and cowardice. They also recall Cerberus, the three-headed dog guarding the entrance to the hell of classical mythology. The triumphant lion-poet here must be understood as allegorical; at the conclusion of "Pleurs dans la nuit" (Tears in the Night), a "real" lion roars, "Forgive me, Lord," as he endures the purgatory of reincarnation (6.6). But as "Les Mages" (The Seers) makes clear in a poem cycle that more than once mentions John of Patmos, author of the Apocalypse, other prophets may not know what they are doing; they may be only involuntary instruments of God (part 3). Implicitly Hugo remains superior to all of them, owing to his lucidity.

When Hugo's lyric self seems a defiant Promethean figure, invading heaven to steal fire from God, the impression misleads. In "Ibo," for example, the poet boasts that he will challenge the terrors of the beyond to bring back forbidden truth from on high and share it with humanity. But the event described is only a plan: it has not yet occurred. Even in that plan, no contact with the truth, to say nothing of God, is ever made. The hero brings back nothing. He only imagines defiance, not even knowing whether God would consider a search for the truth as defiance. When Hugo imagines roaring like a lion at the shadows if they should bark at him as he penetrates the realm of cosmic mystery, he is merely projecting his own hostility on the unknown, unwittingly confronting his own fear. Such psychic projection creates compelling, convincing illusions of the Other whenever we can't observe how the Other actually behaves.

Most ode poets share values with their audience and represent the claims of the established order. Thus they can achieve concision. A cheer is briefer than an argument. But in his exile, Hugo sought to bring enlightenment to the benighted French society that had acquiesced in the foundation of the empire. To explain and justify his unfamiliar ideas concerning punitive reincarnation and universal redemption, he needed a framework larger than that of the traditional ode. Long expository, didactic passages inflate certain odes of *Les Contemplations* (e.g., "Magnitudo parvi" [The Greatness of Little Things], "Pleurs dans la nuit" [Tears in the Night], or "Les Mages" [The Seers]) to several hundred lines. "Ce que dit la Bouche d'Ombre" (What the Mouth of Darkness Says) has nearly a thousand. To shape such gigantic creations, Hugo uses three organizing principles in particular: listing, layering, and progression.

Listing reflects the chaotic enumeration of the inspired ode poet. Revelations flood in from a higher, spiritual source. The jumble that results reflects how this higher order is hidden behind the mask of our material world and is incomprehensible to ordinary people.[10] "Pleurs dans la nuit" illustrates this device in *Les Contemplations*. There it creates a semblance of the chaos of the unredeemed penitential world; it also reflects the unselfconscious state of the poet relaying messages from a supernatural realm. This poem develops the notion of punitive reincarnation as the spirit voices had described it during Hugo's seances in exile.[11] Representing himself here as a passive recipient of revelation, taking dictation from on high, Hugo abandons the surprise ending and restores the traditional order of the four parts of the ode: (a) establishing contact with a higher power, (b) the resulting vision, (c) expulsion of the scapegoat, and (d) affirming heroic resolve. To lengthen the poem, Hugo simply repeats this four-phase cycle several times without clear-cut progression. Such repetition does modify the cycle. The first phase need not be repeated. Once communication with a higher order has been established, it can be taken for granted throughout the remainder of the poem: the sublime poetic diction proves that such communication persists. And the reaffirmation of heroic resolve motivates and merges with the presentation of each new vision. Therefore an ode expanded in this way will not be organized a-b-c-d, a-b-c-d, but instead a-b-c-d, b/d-c, b/d-c and so forth.

"Pleurs dans la nuit" opens conventionally by asserting the poet's unique mission and visionary powers: "Je suis l'être incliné qui jette ce qu'il pense; / Qui demande à la nuit le secret du silence / . . . / Dans une ombre sans fond mes paroles descendent" [I am the bowed being casting forth his thoughts; / Who asks silence's secret of the night / . . . / Into endless shadows my words descend] (729). "Incliné" suggests a person standing above the universe and bending over it in meditation. This poet can converse with vast natural forces such as the night. His words descend toward ordinary beings. His first vision is incomplete: it reveals thesis and antithesis (initial situation and reaction), but not yet a synthesis: "L'être éternellement montre sa face double, / Mal et bien, glâce et feu" [Being forever shows its double face, / Evil and goodness, the ice and the fire] (731). Despite the superficial meaning of "its double face," we are not in a Manichaean world where evil and good are equal as well as opposite forces. The poet dramatizes evil in the poem's fourth section through the description of a funeral procession. But later in the poem, he will resolve the problem of evil by reintegrating it into a larger, redemptive scheme.

The fifth section (732–33) introduces the anti-selves, here people deprived of vision. Seeing in the human condition a prison sentence ending with the void of death, most people remain skeptical and blinkered: "Pour eux, le ciel ment, l'homme est un songe et croit vivre; / Ils ont beau feuilleter page à page le livre, / Ils ne comprennent pas" [For them, God lies; dreaming, we think we live; / In vain they leaf through the book page by page, / They do not understand]. In the first verse, the dislocated rhythm (five plus seven syllables instead of the conventional six plus six) and the 12 plodding monosyllables mirror the infirmity of such skeptics' thought. They cannot hear the message of faith communicated by the natural world everywhere. But the negative conclusion of this fifth section contains a *métaphore maxima* (noun plus noun), which by violating ordinary syntax shifts into a vision limited neither by human language nor by the imperfections of the material world.[12] "Leur âme . . . dans le grelot monde / N'entend pas sonner Dieu!" [Their soul trapped in this sleigh bell world / Cannot hear God ring forth!]. This spatially sublime equation (the spiritual order is as much vaster than the material one as the material order is vaster than a sleigh bell) prepares the visionary expansion of the next section.

The brief sixth section (733–34) restores the plenitude of spiritual vision: "Tout être a son mystère où l'on sent l'âme éclore, / Et l'offre à l'infini [*sic*]" [In each being's secret we feel the soul bloom, / An offer to the All]. Then a vast doctrinal expansion in the seventh section (734–37) outlines Hugo's beliefs concerning punitive reincarnation. He asks God to have mercy on all evildoers, sunk helpless in the prison of the earth. Two metaphors strongly conclude the exposition. They state how God's purpose, sensed by the prophetic mind, subsumes the antitheses of good and evil into an ascension: "Échelle de la peine et de la récompense! / Nuit qui monte en clarté!" [Ladder of penalty and of reward! / Night rising toward the day!] (737). These lines sum up the spiritual meaning of *Les Contemplations*.

The ode cycle begins anew in the eighth section of "Pleurs dans la nuit" (737). We return to a graveside scene, anticipated by the funeral procession of section 4. Prison imagery recurs, associated with the dark void of the tomb. Sections 11 through 13 (739–45) introduce the anti-selves in a new form. They are no longer skeptics but heedless, frivolous, pretentious persons, unaware that "l'aigle trépas" and "le fossoyeur oubli" (the eagle demise and the grave digger oblivion) hover near them; their pyramids will crumble into dust. Note how again two *métaphores maximas* serve to suggest a higher reality. This time Hugo varies the pattern of illumination by eventually granting superior wisdom to the anti-selves rather than to the prophetic poet. When they die and enter the beyond "sous l'immensité qui n'est qu'un œil sublime" [beneath vastness which is a sublime eye] (745), they realize that even the infinity of their imagination contains only a fragment of a total awareness of God. Masks of matter fall, and the unknown is revealed to them.

A third and final form of anti-self, the cynic, appears in the 14th section of the poem (746). During two stanzas, the cynic has his own antiode, affirming ignoble values. Hugo reinforces the second stanza with a phatic (attention-getting) introduction: "Écoutez-le:—Jouir est tout. L'heure est rapide. / Le sacrifice est fou, le martyre est stupide; / Vivre est l'essentiel" [Listen to him:—Pleasure is all. Time flees. / Martyrdom is stupid, sacrifice mad; / To live is the main thing]. Hugo subtly subverts the cynic's observations. Rather than follow them with an indignant outburst, he linguistically encodes the cynic's message so that its emptiness is suggested by the very words that compose it: the internal rhyme "tout, fou," twice echoed in the first verse (Écoutez, jouir) sounds hollow. The syntactic parallelism of these five short sentences (A is B) is monotonous, and the main verb in them, *est* (is), is the most inexpressive and colorless of all possible connectives.

Moving far beyond the cynic's simplistic philosophy, the following sections further condemn it by implication. First Hugo addresses the wind with a series of rhetorical questions that expatiate on the *ubi sunt* topos (15.746–47). An example of this topos is Villon's refrain "But where are the snows of yesteryear?" The 16th section (747–49) then answers the riddle of death by evoking "l'arbre éternité" [the eternity tree] with the great thinkers of human civilization perched among the branches. Death does not kill the spirit. God flows through all being. By calling God "le mot de l'énigme" [the answer to the riddle] the French text associates the answer ("le mot") to the problem of evil with the poet's words ("mots"). The ode's final exhortation metaphorically assimilates humankind itself to language, transforming us into signifiers whose signified is God: "Ne doutons pas. Croyons. Emplissons l'étendue / De notre confiance, humble, ailée, éperdue. / Soyons l'immense Oui" [Let us not doubt. Believe, filling the span / Of our confidence, humble but winged. / Let us be the great Yes] (748).

"Humble, ailée" is an oxymoron: etymologically, "humble" means next to the ground. The believers' faith, expressed through submission to God, exalts them. In this poem, Hugo does pray for and envision an eventual ascension toward God, but it must occur beyond the limits of his narrative: "Un jour, quand souffleront les célestes haleines, / Dieu seul remontera toutes ces urnes pleines / De l'éternelle nuit" [One day, when the celestial breath shall blow, / God alone will bring up all those full urns / From the eternal night] (739).

The structural cycles of "Pleurs dans la nuit" imitate the cosmic cycles of redemptive reincarnation. Cycles imply that we are driven by events beyond our control. In "Les Mages" (The Seers, 6.23), Hugo reasserts control as a spectator if not as an actor. He offers an overview of prophetic genius in history; he presents a self-conscious definition of the role and nature of the poet-prophet; and he deploys a more elaborate structure than cyclical repetition—layering. Layering (which in its most abbreviated form is the chiasmus of which we have already seen so many examples) distinguishes inner from outer worlds, superficial from profound realities. It implies that the poet can discriminate among and evaluate various perspectives on the truth.

An earlier version had distributed six parts of "Les Mages" over three nested layers, thus: ABCCBA.

1. The poet-prophet in society: definition and examples.
2. His visionary powers.
3. Dramatic expectations of a revelation.
4. The Mystery unveiled.
5. The effects of revelation: Liberty and Progress.
6. Redefinition of the prophet as the instrument of social change.

The definitive version in 11 parts retains the same general structure of definition-action-revelation, arranged ABCCBA. But the structure has been greatly enlarged. The original part 4 becomes parts 4 through 8; 5 and 7 are new. Part 5 becomes 9 and 10.[13]

Within each section, chaotic enumeration (a traditional device in the Great Ode) allows for limitless extension while creating the effect of a *kairos,* or sacred supernatural time, knowable only by the visionary. "According to the pattern fixed by Pindar, an ode must be rhapsodic, since this genre in contrast to others calls for the perpetuation, by the work of art, of the poet's original fervor. . . . It is the 'disorderliness' of the chaotic enumerations, reflecting the diversity and fullness of the world, which offered the best approximation of the rhapsodic style of the ode" without subjecting it to the drastic discontinuities of thought or setting used by Pindar and Ronsard (Spitzer 1967, 207). By juxtaposing many disparate historical names, times, and places, Hugo suggests a poetic vision that transcends the limits of ordinary perception.

Examined linearly, the poem moves from the social to the personal to the divine; it then returns in a way that synthesizes the three levels. These correspond to the successive periods of Hugo's fictionalized career: author and politician, exile brooding over his daughter's death, and enlightened prophet. Overtly, on the narrative plane, "Les Mages" presents the visionary as a passive recipient of divine revelation, at times even involuntary and unaware. But the layered structure of the poem does not allow this interpretation of the poet's role to stand where Hugo himself as implied author is concerned. His structural control is too artful, too self-conscious. The notion that he is a Promethean or "demonic" adventurer who triumphs over God, a notion one might superficially derive from "Ibo" (6.2), becomes implausible in the light of his disciplined structure. Similarly to the direct statements of the preceding poem, "Spes" (Hope), the structures of "Les Mages" present the poet as an active, faithful prophet in a blinded world. In other words, "Les Mages" conforms to the archetype of Withdrawal–Enlightenment–Return. Because "Spes" and "Les Mages" received the most recent dates of all the poems (January 1856) when Hugo published *Les Contempla-tions,* the structure of "Les Mages" may well sum up the meaning of the whole collection.

When Hugo does portray the end of time and the ultimate redemp-tion of Satan at the end of "Ce que dit la Bouche d'Ombre" (6.26), he switches from alexandrine rhyming couplets—their open-ended accu-mulability corresponds to the mode of narrative—to *sixains* (six-line stanzas) where the couplets are separated by hexasyllables (six-syllable lines). Thus strophic form imitates the stasis of eternity. But he can describe this extra-narrative world only by creating a paradoxical illocu-tionary mode that combines the presence and the absence, the end and the beginning, of language. The final stanza reads: "Tout sera dit . . . un ange / Criera: Commencement!" [All will have been said . . . an angel / Will shout: "Beginning!"] (822).

Hugo dedicated a poem to his daughter on each anniversary of her death (4 September). And the long poem following the six books of *Les Contemplations,* "À celle qui est restée en France" (To She Who Has Remained in France), is dedicated to, and focused on, Léopoldine. It seems a sequel to "Demain, dès l'aube." Banished from France, Hugo can no longer visit her tomb, but he hopes that his book will fall into her silence like a tear of love. "Qu'elle dise: Quelqu'un est là; j'entends du bruit! / Qu'il soit comme le pas de mon âme en sa nuit!" [Let her say: Someone is there; I hear him! / My book is my soul's footstep in her night!] (4.826.131–32). Like other famous deceased women in men's high visionary literature—Dante's Beatrice, Petrarch's Laura, Goethe's Marguerite—she has become Hugo's psychopomp, a guide for the soul.[14]

Chapter Seven

The Prophet: Paradise Regained

Within the *Contemplations*, Hugo's grief work had helped him move from stunned sorrow through indignant rage before achieving the detached cosmic view of "Mors" (death). Similarly, in the volumes of his collected verse, he moved from the predominantly personal concerns of grieving, commemoration, and autobiography in the *Contemplations* to a sweeping spiritual history of the universe, sketched in the verse trilogy that followed. It comprised *Dieu* (the Creator), *La Légende des siècles* (history), and *La Fin de Satan* (universal redemption at the end of time).

These four works (*Dieu* and *La Fin de Satan* were unpublished during his lifetime) made Hugo the leader of visionary French romanticism, a figure rivaled in European literature only by Novalis and William Blake. Visionary French romanticism was not so much a puddle of "spilt religion" (the British critic T. E. Hulme's trenchant phrase used to disparage romanticism in general) as a series of attempts to rebuild a doctrinal structure to replace what had been leveled during 13 years of revolutionary upheaval. The Catholic Church had been banned, churches desecrated, and priests forced to recant or driven into exile. Those who did not wish to restore an ultramontane church and a divine-right monarchy found that the priesthood of every believer had become a necessity for those who sought a revelation that could replace an apparently moribund Catholic teaching.[1] The leading French pioneer in this movement was Louis-Claude de Saint-Martin (1743–1803), whose *L'Homme de désir* (The Man of [Spiritual] Desire, 1790) and *Le Ministère de l'homme-esprit* (The Ministry of the Spirit-Man, 1802; note the *métaphore maxima* in the title) influenced Nodier and Sainte-Beuve, and consequently, their friend Hugo. Their notion of organic unity and a spiritual evolution of humanity toward reintegration with God is called "illuminism." It has been described in the previous chapter on *Les Contemplations.*[2]

Visionary literature reconfigures old values. Prophets must make two major choices: whether to explain the manifestations of the supernatural, and whether to follow them with a program for reorganizing society. Four literary modes result:

1. Explanation plus program: utopias (e.g., Ballanche's *La Ville des expiations*, or visionary socialism).
2. Explanation without program: romantic epiphany (textual revelations of divinity, such as Chateaubriand's *Atala*, Balzac's *Séraphîta*, Nerval's *Aurélia*, Hugo's *Dieu* or *La Fin de Satan*), or the *merveilleux* (conventional religious visions, or fairy tales).[3]
3. Program without explanation: dystopias run by evil beings (Lautréamont's *Les Chants de Maldoror*). These resemble sadistic sexual fantasies (Sade, Octave Mirbeau, Rachilde), except that the latter are nonsupernatural.[4]
4. Neither program nor explanation: the fantastic in a "pure" nonrationalized form (Mérimée's "La Vénus d'Ille," Robbe-Grillet's *Djinn*, Henry James's *The Turn of the Screw*, Poe's *The Fall of the House of Usher*, Carlos Fuentes's *Aura*). There are numerous intermediate forms between (2) and (4).

Romantic epiphany's absence of program creates a curious lack of closure. The reader does not discover how to apply the enlightenment he or she has received. We simply learn that there is, or will be, a better world.

Dieu

The protagonists of romantic epiphany begin by wandering. At the outset of *Dieu*, Hugo's narrator floats through space "comme une algue qu'entraîne un ténébreux reflux" [like seaweed drawn by a mysterious tide] (945) (creation flowed outward from God; the visionary is being drawn back toward Him).[5]

Like other visionary romantic authors, and like Dante before them, Hugo is in the broadest sense a Protestant: revelation comes to him not through a member of the Holy Trinity, the Blessed Virgin Mary, or a canonized saint, and not through priests, scripture, or sacraments, but through beings not officially part of Catholic dogma and traditions. Christ remains strikingly absent from such romantic epiphanies.

Hugo's narrator in *Dieu* receives eight successive revelations, each from a different winged being. In order, they present the insights of Atheism, Skepticism, Manichaeism, Paganism, Mosaism, Christianity, Rationalism (the longest section), and Light. After each encounter, the poet looks upward, "Et je vis au-dessus de ma tête un point noir" [and I saw a black speck above my head]. In Hugo's artistically self-conscious world, this dark spot is among other things the period at the end of a sentence. Beyond it lies a new beginning.[6] But in its form as a typographical period, this beginning is also already an ending, an advance mention of a frustrated transcendence. It corresponds in Hugo's everyday experience to the black retinal spots that impaired his vision. They came from his habit of staring at the sun. And yet he knew that physical light was only relative. In 1842 he wrote: "I've always felt a painful emotion when reflecting that the normal condition of the sky is night. What we call day exists for us only because we are close to a star."[7]

As ontogeny recapitulates phylogeny, Hugo's journey recapitulates the evolution of human religious thought. The eight progressively refined versions of human understanding of the Godhead form a diachronic system in which Christianity is ultimately superseded both chronologically and philosophically. Like the seven blind men each touching a different part of an elephant, each human religion grasps some aspect of God but can formulate it only in a ludicrously inadequate way.[8]

Unlike most other visionary romantics, Hugo does not pretend to have apprehended absolute truth. The supreme vision of God can occur only after the poem's conclusion, in the darkness of death. The final revelation, entitled "La Lumière" (The Light), expatiates on the topos of inexpressibility. Like the sum of an infinite series, God may be continually approached but never attained. "Il [Dieu] échappe aux mots noirs de l'ombre" [God eludes the shadows' dark words] (Légende, 1104, v. 4).

From Hugo's viewpoint, writing is a vain, paradoxical attempt to structure chaos, to deploy spatial metaphors that may create a clear picture of our epistemological confusion. Richard B. Grant observes that "within each of the sections that proclaim that God does exist in some form [3–8], one finds a consistent pattern on Hugo's part of undercutting or denigrating the positive visions that he has been presenting." Through their multiplicity, the endings Hugo sketched for Dieu form a fourth ending, an implied renunciation of the quest.[9] Compare the ending of "Pleurs dans la nuit" (Tears in the Night), where John of Patmos, the author of the Book of Revelation, ascends on his eagle to see Jehovah:

> Il vit l'endroit sans nom dont nul archange n'ose
>   Traverser le milieu,
> Et le lieu redoutable était plein d'ombre, à cause
>   De la grandeur de Dieu
>   (750)

[He saw the nameless place across which no
   Archangel dares pass;
That fearsome place was all darkness, from the
   Glory of the Lord.]

"Abîme" (Abyss), the last poem in *La Légende des siècles,* also ends in shadow. God says: "Je n'aurais qu'à souffler, et tout serait de l'ombre" [With one puff of my breath, all would be dark] (746).

Death alone offers the supreme revelation, before which the others remain partial and defective. Hugo makes this conclusion explicit in the unfinished section "Le Jour" (Daylight) that he had planned for the ending of *Dieu.* The last being he encounters, enveloped in a winding sheet, tells him:

> . . . —Passant,
> Écoute.—Tu n'as vu jusqu'ici que des songes,
> . . . .
> Mais maintenant veux-tu d'une volonté forte
> Entrer dans l'infini, quelle que soit la porte?
> . . . .
> . . .—Oui, criai-je.—. . .
> Il me toucha le front du doigt. Et je mourus.
>   (1113–14)

> [Passer-by,
> Listen.—So far you have seen only dreams,
> . . . .
> Now with a firm resolve will you enter
> The infinite, through no matter what door?
> . . . .
> —Yes, I cried.— . . .
> He touched my forehead lightly. And I died.]

Earlier visionary romantic works introduced a personified human audience to whom the prophet could transmit revelation. Chateaubriand's Chactas, in *Atala,* survives for decades so that he can relate his mystical experiences to René. As a result, Chactas may reorient René away from his morbid fantasies of incest and toward the spiritual order. Balzac's Wilfred and Minna, in *Séraphîta,* return from the angel's side to invite the atheistic Pastor Becker—who has believed Séraphîta insane—to join them on their journey toward God. But Hugo, like Nerval, has freed himself from the lingering concern for verisimilitude inherited from the eighteenth century: the continuity of revelation will now depend not on a personified but on an implied audience. The corroboration created by an intermediate layer of narration (by the visionary relating his or her experience to another fictional character) is sacrificed to gain greater immediacy. Hugo, confidently adopting the prophetic voice whose statements are true by virtue of being enunciated, tells of his own death as unselfconsciously as did Moses in the Bible. Hugo writes from a doubly marginal position—in exile, and in communion with the supernatural. But unlike most other romantics, he advances a solution to the problem of alienation: that we should join with him and God alike, in an all-encompassing faith for the modern age.

La Légende des siècles

Hugo had been preparing all four of his great visionary poems—*Les Contemplations, Dieu, La Légende des siècles,* and *La Fin de Satan*—at the same time. His work on the latter three intensified once he had completed *Les Contemplations.* However, it was only *La Légende des siècles* that he then began preparing actively for publication. Concerned with marketability, his Belgian publisher Hetzel had encouraged Hugo to write more epic rather than prophetic poems. So he compromised his prophetic vocation to write "little epics." In them, he creates a largely fictionalized history to illustrate the influence of Providence in human affairs. He emphasizes stories from the Old Testament, Greek myth, the European Middle Ages, the Renaissance, and the French Revolution. He does not follow a strict chronological progression or try to link one poem explicitly with the next.

The last five poems combine a quasi-Enlightenment myth of social and scientific progress—knowledge dispels injustice—with an apocalyptic vision. At first glance these two motors of history, Providence and technology, seem mutually incompatible. But Hugo suggests that as society becomes increasingly enlightened, its efforts will converge ever more closely with the flow of our spiritual destiny, hastening the consummation of the latter.

The *petite épopée,* or "little epic," the short narrative verse genre, was so named in the seventeenth century. Interest in it had been revived by two publications in 1819: André Chénier's *Bucoliques* and the Amédée Pichot translation of Byron's *Tales.*[10] Alfred de Vigny, for a time a close friend of Hugo, was the first prominent French romantic author to take up the genre in his *Poëmes antiques et modernes* (1826) and later in his *Destinées* (1864; most were published individually in journals before Hugo began to write the *Légende*).

One must realize, however, that Hugo's primary model was one he had known since childhood: Ovid's *Metamorphoses.* From the Middle Ages through the nineteenth century, privileged young males studied at least seven years of Latin. Their major classroom texts were Vergil's *Aeneid,* Horace's *Odes,* and Ovid. Himself inspired by the Greek author Hesiod's cosmogony, *The Works and the Days,* Ovid wrote a long cycle of short narrative poems. They run from the creation of the world through a condensation of the *Iliad* to what Ovid presented as the climactic reign of Augustus Caesar, his patron. Ovid and Hugo's versions differ from other models of the *poëme* because they involve metamorphoses caused by the active intervention of personified supernatural forces. In Ovid, however, the transformations usually involve ontological degradation: "demotion" from human to animal or plant. Occasionally, instead, they involve apotheoses that change a hero such as Hercules into a demigod (see Ovid, book 9). But Hercules' transformation is routinized: the gods welcome him among them after a discussion and a vote. And his ascension remains an individual honor; it is not an allegory of a general human capacity for transcendence. Moreover, however much Ovid's characters are transformed, metamorphosis in his poems leaves them as familiar entities—for instance, trees or animals—in a familiar world.

In contrast to Ovid, Hugo describes transformations that recreate his characters in unprecedented forms; once changed, moreover, they find themselves on the stage of a previously unknown world. A visionary, Hugo models himself consciously on the Old Testament prophets. The inevitable redemption of humanity is his ostensible theme.[11] Ovid is content to claim that the rule of the man-god Augustus fulfills our destiny: the privilege of contemplating the emperor is enough. Hugo promises that some day we shall all become like gods.

Thus he demythologizes the individual in favor of the collectivity. Even the Blessed Virgin Mary is affected. The papal bull "Ineffabilis" of 1854 had proclaimed the doctrine of the Immaculate Conception: unlike any other mortal, Mary was conceived free from Original Sin so that she might be a fit vessel for the embryo of Jesus Christ. But "Le Sacre de la femme," the first poem of *La Légende* after Hugo's introduction, replaces Mary with Eve. In Genesis, the Fall and the expulsion from the earthly paradise occur before Eve conceives any children. Unlike Mary, the Catholics claim, we all are conceived in sin; "inter fæces et urinam nascimur" [We are born between feces and urine]. But in Hugo's version, Eve becomes pregnant before the Fall. He describes a day when in the eye of nature she suddenly appears more august than her spouse.

> Pourquoi ce choix? pourquoi cet attendrissement
> Immense du profond et divin firmament?
> Pourquoi tout l'univers penché sur une tête?
> Pourquoi l'aube donnant à la femme une fête?
> . . . .
> Un long rayon d'amour lui venait des abîmes,
> De l'ombre, de l'azur, des profondeurs, des cimes,
> De la fleur, de l'oiseau chantant, du roc muet.
> Et, pâle, Ève sentit que son flanc remuait.
>
> (24)

> [Why this choice? Why this immense tenderness
> From the profound and divine firmament?
> Why all the universe bent toward one head?
> Why the dawn giving the woman a fete?
> . . . .
> A beam of love came to her from the depths,
> From shadows, azure skies, abysses, crests,
> From flowers, from birds' songs, from silent rocks.
> And, pale, Eve felt a quickening in her womb.]

Since we are all born innocent, Hugo implies, not tainted with Original Sin ("In Adam's fall, we sinnéd all"), we all are redeemable.

The second poem, "La Conscience" (Conscience), stresses how God's relentless pursuit of the sinner gives even the most wicked the possibility of receiving grace. Hugo elsewhere equates conscience with God; here he describes Cain's perverse attempt to flee conscience. He freely adapts Genesis 4:8–12. In the Bible, God discovers Cain's murder of his

brother Abel, curses Cain, and drives him from the fertile land, condemning him to be forever a wanderer. But at Cain's request, God
marks him with a sign of divine protection, so that he, although an
accursed being, will not be struck down by whoever sees him. Then
Cain retires to the land of Nod and founds a family. In "La Conscience,"
however, by the time Cain murders Abel he already has a tribe of
descendants, children and grandchildren. They flee from before God's
presence for a whole day. But Cain still sees the eye of conscience glow-
ering at him from the sky. He flees again, for a whole month, until he
reaches the shore. Then he hides inside a tent; next, behind a wall; after
that, inside a demonic city; and finally, inside a tomb. These six
attempts to escape awareness of his guilt prove fruitless. The succes-
sively more elaborate shelters inside which he tries to hide suggest the
technological evolution of his society; but such material progress leads
only to death (symbolized by Cain's final refuge, the tomb), and one
finds divine judgment even there.

Throughout *La Légende des siècles*, Hugo describes how social outcasts
("Un voleur à un roi," "Les Quatre Jours d'Elciis, série 3: La Vision de
Dante," "Masferrer," and "Welf, castellan d'Osbor"), animals ("Le Cra-
paud," "Le Lion d'Androclès"), and even inert matter ("L'Aigle du
casque," "La Colère de Bronze," "La Paternité") suddenly reverse roles to
judge and punish their social or ontological superiors. (Titles in order: A
thief to a king; The Four Days of Elciis, Series 3: Dante's Vision; Masferrer; Welf, proprietor of the castle of Osbor; The Toad; Androcles' Lion;
The Wrath of Bronze; Paternity). The archetype of Inversion in these
examples also foreshadows our salvation through the gratuitous power
of grace.

In contact with a supreme truth, Cain interprets it wrongly. But the
inescapable eye means that the possibility for repentance, contrition,
and atonement is always there. In the Bible, Genesis 6–8 relates the
destruction of the race of Cain by the flood. More optimistic, Hugo tacitly spares Cain's race so some may be redeemed. His description of
Cain's grand-daughter Tsilla, blond and gentle as dawn, portends a reconciliation.

To be enlightened, however, humans must expose and reject the false
gods of monarchy and imperium. They have an innate sense of awe, but
they must direct it aright. Hugo was to explain, in *L'Homme qui rit* (The
Man Who Laughs, 1869), that those who think they are praying to
Jupiter often are really praying to Jehovah. The title of the masterpiece
in *La Légende des siècles*, "Le Satyre" (419–30) suggests the equivocal

character of Olympus. The protagonist's name, a homonym, means both "satyr" (le satyr) and "satire" (satire; calling into question the established order of things). Half-man, half-goat, he deconstructs the opposition of human and bestial. The whole poem illustrates the archetype of Inversion: at the beginning, the gods of Olympus are the faun's masters; at the conclusion, he is theirs. When this creature, unknown to the gods although they know so many satyrs, is caught on Olympus by Hercules and brought before them, his occupation is announced in a silent pun that contains the satyr's unrecognized potential: "Il était voleur" [he was a thief/someone who flew]; implicitly, "who rose above his level." The first section after the prologue, "Le Bleu" (The Blue), describes the official heaven of the ancient Greek and Roman gods. As the satyr begins to sing in the second section, "Le Noir" (The Black), at Jupiter's inquisitive request, he gradually grows larger. He stands for the Renaissance and the Reformation, for challenges to the fatalism of ancient polytheism and to the dogmas of Catholicism. The third section, "Le Sombre" (The Shadowy), depicts human speculation overcoming original sin. And in the fourth section, "L'Etoilé" (The Starry [realm]), the satyr finally becomes larger than Olympus itself, declaring in an awesome voice: "Place à Tout! Je suis Pan; Jupiter! à genoux" [Make way for the World-All! Jupiter! on your knees] (430). Typically for romanticism, the sequence of section titles (The Blue, The Black, The Somber, The Starry) reflects a false consciousness yielding to a true one as day gives way to a night in which the material order has become invisible, but where a higher truth can be seen.

Some critics have erroneously identified Hugo's religious position here as pantheism. That system, asserting that "the world is God's body," would preserve the hierarchy where God as mind is superior to Creation. Instead, Hugo proclaims panpsychism: all creation contains a spark of soul that allows one to intuit God. The satyr would be the world-soul. The dramatic conclusion to the Légende, "Plein Ciel" (The Plenitude of Heaven), uses the image of a dirigible—a recent invention—to symbolize how material progress can lead to the conquest of the unknown. As Hugo said in 1867, "the day when the first airship takes flight, the last tyranny will retreat beneath the earth."[12]

La Fin de Satan

La Fin de Satan (The End of Satan) tells of an exile happily returning to his native land. Hugo enriches the motif of a struggle between Satan and God, followed by a reconciliation, with both historical and eschato-logical meanings. Social tyranny yields before the progress of liberty, whose culmination was the fall of the Bastille. Creation, which God has had to detach from Himself to allow it an independent existence, will be reintegrated into the divine essence. Since 1821 Hugo had believed that human history reflected a spiritual drama of the passage from the lost Eden to Paradise Regained. He had imagined that postlapsarian human-ity was the great exile, and the visionary poet a fallen archangel who remembers heaven. Satan himself appeared in Hugo's earliest verse, and the poem "The Antichrist" of 1823 anticipated an "End of Satan."[13]

But Satan in Hugo's mature work represents a flagrant exception to the cosmology of the Great Chain of Being. He had enjoyed a direct vision of God but yet revolted. Exiled to the depths of hell, he neverthe-less (like Milton's Satan) remains able to assail God indirectly, through Creation. This extraordinary twofold capacity for independent action was overdetermined. For aesthetic reasons, Hugo needed a dramatic mover to create incidents and to drive the action of the narrative poem. For the sake of morale, Hugo—like other political or religious true believers—needed to insist on the absolute truth of his moral vision and on the inevitable triumph of his cause. The very strength of this convic-tion made it difficult for him calmly to await the arrival of a better age. As a crystallization of the author's impatience, Hugo's Satan can account both for the presence of evil on earth and for the delays that allow this evil to endure too long. In real life, Hugo was the political Satan, condemned and exiled. *La Fin de Satan* reverses these roles: Napoleon III becomes Satan's minion, waxing fat off the proceeds of injustice; Hugo, as God's prophet, announces the end of empire. The precarious equilibrium of this emotional solution would however be endangered if the emperor offered Hugo amnesty, officially mending the absolute rift between imperialists and republicans.

Like others who find themselves in an emotional impasse, Hugo had adopted two opposing solutions to establishing his moral superiority to Napoleon III. In *Les Châtiments,* he played the role of God, assigning the emperor to a satiric, poetic hell. But the emperor continued to reign. So in *La Fin de Satan* Hugo anticipated a universal spiritual regeneration that would make all worldly kingdoms fade to insignificance. Yet he could not overcome his desire for vengeance. This emotional ground-swell, running counter to the ostensible topic of reconciliation, provoked excessive grandiosity in Hugo's fictional portrayal of the Devil. Satan's elder daughter, the angel Liberty, recalls a period when he was more splendid than all the other angels and when the elements of the cosmos had mistaken him for God (928). The angels remain fascinated by his memory: "Ils songeaient à Satan dont la blancheur fatale, / D'abord ravissement, puis terreur du ciel bleu, / Fut monstrueuse au point de s'égaler à Dieu" [They mused on Satan whose fateful whiteness, / At first heaven's delight, and then its dread, / Was so monstrous it equaled that of God] (808). Thus Hugo allows his own historical role as a condemned rebel to contaminate the viewpoint of the epic narrator who condemns. This confusion crops up elsewhere.

The very description of the Fall betrays that both Hugo and Satan feel a repressed yearning for their homeland. Never had another author recounted it with so many incidents. Satan struggles to stop falling and to climb back up toward the light. Now a Fall like that in Dante or Milton, where only the result is shown, implies that damnation is definitive, is a fait accompli. On the contrary, the enumeration of the stages of the descent in Hugo, each accompanied by the ever more intense suffering of privation, already hints at a possible itinerary of return. From the beginning, when the archangel, "drawn by the weight of his crime" (768), sinks into the abyss, one can guess that he will finally free himself from this weight. It seems not an integral part of his soul, but oppressive extra baggage. All Satan needs to do is set it down.

In short, orthodox damnation entails the loss of one's free will. Devils can no longer do anything but evil. God, who decrees the good, nevertheless allows evil to act provisionally, in the unwitting service of an ulterior, greater good (the doctrine of "permissive evil"). In Hugo's poem, on the contrary, it is Satan who both decrees evil and finally allows the good to take place on the earth. He takes the initiative, as Liberty's appeal to him shows:

> Je viens te prier, toi qu'on proscrit. . . .
>
> . . . J'agenouille
> La lumière devant ton horreur, et l'espoir
> Devant les coups de foudre empreints sur ton front noir!
> . . . .
> Oh! laisse-moi rouvrir les portes sépulcrales
> Que, du fond de l'enfer, sur l'âme tu fermais.
> Laisse-moi mettre l'homme en liberté. Permets
> Que je tende la main à l'univers qui sombre.

· ·
Dieu me fit Liberté; toi, fais-moi Délivrance!
                                             (927–31)

[I've come to beg you, you the exiled one. . . .
. . . I bow down
The light before your horror; I bow hope
Before the lightning scars on your dark brow!
· ·
Oh! Let me reopen sepulchral doors
That you closed on the soul, from depths of hell.
Let me set humanity free. Allow
Me to stretch my hand to the sinking world.
· ·
God made me Liberty; make me Release!]

The whole long speech adopts this pleading tone, and once Satan says
"Go!" he unleashes the mechanism of universal redemption.

Certainly Satan has limits in hell. He must remain alone in total
darkness. Only in dreams sent by God can he communicate with
heaven. The evil he inflicts on humans makes him suffer too. Yet he has
extraordinary powers that seem even divine. The power of his Word creates ex nihilo, albeit involuntarily. His four cries of despair and defiance
as he falls are transformed into Cain, Judas, Barabbas, and the city of
Sodom. Once Satan reaches the bottom, he molds the ghoul Lilith, his
younger daughter, from the shadows. (Contrast with this premeditated
act the surprise and distress of Milton's Satan in *Paradise Lost* when he
meets Sin and Death, the involuntary consequences of his previous acts.)
Then Satan establishes mysterious links with the earth.

Sometimes Lilith acts independently, for example when she saves the
nail, the club, and the stone Cain used to murder Abel. She knows that
future human generations will use them to found war, capital punishment, and prison. In this instance, Satan must await her report to learn
what she has done. At other moments, however, he seems immediately
aware of terrestrial happenings. His laughter bursts like thunder when
the people choose to save Barabbas rather than Christ. And yet humanity is fully responsible for the Crucifixion (870, 877–78, 888).

When Satan learns of the creation of the first man, he has no need to wait for the assent of Adam's free will to spread moral evil over the earth. Noah explains that Lilith seduced Adam before Eve even appeared (774; a cabalistic tradition). In a passage added to the 1854 original in 1860, Satan characterizes himself as a cosmic principle opposed to and in some ways in control of God:

> Je contrains l'océan, que Dieu tient sous sa loi,
> Et la terre, à créer du chaos avec moi.
>
> ·
>
> Jéhovah frissonant sent aujourd'hui partout
> Une création de Satan sous la sienne;
>
> ·
>
> Je veux le torturer dans son oeuvre .
>
> (902–3)
>
> [I force the ocean, subject to God's law,
> And the earth, to create chaos with me.
>
> ·
>
> Shivering, Jehovah feels everywhere
> Satan's creation underneath his own;
>
> ·
>
> I want to torture Him through what He's made.]

Despite such passionate defiance, Satan's eventual conversion can be foreseen even during his fall, when he realizes that he cannot be self-sufficient. To have light, he depends on the one remaining visible star. In vain, he begs it desperately not to go out (770). Later he admits the crime of envy (889). His spiritual reascension is suggested by the series of entities addressed in his apostrophes in the section "Hors de la Terre" (Outside the Earth) parts 3 and 4. First he calls out to the night and the void around him, but later, to the light and life of the Creation. In the eighth part of his monologue, he humbles himself by asking forgiveness not only of God but also of all nature, because he has sowed evil everywhere. He finally feels compassion for those he has afflicted and senses that he can alleviate his own suffering if he stops doing evil (911). His strongest argument for mercy derives from his newfound humility: eternal damnation would set limits on the light and love of God by reserving a dark corner in the universe (904). To argue that his eternal damnation would make him equal to God's eternal blessedness, however, seems an attitude remote from Christian resignation.

In any event, the process of his external redemption begins soon afterward. The angel Liberty, born of the one feather fallen from Satan's wing at the moment of his expulsion, and allowed to remain in heaven, descends toward her father. She represents the spark of divinity, the possibility of efficacious grace, that persists in the worst of creatures. She confronts Lilith, who represents Satan's capacity to choose evil, as Liberty represents his capacity to choose the good. According to Hugo's mythology, Lilith and Liberty cannot coexist in the same place at the same time; Liberty's radiance makes Lilith fade into nothingness. Good and evil struggle in Satan's mind, but finally he allows Liberty to rescue humanity. She does so by destroying the prison of the Bastille. By allowing others to become free, Satan has freed himself.

God seems curiously passive in this epic, but that is because Hugo tells the story lyrically rather than narratively. He implies causality by simple juxtaposition. In the scene following Christ's death, for example, Satan confesses his love for God. We understand that Christ's self-sacrifice has contributed to the Demon's salvation. The interior monologue that expresses Satan's crisis of conscience here is three times interrupted by hymns that other beings address to God: birds, then stars, then angels. This progression traces an ascent that is both spatial (higher and higher in the air) and ontological (higher and higher on the Great Chain of Being); it foreshadows Satan's own.

For reasons both aesthetic and personal, Hugo never completed his mystical poem. He had trouble preserving coherence while shifting the setting continually between hell and earth. Milton had solved this problem in *Paradise Lost* by closely following the biblical account, and by using an archangel's prophetic vision to relate the postlapsarian fortunes of humanity. But Hugo never reached a clear understanding of the relationships between those two domains and never specified exactly what share of responsibility Satan, Lilith, humanity, and God each had for the existence of evil. Then, where narrative progression was concerned, the taking of the Bastille (a section never completed) risked being anticlimactic after Nimrod's world conquest and Christ's passion in the first two historical sections. Hugo would find a much better solution in *Les Misérables*. There he concentrated on terrestrial events, so that Jean Valjean's redemption symbolized Satan's, rather than the contrary. The anagogic strand of the novel leads from the everyday to the cosmic.

From Hugo's militant political viewpoint, *La Fin de Satan* risked having undesirable consequences; it risked encouraging an attitude of passive waiting ("attentisme") among French people under Napoleon III, since all decisions were made in the beyond. Hugo's cosmology had assimilated hell to the Catholic purgatory. Bringing that purgatory to earth in *Les Misérables* would transform the notion of involuntary expiation into an exhortation to social action aimed at relieving suffering.

Hugo had at least two poets in him: the passive visionary (see "Les Mages" in *Les Contemplations*) and the militant, satiric rebel. Perhaps unconsciously, Hugo identified the latter with a Satan who would refuse amnesty. As long as Hugo had little hope of an acceptable political pardon and a dignified return to France, he did not suffer the temptations of compromise and submission. Thus he could contemplate Satan's repentance and redemption with detachment, feeling himself dissociated from any such drama. The story of Satan's pardon expressed a repressed desire for reconciliation and return to the homeland, nostalgia Hugo was too proud to admit to himself. But as his exile dragged on, and as his family left him alone more and more often, the intensity of his nostalgia grew: Satan's redemption, only an episode in the *Contemplations,* becomes the exclusive subject of *La Fin de Satan.* When hope dawned, continuing to compose the latter poem became too painful.

Some dates will clarify the situation. *La Fin de Satan* was composed in 1854 and expanded from 1859 to 1860. As early as October 1849, Hugo in his role of peer of France (roughly analogous to senator) had opposed some of Napoleon III's policies. Knowing there was a warrant for his arrest, Hugo fled the country in December 1851, shortly after the coup d'état. But in January 1852, his sons were released from prison. In April, the government was rumored to be offering Hugo a safe-conduct pass for his return. He refused. On 2 December 1852, the first anniversary of the coup d'état that founded the Second Empire, the French government offered a full pardon to any émigré who promised to stop opposing the new regime. At that time, Hugo was busy composing *Les Châtiments;* the force of his anger sustained him. After a few years in exile on an island in the English Channel, however, Hugo's family started to become bored in their isolation. In the winter of 1858, his wife and his daughter Adèle left Guernsey to spend some time in Paris. From that time on, they would make increasingly prolonged trips to France. Starting in 1859, Hugo's sons accompanied the rest of the family. The poet sometimes remained alone. During the summer of 1859, the French government renewed its offer of amnesty. The temptation became so great, one must suppose, that in April 1860 Hugo defended himself against it by solemnly swearing never to return to France. Eleven days later, he had definitively abandoned *La Fin de Satan,* a poem about a happy return from exile. Feverishly, he turned instead to *Les Misérables,* a 1,500-page novel he would finish 14 months later.[14]

As soon as the empire fell, Hugo hastened to France. Aged 68, he even tried to volunteer for combat against the Prussians. Now he could consciously identify himself with Satan without being untrue to himself by musing about a humiliating political submission. In *Toute la lyre* in 1874, he could therefore describe himself as a fallen archangel "Rongé du noir regret du firmament vermeil" [Consumed with longing for the crimson firmament] (5.36). But the exile of which he now speaks, as at the beginning of his career, is that of all humanity, chained to the world of matter and illusion, far from the Godhead until the universal redemption at the end of time.

Chapter Eight
The Masterpiece: *Les Misérables*

Hugo's Social Views

Admired for his poetry and respected for his theater, which provided the main impetus for the militant romantic movement from 1827 through 1838, Hugo as a novelist has been severely underrated. *Les Misérables* (The Underclass) in particular may be more than his masterpiece: it may be "the great French novel" of the nineteenth century. Its sweep rivals Melville's *Moby Dick,* Tolstoy's *War and Peace,* and Manzoni's *The Betrothed.*

After completing his great visionary poem cycles, Hugo turned eagerly to writing *Les Misérables* (1862). He finished the vast novel in 14 months. Its initial inspiration was probably his *Dernier Jour d'un condamné à mort* (The Last Day on Death Row, 1829). There Hugo dramatized the plight of prisoners in the galleys at Toulon, especially one sentenced to five years for stealing a loaf of bread.[1] Hugo insists on extenuating circumstances, notably, on the brutalization of the poor by society. "There but for the grace of God go I," might be his hypogram, the matrix of his meaning.[2] With it he, like his contemporary Charles Dickens, deconstructs the simplistic dichotomy of innocence and crime that allows us to evade social responsibility.[3] Hugo's attribution of near-satanic resentment to Jean Valjean seems overblown when we consider his behavior. His only actual crimes are two acts of petty larceny, plus a third of which he is falsely accused (stealing a loaf of bread, a coin, and some apples), but Hugo is making the point that he made in *Claude Gueux:* harsh law enforcement breeds the monsters it wants to eliminate (Grant, 157–58).

Hugo himself had been a prisoner of conscience since 1851, remaining in voluntary exile because he refused to accept Napoleon III's empire. Compensating for his exile in his thoughts, he makes a mental return to Paris, where he situates his epic novel, *Les Misérables.*[4] The loving precision of his detailed Parisian topography there combines the realistic with the nostalgic. Frequently he describes a vanished scene and

adds that he's not sure what one would find there now. "[The author]
doesn't need to say he loves Paris; Paris is the birthplace of his intellect.
Today demolitions and reconstructions have made the Paris of his youth,
that Paris he religiously bore away in his memory, a Paris of former
times. But let him speak of that Paris as if it still existed. He doesn't
know the new Paris, and he is writing with the [image of the] former
Paris before his eyes, an illusion that is precious to him"[5] (1.5.1.478).
Hugo's reminiscences of Paris often carry an implied symbolic commentary on how ephemeral neighborhoods and monuments can be. For
example, see the passages concerning "l'éléphant de la Bastille"
(4.6.2.485, 495). The beast of the Bastille prison that swallowed innocent people before the Revolution has been transformed into an avatar
of the whale that God sent to preserve Jonah. Napoleon I had had that
monumental plaster elephant statue built—it stood on the site of the
former Bastille from 1814 to 1846—to embody the idea of the might of
the French people, but "God had made of it something greater; He
housed a child there" (488).[6] Today (in 1862) that grotesque reminder of
Napoleon has vanished, Hugo observes. Similarly, the narrow, crooked
streets near the Corinth Restaurant, where the rebels of 1832 led by
Enjolras made their last stand behind a barricade at the social climax (as
opposed to the climax of the personal drama) of Les Misérables, have been
straightened and widened until no trace of the original site remains
(4.12.1.110–13).

The Plot

The plot of Hugo's sprawling, sentimental novel focuses on the redemption of the convict Jean Valjean: first through a bishop's Christian love
for him, and then by Valjean's love for the orphan girl Cosette.[7]
Although he literally cannot live without her, he eventually relinquishes
her to the man she loves.

   Elements of the detective story (the police investigator Javert's unre-
lenting search for Jean Valjean, and depictions of the underworld)
remind one of nothing so much as a Dickens novel such as Oliver Twist
or Our Mutual Friend. Both Hugo's and Dickens's major theme is that
poverty dehumanizes. Some, like the criminal anti-father Thénardier,
become indifferent not only to the sufferings of their victims but even to
the survival of their own children. When his two youngest boys disap-
pear, he makes no effort to locate them. And he does not care whether
his older daughter Éponine will be killed by other members of his gang

for interfering in a burglary. Others such as the police detective Javert, born to a prostitute in prison, and without any family himself, react with uncompromising moral brutality toward the accused.

Dickens and Hugo want to excite our compassion. But their benevolence is paternalistic, and their modest proposals for the voluntary, partial redistribution of wealth—as in Dickens's *A Christmas Carol*—could not threaten well-to-do readers. Aside from his steadfast opposition to capital punishment, Hugo offers no practical solutions for reforming the police, the courts, or the prisons. He simply tries to stimulate our moral sensibilities as Fantine's misadventures and steadfast love for her child stimulated the moral sensibilities of Jean Valjean. Hugo intends the reformed convict to serve as a model for us as Valjean comes to know God, whom Hugo equates with conscience. His message is that of the Gospels: "Inasmuch as ye have done it unto one of the least of these my brethren, ye have done it unto me" (Matt. 25:40). Eventually, Hugo will explicitly compare Valjean to Christ.[8]

A poor young tree pruner at the outset of the story, Jean Valjean is supporting his widowed sister and her seven children. One winter, lacking work, and fearing that his relatives will starve, he breaks a bakery window to steal a loaf of bread. He is sentenced to five years in the galleys at Toulon. Four times he tries to escape. Each time he is recaptured, and his sentence is eventually extended to 19 years.[9]

His incarceration began in 1796, when Napoleon (who is just his age) first assumed a share of governmental leadership. Valjean's release in 1815 corresponds to that of the French people, freed from the tyrannical leadership and bloody wars of Napoleon I.[10] The individual spiritual drama reflects French history.

Valjean has become deeply embittered against society because of his excessively harsh punishment. After his release, this attitude is promptly aggravated: his ex-convict's yellow passport makes everyone scorn and reject him. Only a saintly bishop, Monseigneur Myriel, is willing to give him lodging for the night. But Valjean cannot resist stealing the bishop's last remaining luxuries, his silver place settings. Valjean flees in the night. He is arrested and brought back, but the bishop saves him from imprisonment by saying he had given the place settings to Valjean. The bishop then adds two silver candlesticks, which his guest had "forgotten." As Jean Valjean is released, and about to set off again, the bishop whispers in his ear that he has purchased Valjean's soul with his gifts, and that Valjean has promised him henceforth to embrace the good.

Hugo's depiction is not simplistic; the bishop's beneficent influence will work progressively but intermittently on Jean Valjean. On the road north, impulse and residual rage lead Valjean to steal a coin from a little chimney sweep (a crime that will pursue him for the remainder of the novel), but then he repents and resolves to lead a virtuous life. He cannot forget the bishop's act of kindness. "He fought against this heavenly indulgence with his pride, which is like the stronghold of evil within us" (1.2.13.139). An inner voice tells Valjean that he must choose between virtue and crime. He is obliged to judge himself; he exclaims: "Je suis un misérable!" [I am an abominable man!] (139, 141). The inner image of the bishop's virtue makes the old self-image of the hardened, vengeful criminal fade away as if Jean Valjean could contemplate Satan illumined by the glow of paradise (142).

Incognito in a northern village, Valjean becomes the benevolent mayor "Monsieur Madeleine." His name alludes to Mary Magdalene, the archetype of repentance. With Madeleine's career, Hugo illustrates a paternalistic "trickle-down" theory of social progress: all redistribution of wealth is voluntary. He ensures the prosperity of an entire community by inventing a superior method for manufacturing glassware. Despite his modest protests, in time he is elected mayor. His period of achievement in this role, from 1815 to 1824, coincides with the first and relatively more liberal period of the French Restoration under Louis XVIII.

Meanwhile Fantine, a young working woman impregnated and then abandoned by her cynical Parisian lover, has returned to her hometown to find work. Hugo has not received due credit for anticipating the naturalist movement in the chapters devoted to her life both in Paris and in her hometown. I would define naturalist literature as treating the working classes seriously and tragically while emphasizing the influences of heredity and environment. Naturalism tends to depict drudgery. In the Paris scenes, however, Hugo depicts the *grisettes* (young women who wore gray smocks at their jobs, and who were stereotypically easy targets for seduction) at play rather than at work. And he emphasizes the inequities of their sexual exploitation by middle-class men in a way Zola, with his sexual insecurities, could not (cf. Zola's *Nana,* 1880, depicting female sexuality as a monstrous source of social corruption).

To be hired, Fantine—although a devoted mother—must conceal her illegitimate child, Cosette.[11] Fantine innocently lodges the child with the evil Thénardier couple and their pampered daughters, Éponine and Azelma.[12] Unknown to Fantine, Cosette is starved, overworked, beaten, and terrorized. When the manager of M. Madeleine's glassworks factory learns of Cosette, he fires Fantine. She must turn to prostitution to support her child.

Eventually M. Madeleine learns of this situation and promises to reunite Fantine with her child and to care for them both. Ordering her release when she is unjustly accused of assault, he alienates the local police inspector, Javert, who has already sensed something suspicious about M. Madeleine. And soon his conscience compels him to denounce himself when an innocent vagrant, Champmathieu, is falsely accused of stealing apples, mistaken for Jean Valjean, and about to be sentenced to life in the galleys. (This episode may reflect the historical Hugo's decision to "go public" with his opposition to the coup d'état of Napoleon III, knowing that he would therefore face a possible lifetime in exile, when it would have been much more comfortable and convenient to keep silence.)

Valjean has time to hide the fortune he made legitimately in glassware, but the rigid Javert will not allow him to bring Cosette to Fantine before she dies. Jean Valjean returns to prison in 1824, the year when the reactionary monarch Charles X took power. On the spiritual plane, Valjean's renunciation of his freedom saves him from self-righteousness, the first danger of loving one's fellow humans: having done good, one feels superior. One must learn to relinquish this prideful, alienating sense of superiority.

Considered in isolation, the generalizations with which Hugo characterizes the moral dynamics of his novel later in the story make its outcome seem inevitable: "The book the reader holds at this moment is from end to end, as a whole and in its details, whatever may be the interruptions, exceptions, or momentary weaknesses, the march from evil to good . . . from the void to God. The point of departure: matter; the point of arrival: the soul. The hydra at the beginning, the angel at the end" (5.1.20.269–70). In its details, however, Hugo's moral vision remains too complex to let us assume that even the most saintly influences or the firmest resolve makes anyone's regeneration a certainty. When Valjean begins actively practicing Christian charity, this new vocation provides him with the rationalizations—based on the importance of his service to others—that almost overwhelm him. The obscure old tree pruner Champmathieu seems expendable, whereas if "M. Madeleine" is arrested, as Valjean knows, the community he has nurtured will collapse. The accidental delays he encounters while rushing to the final session of Champmathieu's trial tempt Valjean to give up his attempt at exonerating his substitute. He could say he had tried everything in vain (the possibility of his disclosing his identity *after* Champ-mathieu's sentencing never is raised).

To escape once more from prison, Valjean feigns a drowning accident; believed dead, he returns to Paris, where all the major characters will converge. With a note from Fantine authorizing him to take Cosette, he reclaims her from the Thénardiers. He brings her to hide with him in Paris. But Javert has been reassigned there and recognizes him. Pursued by Javert, Valjean finally manages to find a haven in a convent as an assistant gardener. (The regular gardener who lets him stay is a man whose life Valjean once saved.)

Valjean raises Cosette like a daughter, and they love each other deeply. He is consoled by the thought that she will always stay with him because she will grow up ugly. Through Bishop Myriel, Valjean learned of virtue; but through practicing virtue, he risks falling prey to pride. The accident or providential intervention (the many apparent coinci-dences in Hugo's novel constitute an indirect attempt to persuade us that God intervenes in human affairs, while preserving the imperatives of human commitment and responsibility in the overt rhetoric of the narrator) that leads Valjean to the safe shelter of the convent saves him from pride: he must compare his involuntary sufferings as a victim of social inequities and as a convict to the voluntary, altruistic suffering of the nuns (2.8.9.97–101). Their example foreshadows Valjean's volun-tary self-sacrifice.

Through Cosette, he has learned of love; but his love remains selfish (2.4.3.470, 472). It is indispensable for him. The narrator speculates that Jean Valjean might have needed Cosette's daughterly love to perse-vere in virtue. As mayor, he had learned much more than before about social injustice; he had been sent back to prison for doing good; he needed the support of Cosette's dependency to keep him morally strong (472–73; cf. 4.3.5.423). She is schooled in the convent. To prevent her pursuing a false religious vocation, Valjean leaves after seven years, and they live in seclusion. Meanwhile, the Thénardiers as well have come to Paris to join the underworld.

Becoming a beautiful young woman, Cosette attracts the attention of a poor young man, Marius. He has been estranged from his royalist grandfather because of his loyalty to his deceased father, a heroic colonel under Napoleon. By moving across Paris, Jean Valjean manages to elude Marius. As yet unrecognized by Thénardier, however, Jean Valjean nev-ertheless attracts his attention by generously giving alms. With the aid of the formidable Patron-Minette gang, Thénardier tries to kidnap

Cosette to hold her for ransom. By coincidence, Marius lives next door to the Thénardiers. Learning of their plan to kidnap and torture Jean Valjean to force him to write a letter that will lure Cosette into their ambush, Marius denounces them to Javert. But then he learns that Thénardier is the man who had saved his father's life at Waterloo (inadvertently reviving him by stealing the valuables from his unconscious body, left for dead). The dying wish of Marius's father is that his son will find and repay Thénardier. Therefore Marius feels a sacred obligation to help him under any circumstances.

Thénardier's daughter Éponine has fallen in love with Marius. She and her family had persecuted Cosette when she stayed with them as a paid boarder and, in effect, as a slave. Now, although Cosette never becomes aware that Éponine has moved to Paris, the roles have been reversed. Devoted without hope of reward, and self-effacing, Éponine helps Marius find Cosette again. Cosette and Marius fall helplessly in love and meet at night in Cosette's garden for a chaste but passionate romance. When Thénardier's gang stakes out Valjean's isolated new residence—without realizing that it belongs to their former intended victim—Éponine drives the gang away and anonymously warns Valjean to move. Valjean plans to flee to England. An accident prevents Cosette from telling Marius where she is going. In despair at not finding her at home, he plans to seek death on the barricades of the insurrection of 1832. As he joins his republican friends there, a sudden political illumination makes his commitment to their cause authentic.

Meanwhile Jean Valjean has discovered the imprint of Cosette's desperate note to Marius on her blotter. He hates Marius for threatening to take away the only person he has ever loved; Valjean must now overcome the second trap of loving. When you love, you can feel a claim on those you love; you must renounce possessiveness and set them free. After an intense inner struggle, Valjean goes to the barricade to protect Marius. Realizing that Marius and she love each other, "he who had finally come to believe himself incapable of wishing anyone ill, there were times when he felt reopening and rising up against that young man those old depths of his soul where there had once been so much rage" (4.3.7.430).

The loss of the person one loves, Hugo says later, is the cruelest, the only true ordeal (4.15.1.181). Having discovered that Cosette adores Marius in turn, Jean Valjean "felt right down to the roots of his hair the enormous reawakening of selfishness, and his ego howled within his spiritual abyss" (4.15.1.182). That man who had devoted so much effort to spiritual perfection looked within his soul and saw the specter of hatred there (183). Hugo does not reproduce the inner debate that leads Valjean at last to the barricade to watch over Marius and eventually to save his life—binding his wounds, carrying him to safety and to medical treatment, and in effect hiding him from prosecution or summary execution for treason. Conscience has its mysteries, Hugo implies.

Éponine simultaneously illustrates a poignant but limited version of sacrifice. Knowing Marius cares only for Cosette, in the name of his friends she summons him to the barricade where they will be fighting, hoping he will die there. But she wants to die first. Disguised as a young worker, she saves Marius by throwing herself in front of a bullet aimed at him.

Meanwhile, behind the barricade, Javert has been unmasked as a police spy. Valjean asks permission to be the one to execute him but then secretly sets him free. When the barricade falls to the government troops and Marius collapses wounded and unconscious, Jean Valjean manages to escape through the sewers. He risks drowning or suffocation in the muck as he carries Marius for four miles on his shoulders.[13] At the locked exit, Valjean meets Thénardier, who has taken refuge there from Javert. Thénardier does not recognize Valjean. He thinks that Valjean has killed Marius for his money, and demands all Valjean's cash in exchange for opening the sewer gate with his skeleton key so that Valjean can escape. Thénardier hopes to distract the waiting Javert by giving him a substitute fugitive. But Javert, who owes Valjean his life, feels morally obligated to let him go. Torn by his unresolvable conflict between religious and legal duty, Javert kills himself.

Marius is nursed back to health by his grandfather, reconciles with him, and marries Cosette. Valjean has given them all his fortune. The moral climax of the novel is Jean Valjean's inner struggle during the wedding night. Should he confess to Marius that he is an escaped convict and withdraw from Cosette's life to spare the young couple the shame of his possible denunciation and arrest? "He had reached the ultimate crossroads of good and evil. That shadowy intersection lay before his eyes. Once again, as it had already happened to him at other painful and critical moments, two paths lay before him: one was tempting, the other fearsome. Which should he take? The fearsome path was advised by the mysterious finger that we all see every time we stare into the darkness. . . . We can never find an end to conscience. . . . It is bottomless, since it is God" (7.6.4.413 –15). Hugo, like the romantic Lamartine in his epic poem *Jocelyn,* implies that human love tempts us to become isolated in the egotism of earthly happiness. It is sacrifice, not human love alone, that brings us closer to God.

On the next day, Valjean confesses secretly to Marius that he is not Cosette's father, and that he is an escaped convict. Marius, believing that Valjean's fortune was stolen, does not touch it. And believing that Valjean killed Javert at the barricade, Marius only reluctantly allows him to see Cosette in the anteroom to his grandfather's house. Realizing he is unwelcome to Marius, Valjean stops coming, stops eating, and wastes away.[14]

Now Thénardier unwittingly serves as the instrument of Providence. He comes to Marius to extort money from him by revealing the "secret" that his father-in-law is an escaped convict who has recently killed a man (meaning Marius himself). Inadvertently he reveals that Valjean neither made his fortune illegally nor killed Javert: indeed, he is the one who saved Marius. The latter discharges his debt of honor to Thénardier, sending him to America, where he will become a slave owner.[15] Marius and Cosette rush repentantly to Valjean's bedside; they arrive too late to save him. But they beg his forgiveness and he dies happy in one of the most pathetic scenes in literature, which is also an optimistic rewriting of the death scene in Balzac's *Le Père Goriot (Old Goriot)*.[16]

The Archetype of Inversion

Throughout *Les Misérables,* Hugo frequently suggests the archetype of Inversion.[17] They who humble themselves shall be exalted. Jean Valjean socially humbles himself in others' eyes by confessing his identity as an escaped convict. He physically lowers himself by descending into the sewers of Paris to carry the wounded, unconscious Marius away from the barricades. But this physical descent exalts him spiritually. As many commentators have remarked, his dark night of the soul will lead to his total regeneration as well as to a reconciliation with his grieving, admiring son-in-law and adopted daughter.

The archetype of Inversion shapes characters and destinies other than Jean Valjean's in *Les Misérables*. In its negative form, Inversion means that what had seemed good, proves bad. Hugo invokes this form of the archetype to characterize the police agent Javert when he learns that M. Madeleine, who earlier had humiliated him, is really the ex-convict Valjean. "A monstrous Saint Michael," Javert is both imposing and hideous: "The honest, pitiless joy of a fanatic in the middle of committing an atrocity preserves some kind of lugubriously venerable radiance. . . .

Nothing was as poignant and as fearsome as that figure, where one could see what you might call all the evil of the good" (1.8.3.319–20). The sinister, deformed grandeur of Thénardier's visionary painting of Napoleon may be another example of this phenomenon, of a spider's ambition to rival the sun (3.8.6.275).[18] It seems as if Thénardier, by capturing the emperor's image, were trying to appropriate for himself the soul of Napoleon's genius.

In its positive form, Inversion means that what seemed bad, proves good. The Beatitudes from Christ's Sermon on the Mount (Matt. 5:2–12), and the Passion itself (Matt. 27–28; Mark 15–16; Luke 23–24; John 19–20), are outstanding examples. Appropriately for his tidy structural sense, Hugo frames his epic novel with nesting layers of inversions. At the beginning and the end, we learn that humility can lead to spiritual exaltedness (in Bishop Myriel, then in Jean Valjean). In fact, the novel is framed by two rejections of Jean Valjean as a convict (by society in general, and then by his son-in-law, Marius). In the middle, Javert's bad excess of goodness is followed by his shocked awareness of the possible goodness of badness as he learns of Jean Valjean's moral sublimity. He then intuits "some sort of justice according to God, working counter to justice according to human beings. . . . the monstrous could be divine" (5.4.1.352).

Near the end, having won his last spiritual battle by confessing his past to Marius, Jean Valjean speaks for the author as he explains that "to respect myself, I must be despised. Then I hold my head high. I am a convict who obeys his conscience. I know all too well that it's not plausible. But what can I do? It's so" (5.7.1.425). The word "ressemblant" echoes Hugo's pirouette at the beginning of the novel as he concludes his idealized moral portrait of Bishop Myriel—"We don't claim that it's plausible; we'll say only that it's a good resemblance" (1.1.2.33). This subtle, nearly subliminal association of the two men reminds us of Myriel's enduring moral influence on Valjean. Switching from the author's voice to the hero's voice in the second of these scenes makes the novel's moral import more immediate at the climax. Hugo had summed it up not many pages earlier: "For those of us who prefer martyrdom to success, John Brown is greater than George Washington" (5.1.20.265). His motto might be Rousseau's: "Vitam Impendere Vero" [to sacrifice one's life for the (cause of) truth]. This resolve is the essence of the moral sublime.

Unlike his contemporaries Baudelaire, Rimbaud, and Verlaine, Hugo has received little credit for preparing the religious revival in French letters during the first half of the twentieth century. Like Claudel (who detested Hugo), Mauriac, or Bernanos 30 to 90 years after him during the Catholic Renaissance, Hugo in 1862 dramatizes his heroes' relentless pursuit by conscience, meaning our instinctive awareness of God. "To write the poem of the human conscience, were it only the conscience of a single person . . . would be to blend all epics into a higher, definitive epic. . . . There you find, underneath an external silence, battles between giants as in Homer, struggles with dragons and hydras and clouds of phantoms as in Milton, visionary spirals as in Dante. What a shadowy thing is this infinity that every person bears within" (1.7.3.248).

Artistic Self-Consciousness: The Art of Hugo's Digressions

The plot summary of *Les Misérables* suggests a melodramatic thriller by Dumas *père* or Eugène Sue. Hugo adopts many conventions from that genre: the evil master of disguises, the mysterious fugitive, daring escapes, self-sacrifice in the name of love. And for whatever reasons, critics seem inclined to condemn as symptoms of Hugo's superficiality the same such motifs and devices that they accept without question and even admire when reading Balzac or Stendhal. But artistic self-consciousness in Hugo is no less intricate than in other great writers; his political experience often is broader than theirs; and his range of characterization (although his novels lack self-confident, assertive women such as Stendhal's Mathilde or Lamiel, Balzac's Eugénie Grandet, or the villainous Cousine Bette) is unquestionably richer. An overview of Hugo's novelistic imagination provides a good starting point for an attempt to do him justice. He combines elements from other traditions into a structure more imposing than those traditions themselves: he possesses a preeminently synthesizing imagination.

This gift shows in the generalizations and aphorisms one finds on nearly every page of *Les Misérables*. Consider the introductory story of the bishop of D——. Hugo observes in passing that "true or false, what is said of people often has as large a place in their lives and especially in their destinies as what they do" (1.1.1.25). And two pages later: "It seems a woman must be a mother to be venerable [instead of merely 'respectable']" (27). Again, "there is always even more wretchedness at the bottom of society than fellow-feeling at the top" (33). Hugo's generalizations, like La Rochefoucauld's two centuries earlier, reflect the traditional belief in a "human nature" that remains invariable, and that implicitly makes the universe revolve around human beings. But Hugo always roots his aphorisms solidly in a social context. He sees people as a medley of potentialities; he emphasizes personal responsibility; yet he understands that the outcome of people's lives often depends on chance, on Providence, or on how they are treated by others. The distinction between the two writers becomes clearer through a brief comparison. Consider La Rochefoucauld's famous maxim: "L'hypocrisie est un hommage que le vice rend à la vertu" [Hypocrisy is a form of respect that vice pays to virtue]. It describes an abstract, unvarying relationship among abstract nouns—hypocrisy, vice, virtue. As we see in the foregoing examples, Hugo, in contrast, describes relationships among real people (what is said or felt about them by others) and the contingencies of individual existences: social (one's reputation), biological (e.g., being a mother), and financial (wealth or poverty). At the same time, in his political subtext, he implicitly urges the French bourgeoisie to stop supporting Napoleon III through their passive acquiescence to the empire, and to strive for the restoration of the republic.[19]

Hugo's historical and cultural digressions set the stage for the characters, explain the limits of their possibilities, and often hint at, foreshadow, or symbolize what he sees as an overarching spiritual odyssey of Fall and Redemption. Unless we sin in thought or deed, as even Bishop Myriel (his name a near-anagram of *lumière*—light or illumination) will do, we cannot benefit from grace and ascend nearer God. William Blake's scandalous slogan "Damn braces; bless relaxes," like Johann Wolfgang von Goethe's concept of Faustian striving and erring as essential to spiritual progress, are earlier, condensed versions of Hugo's theme. These writers do not rebel against God; they reject society's image of a God who demands self-righteousness and conformity.[20]

The most important of Hugo's excursuses within *Les Misérables* are 10 sections concerning (1) "L'Année 1817" (The Year 1817, 1.3.1.); (2) "Histoire d'un progrès dans les verroteries noires" ("The History of an Improvement in the Manufacture of Small Glassware," 1.5.1); (3) "Waterloo" (2.1); (4) the Convent of the Perpetual Adoration (2.6–7); (5) the street urchin (3.1); (6) the underworld (3.7.1–2); (7) King Louis-Phillipe (4.1); (8) slang (4.7); (9) the origins of the insurrection of 5–6 June 1832 (4.10); and (10) and the sewers of Paris (5.2). These sections contrast social irresponsibility with social responsibility (1, 2), material pomp and spiritual grandeur (3, 4), the symptoms of social dysfunction in the child and in the adult (5, 6), the summit and the nadir of society (7, 8), and political and metaphorical analyses of social corruption (9, 10). Critics who erroneously believe that Hugo is always tugging at our sleeve and bellowing a moral message in our ear—that he can communicate only through bombast—should ponder the tacit social commentary conveyed by his careful structuring of these 10 digressions.[21] Each of the first three sections of the novel contains two; the one exception—three digressions in part 4 and only one in part 5—can be explained by Hugo's desire to prepare a climax with a story uninterrupted for the last 200 pages.

"The Year 1817" characterizes the immoral frivolity of the early Restoration period. The remainder of the first part details the horrific consequences of such behavior for the single mother Fantine. The second digression, on the manufacture of glassware, explains how responsible, enlightened capitalism can enrich an entire society—although blind social prejudice against unwed mothers prevents Fantine from benefiting. Throughout, the contrast between reputation and reality underlines social injustice. Hugo shows as much as he tells his opposition to the sexual double standard, and to treating prostitutes as criminals while their clients go free. The wealthy young men of 1817 who abandon their mistresses are respected; their victims are not. Fantine as a streetwalker is despised; M. Batambois, who assaults her by shoving snow down her dress, seems exempt from the law: later, indeed, we find him serving on a jury. Jean Valjean, the escaped convict, is considered a menace to society: but disguised as M. Madeleine, only he can ensure the prosperity of an entire community.

In part 2, Napoleon's self-aggrandizement, disastrous for France, contrasts with the nuns' total self-abnegation. Hugo implies that both attitudes are excessive; but from Jean Valjean's viewpoint, the nuns provide a startling lesson in self-sacrifice beside which his sufferings as a convict appear relatively mild. Part 3 compares the present of abandoned children to their future: the generous-spirited street urchin Gavroche, not yet brutalized by hunger and cold, to the immoral, savage underworld that he eventually would have little choice but to join.

Part 4 contrasts the summit of society, the king, whose conspicuous display creates an icon of social value, with the concealed base whose members are linked by their slang. In a particularly supple movement of thought, Hugo first seems to use a naive reductio ad absurdum to recommend slang as a legitimate object of study. All trades and professions, he says, have their own slang. But then, in a characteristic pirouette, he distinguishes *argot* from other jargons as the language of extreme poverty and a "langue de combat," a means of aggression through language (4.7.1.9). Language is an aspect of culture, however, Hugo claims, and studying it serves civilization. Through a further distinction, he avoids limiting thieves' cant to one dialect. Several interesting passages treat the differences between slang from different regions of Paris. The author, who claims to know them all, indirectly claims the gift of tongues that ensures universal communication. Nothing human, he implies, no language, high or low, is alien to him. His linguistic virtuosity recalls that of Bishop Myriel, who from the beginning is admired and has access to all his flock because he knows the patois from the various regions of southern France. These gifts of tongues recall Pentecost; the apostolic mission that followed; and, by association, a spiritual meaning latent in the novel.

The last pair of digressions depicts the insurrection of 1832 as resulting from social unrest caused by the unfair treatment of workers, and juxtaposes it with a discussion of the sewers, the physical underpinning of Paris and its culture. Hugo draws an implicit parallel. Unless the sewers are studied, rebuilt, and cleaned out, he argues, they will overflow into the streets above as they have done before. Unless we pay attention to the people, they will rise in rebellion. Flushing fecal matter into rivers poisons our environment and wastes a precious potential resource, Hugo claims; likewise, he implies, locking the poor in prisons poisons society and wastes great potential resources. The naïveté of our wishing always to remain clean and decent by suppressing human waste products is exposed when they contaminate the remainder of society.

Flushing away human wastes symbolizes attempting to conceal all social problems through incarceration—and creating the specious impression that society is making progress by merely changing the words used to refer to our instruments of control. Hugo skewers the euphemistic pseudo-progress that claims to be advancing toward humanitarianism while changing nothing but the words—or worse yet, the arrangement of the words—that describe social conditions: "Formerly those harsh places where prison discipline isolates an inmate were composed of four stone walls, a stone ceiling, a stone floor, a folding bed, a barred skylight, a door reinforced with iron, and were called *dungeons;* but the dungeon came to be considered too horrible; now it's made of an iron door, a barred skylight, a folding bed, a stone floor, a stone ceiling, and four stone walls, and it's called a *punitive detention cell"* (4.6.3.496).

Syllepsis: A Signpost to Mystery

Hugo's synthesizing imagination associates the material with the spiritual by using syllepsis as a signpost to mystery. This figure of speech uses the same word with two radically different meanings in different contexts; the archetype of Inversion, a more fully developed equivalent of syllepsis, suggests that apparently contrasting values are actually the same phenomenon viewed from opposite directions. Hugo prepares us to understand his first prominent use of syllepsis in *Les Misérables* by introducing it with its expanded form, thematic inversion. Impoverished from having given alms, Bishop Myriel rides into the town of Senez on a donkey. He sees that the mayor is scandalized by his humble mount and hears several bourgeois laughing at him. "I see why you are scandalized," Myriel retorts, "you think it's quite prideful for a poor priest to ride a mount that was Christ's [entering Jerusalem on Palm Sunday]. I assure you that I did so from necessity, not vanity" (1.1.3.33–34). A page later, Myriel introduces syllepsis through a pun. Teasing his servant Madame Magloire for calling him "Votre Grandeur" [Your Greatness], he asks her to bring him a chair so that he can reach a book on a high shelf, because "my Greatness/height [ma grandeur] doesn't reach to that board" (1.1.4.35).

The same interplay of material and spiritual reappears in a double meaning when Jean Valjean, at Champmathieu's trial at the time of the Restoration, notices a crucifix on the wall of the courtroom. There had been none when he was tried in 1796: "When he was sentenced, God [the physical representation of Christ; the spirit of God] had been absent" (1.8.9.295). Again, when Cosette and Marius are married on Mardi Gras, a carriage full of ribald maskers hired by the government watches their wedding procession go by, and one of them observes "a false *noce* [wedding procession]. We are the real *noce* [bawdy orgy]" (5.6.1.398). The riffraff in the carriage consider their material celebration more authentic than a spiritual one. Still later, when Marius offers to use his grandfather's influence to secure a pardon ("grâce") for Jean Valjean, the ex-convict answers, "I need only one kind of pardon/grace, that of my conscience" (5.7.1.427–28). Human and divine law contrast.

The predominant syllepsis, of course, is that of the title: "misérable" means both "a member of the underclass" and a morally degenerate person. Poverty often brutalizes people, as Hugo is well aware, but he carefully distinguishes material from spiritual disgrace. Once a character identifies himself as a "misérable" (it is only men who do so in this novel), the term already reveals a self-awareness that anticipates regeneration. Once you acknowledge that you are a reprobate in Hugo's world, you wish to start becoming something better. In the context of the novel, the title connotes both the spiritual hypocrisy of blindly condemning others and the enlightenment of morally condemning oneself, which is the starting point on the road of redemptive contrition. Sinners all, we are invited to emulate Jean Valjean. Key words have exceptional importance in Hugo because of the organic worldview that he shares with many fellow romantics: like chromosomes in a living cell (a concept, of course, unknown at the time) each part of Creation reflects the whole, and all is evolving toward an ultimate atonement with God.[22]

By naming four of the five parts of the work after individuals—Fantine, Cosette, Marius, "L'Idylle rue Plumet et l'épopée rue Saint-Denis" (The Love Story of Plumet Street and the Epic of Saint-Denis Street), and Jean Valjean—Hugo links social lovelessness (our lack of *caritas* or commiseration) to our individual, imperative need for love. In order, the four characters named are the working woman fallen to the status of a prostitute to be able to support her daughter; the daughter, rescued from the abusive Thénardiers by Jean Valjean; the young man who loves her, and who as an admirer of Napoleon has been rejected by his monarchist grandfather; and the redeemed ex-convict. The first and last of the four individual names refer to persons of the older generation (symbolizing the social past), who die because they have no one to love them; the middle two names designate people of the younger generation (symbolizing the social future), who survive because they are loved. The remaining section, on "L'Idylle" (meaning, in French, "love story" or "love interest"), deconstructs the simplistic dichotomy of past and present by contrasting self-absorbed young love with idealistic self-sacrifice in the interests of humanity. We need to be loved both as humans and as ourselves.

Hugo and the Idealistic Novel

A useful starting point for vindicating the aesthetic merits of *Les Misérables* is a provocative distinction made by Naomi Schor in her attempt to rehabilitate the novels of George Sand. Schor divides nineteenth-century French novels into two contrasting strains, the realistic and the idealistic. She claims that the idealistic tradition, familiar at the time and whose chief representative was Sand, has been largely forgotten. Sand's originality, Schor claims, marginalized her.[23]

Valuable as Schor's concept has been in reviving interest in Sand, it unfortunately tempts her readers to slip back into a gender-based essentialism: women can be altruistic, but men cannot. Schor wants to dramatize Sand's achievement, and to that extent her formulations are entirely legitimate; but her view is too limiting in the larger contexts both of romanticism and of the nineteenth century. Balzac, Senancour, Gautier, and even Zola wrote idealistic novels; Stendhal's contain idealistic strands; Flaubert's *Trois Contes* correspond to this genre, and there his "Un cœur simple" (A Simple Heart), a tale of obscure sainthood, was inspired by, and written *for,* George Sand.

Enumerating examples and counter-examples, however, will not explain Hugo. More important is that *Les Misérables* deconstructs the opposition of real and ideal by synthesizing them. Hugo's novel repeatedly refers to Providence, grace, prayer, redemption, and the afterlife. The immortality of the soul is suggested by scenes in which, shortly after they have died, both Fantine and Éponine can understand comforting words said to them, or feel a chaste kiss, and thus can be at peace (1.8.4.324; 4.14.6.171). Indeed, *Les Misérables* ends by explicitly affirming the afterlife, with this sentence referring to Jean Valjean: "No doubt, hidden in shadow, some great angel stood with wings unfurled, waiting for the soul."[24]

Supererogation, the transference of merit beyond what is required for one's own salvation (in French, *réversibilité,* as in the title of Baudelaire's poem in *Les Fleurs du Mal*), provides a guiding thread in *Les Misérables.* Supererogation is a dynamic mode of Inversion, a way of integrating belief in free will with a providentialist fatalism. The first example in the work occurs in the "Conventionnel" G—— (a representative of the assembly that dissolved the monarchy, and of which a majority excluding G—— condemned Louis XVI to death). He humbles Bishop Myriel, who recognizes the moral excellence of his devotion to humanity and kneels before him to ask his blessing. "Nobody could say that his encounter with that mind [le Conventionnel's] did not play a role in [the Bishop's] approach to perfection" (1.1.10.70–71). The blessing is later transferred—so to speak—from Myriel to Valjean, saving the ex-convict from further hatred and crime: "Jean Valjean, my brother, you no longer belong to evil, but to good. It's your soul I am purchasing for you, I'm drawing it away from dark thoughts and from the spirit of perdition, and I'm giving it to God" (1.2.12.134). Valjean symbolically transfers his own excess of merit to the dying Fantine, assuring her that since her motivation for prostituting herself was her pure wish to provide for her daughter, she remained innocent in the eyes of God. And in the final scene, the repentant Marius, kneeling at the dying Valjean's bedside to ask his blessing, recalls the initial scene between the Conventionnel and Myriel.

Hugo broadly signals the presence of supererogatory merit in his characters. First he compares Bishop Myriel to Christ: "When examples were lacking he invented parables, going straight to the point with few words and many images, with the very eloquence of Jesus Christ, full of conviction and persuasive force" (1.1.3.35). Not long afterward, the as yet unredeemed Valjean is sleeping in the bishop's house. When Valjean wakes in the middle of the night, Hugo explains that his unusual last name probably came from the colloquial contraction "v'là Jean" [There's John]. The phrase recalls Pilate's *ecce homo* [There is the man], spoken when he has Christ wearing the crown of thorns brought out to the Jewish priests who have accused him (1.2.6.100; John 19:5): it suggests a person condemned according to one law, and destined for suffering, but who will be redeemed according to a higher law. At the moment, Valjean outwardly remains quite unregenerate, but the bishop's kindness has already begun to work within his soul.

Hugo picks up the comparison between Valjean and Christ during another night, years later, when the ex-convict struggles against the temptation to allow Champmathieu to be condemned in his place: "Thus this unfortunate soul struggled in anguish. Eighteen hundred years earlier, the mysterious being in whom all the holiness and all the suffering of humanity are summed up had, also, while the olive trees shivered in the fierce wind of the infinite, for a long time pushed aside the fearsome chalice that appeared to him trickling with shadows and overflowing with darkness in the starry depths" (1.7.3.264). Hugo reintroduces the image of the chalice in the title of book 7, part 5, "La Dernière Gorgée du calice" (The Last Draught from the Chalice), and affirms Jean Valjean's total transformation unequivocally from Marius's point of view: the young man begins to recognize Valjean's absolute, self-sacrificial goodness: "The convict was becoming transfigured as the Christ" (5.9.4.479).[25]

Hugo blurs the distinction between Providence and will (in a narratologist's language, between "event" and "act") because he believes that these forces work together. As he describes it, the whole story hinges on the slightest circumstance: if Mme Thénardier had been standing instead of sitting when Fantine first saw her, Fantine would have noticed the innkeeper's colossal size, like that of a strong woman in a carnival, and hesitated to confide her daughter Cosette to her: "A person who is seated instead of standing, destinies hinge on such things" (1.4.1.178). The outcome of the Battle of Waterloo similarly depends on a combination of unpredictable circumstances (2.1.5.346; 2.1.8–9.356–62). Again by chance, Jean Valjean takes refuge with Cosette in what proves to be a convent, where the gardener owes Valjean his life. And destiny brings Cosette and Marius together, Hugo says in so many words; once they are ready, they fall in love at a glance (4.3.6.425).

Chance seems to reflect a hidden divine intentionality preserving the possibility of freedom, whereas necessity results from human evil and error. But we are mistaken if we hold God, rather than ourselves, responsible for political events. The cynic Grantaire whimsically complains: "Well now, so there's going to be another revolution? I'm astonished that the good Lord should have such limited resources. At every moment, He has to set about greasing the tracks of events again. Something's sticking, it's not working. Quick, a revolution. The good Lord's hands are always black with that nasty sort of grease" (4.2.2.188). But where society is concerned, Enjolras, the idealistic leader of the insurrection of 1832, adopts a more responsible, proactive view. "The law of progress is that monsters give way to angels, and that Fatality dissipates in the face of Fraternity" (4.12.8.142). Suffering, violence, and injustice will be eliminated by *philia,* by a community of active mutual concern. Hugo, nevertheless, offers a realistic image of political change: one finds only a few committed militants on either side; others are drawn in through love, affection, anxiety, greed, or hatred.

Once he has been redeemed, Jean Valjean's attitudes are shaped by his overarching faith in Providence, by an active passivity that blends act and event. His conviction that God is with him is explicit in the sewers (5.3.1.304–6), and the narrator endorses his view. "Sometimes happenstance compels us to assume duties," he says during his confession to Marius as he tries to explain how a brutal convict could become a loving father to an orphan girl (5.7.1.425). The melodramatic convergence of the destinies of the orphan Pip and the escaped convict Magwitch in Dickens's *Great Expectations* (1861; see chapters 54 and 56), comes to mind: there too, the orphan appreciates his benefactor's devotion only as the latter dies.

Hugo's own faith in Providence appears in the parallels he implies. Devoting his life to Cosette allows Jean Valjean to atone for his crime toward another child, the little chimney sweep. "M. Madeleine" cannot fully assuage his guilt by giving alms to chimney sweeps who pass

through his town. The opportunity for a definitive expiation—first res-
cuing Cosette and later accepting her loss—is presented to him as if by
accident. Marius is redeemed when he manages to arrive at his surrogate
father-in-law's bedside before Jean Valjean dies, whereas he did not
arrive at his real father Pontmercy's bedside on time, being too indifferent to check into the coach schedules. Such interconnected motifs contribute to the structural rhetoric of the implied author, whose plot seems
to reflect a divine plan. Each structure in *Les Misérables* always contains a
strand of actual or potential redemption.

The Realism of Hugo's Moral Vision

So far we have been characterizing Hugo's idealism. In general, critics
are aware of it, if not of its place in a broad tradition. But they have been
less aware of his realism, and still less aware of how realism and idealism
in Hugo are interconnected. He is not vapidly optimistic; his concept of
Providence always preserves a dimension of human responsibility that
can alter an outcome. The three "fatalities" he identifies in the preface to
Les Travailleurs de la mer (that of nature in *Les Travailleurs de la mer,* that
of religious dogma in *Notre-Dame de Paris,* that of social inequities in *Les
Misérables*) are expressions of unreasoning instinct (recall that for Hugo,
nature is sentient). Humans must remain in an unenlightened state to
be able to exercise free will and work out their redemption. Hugo's
moral complexity appears when he describes how Jean Valjean learns to
read and write while in prison. Although Hugo associates education
with the light that dispels darkness, he acknowledges that education can
reinforce evil by empowering the evildoer: "He went to school at age
forty, and learned to read, to write, to do arithmetic. He sensed that to
strengthen his intellect was to strengthen his hatred. Sometimes, education and enlightenment can serve as an extension [like an extra leaf in a
table] for evil" (1.2.7.117). On the contrary, even the arch-villain of the
novel, unlike the villain of melodrama, might not have become irreme-
diably bad:

> Thénardier was one of those dual beings who sometimes pass among us
> unrecognized and disappear without having become known, because des-
> tiny has shown only one side of them. The fate of many people is to live
> half-submerged in this way. In a calm, monotonous situation Thénardier
> had everything necessary to act like—we won't say, to be—what society
> has generally agreed to call an honest businessman, a solid middle-class
> person. Simultaneously, given certain circumstances, certain shocks that

could stir up his lower self, he possessed all the qualities needed to become a scoundrel. He was a shopkeeper with a monster inside. (2.3.9.456–57)

Hugo depicts his characters' moral progress realistically: revelation comes to them in stages, not total and instantaneous like the vision to Saul on the Damascus Road (Acts 9:1–20). Jean Valjean illustrates spiritual progress; Marius, political enlightenment. Raised an unreflective royalist (like Hugo himself, who lends some of his life story to this character), Marius discovers too late how much his father had loved him. He learns to admire Napoleon, the master whom his father served. "His ideas underwent an extraordinary change. The phases of this change were numerous and successive" (3.3.6.159). Many people in his generation, Hugo adds, underwent similar transformations in their political outlook. Marius now realizes that the republic restored their civil rights to the masses, and that the empire restored the rights of France in Europe. He could not but approve. What had seemed the fall of the monarchy now appeared to him the rise of France. What had seemed sunset proved to be the dawn (163).

When Marius begins associating with the republican "Amis de l'A B C" (Friends of the Alphabet/of the "Abaissé" [the oppressed masses; the pun implies that education fosters social progress]), he is startled by their lack of veneration for Napoleon. "Having abandoned his grandfather's opinions to adopt those of his father, he had believed himself settled in his mind; now he suspected, uneasily and without daring to admit it to himself, that he was not. The angle from which he viewed everything was again beginning to shift" (3.4.3.192). At length he forces the issue, addressing his new friends with a lyrical encomium of the emperor: "To vanquish, dominate, strike like thunder, to be in Europe a kind of nation gilded by glory, to sound a titanic fanfare in history, to conquer the world twice, by conquest and by dazzling others, that is sublime; and what could be grander? —To be free, said Combeferre" (3.4.5.202–3). Hearing this retort, Marius feels what the earth must feel when it is pierced by an iron rod so that the grain of wheat may be deposited in it, Hugo explains: only the wound. The quickening of the seed and the joy of bearing fruit come only later (6.203–4). The adversity of poverty will temper his soul (3.5.1–5.207–23).

The crucial moment of Marius's political evolution arrives as he prepares to join his friends at the barricade. He mistakenly thinks Cosette has abandoned him; he wishes to die. But he feels shame when imagining how his father would feel: a hero, who had often risked his life for France, would abhor the son who contributed to plunging his country into civil war (4.13.3.149–55). Stimulated by imminent death, Marius has a sudden illumination. Because of the insurrection he will join, "France will bleed, but liberty will smile" (152). A war against injustice cannot be defined by national boundaries. "In short, to reestablish social truth [human equality], to restore the throne [of France] to freedom, to restore the people to the people, to restore sovereignty to humanity . . . what cause more just, and in consequence, what grander war?" (154).[26]

When the novel ends, Marius has just learned to recognize the spiritual grandeur of Jean Valjean, but he has not yet learned to apply that lesson to society: "He found it self-evident that certain violations of written law should be followed by eternal punishment, and he accepted, as an instrument of civilization, social damnation. He was still at that point, except that his opinions would inevitably evolve later, since he was naturally good, and fundamentally composed entirely of latent progress" (5.7.2.439). After the death of Marius's political companions on the barricade, he never mentions them again. Has he forgotten them and their cause?[27] Hugo leaves Marius morally unfinished in the novel, as he leaves the work of revolution politically unfinished. By selecting the abortive uprising of 1832 as his subject, Hugo avoids a triumphalist perspective that would leave us satisfied that no further progress toward justice was necessary. Such open-endedness solicits our involvement in the society and politics of the future. Losing a battle—the situation in which the exiled Hugo finds himself—does not mean losing the war. Enjolras's metaphor that a revolution is a toll implies not only that rebellion has its costs but also that when you have paid them, you have not yet crossed the bridge (5.1.5).

Hugo's Political Views

Regarding social progress in general, Hugo is optimistic. He shows Jean Valjean, alias M. Madeleine, reading at every meal. Hugo himself once claimed that 20 years of good free mandatory education would be the last word and raise the dawn. Having become a utopian socialist like M. Madeleine, Hugo thinks that salaries will increase naturally as do profits, and that the dynamism of capital expansion will naturally resolve the problems of workers' conditions. To be fair to Hugo, one must realize that in 1862 an organized proletariat had not yet formed, although it was foreshadowed by a workers' uprising in Lyons in 1832. Labor union movements as such had not yet developed. Hugo still thinks that guidance and enlightenment must descend on the people from "above," from the intelligentsia.

Hugo often plays with the reader, drawing us into making hasty, conventional judgments that seem to agree with his. He then withdraws from such positions with a pirouette, leaving us to confront our own superficiality. After admitting that the rabble (*la canaille*) sometimes fights blindly against the common good, he says that he uses words such as "rabble" only with pain and respect, "for when philosophy gets to the bottom of the facts to which such words correspond, it often finds greatness next to wretchedness there. . . . The rabble followed Jesus Christ" (4.1.1.196).

Nor does he blindly espouse one political solution as definitive. Instead, his trenchant political analyses reveal the aporias, the unresolvable difficulties one encounters by adopting either of two opposed positions, which as it happens are those of liberal Democrats and conservative Republicans in the United States today:

> All the problems that the Socialists address can be reduced to two main problems. First problem: To produce wealth. Second problem: To distribute it. . . .
> England resolves the first of these two problems. She creates wealth admirably well; she distributes it badly . . . [She has] an ill-composed grandeur made up of every material element but lacking any moral element.
> Communism and land reform believe they can solve the second problem. They are mistaken. Their [egalitarian] distribution kills [incentive for] production. Sharing equally eliminates the spirit of competition. And consequently, the desire to work. It's a distribution accomplished by the butcher, who kills what he divides. (4.1.4.369–70)

Hugo suggests a balance of these two extreme solutions, socialism and mercantilism.

Thus he characteristically deconstructs naively categorical views that risk blocking compromise and solution. He contests the dichotomies of middle class and lower class, of police and criminals. He argues that the bourgeoisie is simply the materially satisfied portion of "the people," and that on the other hand the mob can betray the best interests of "the people" through unthinking violence (4.1.1.357; 4.10.2.78). He explains that Javert's unreasoning moral rigidity prevents him from realizing that the police are always infiltrated by criminal double agents such as Claquesous, who disappears from the police wagon while on the way to prison: "Did that sphinxlike man have his forepaws in crime and his hind paws in authority? Javert wouldn't hear of such combinations, but there were other inspectors on his squad, perhaps more knowing than he although he outranked them, and Claquesous was such a villain that he could be a very fine agent" (4.2.1.394).

Similarly, Hugo attacks the divine-right monarchists for criticizing the king because he is insufficiently royalist, and the pope because he is insufficiently papal. Such fanatical supporters undermine their cause. They prevent their leaders from making the adaptive compromises that would allow them and the institutions that they represent to survive.

Insofar as he represents the working classes enslaved by the ancien régime, Jean Valjean had in Hugo's eyes been too brutalized and debased to enter the current of historical progress through militant political action. But his destiny prefigures an eventual reconciliation of social classes foreseen by Hugo: the ex-convict presides over the marriage of Cosette—the proletarian daughter of a prostitute—and Marius, the aristocrat adopted by the bourgeois Gillenormand. Nevertheless, Cosette herself does not participate in, or even know about, the insurrection. Hugo implies that we must await Cosette and Marius's children (foreshadowed by the courageous street urchin Gavroche killed fighting on the barricades) to find a full embodiment of the spirit of the new France.[28]

Why choose the obscure revolt of 1832 rather than the glorious revolution of 1830 as the historical crux of the novel? Hugo was struck by the historian Louis Blanc's account of the 1832 uprising. He borrowed most of his facts from Blanc. Creating a practical manual for revolutionaries or celebrating a particular historical triumph interested Hugo less than providing a symbolic illustration of the French people struggling toward the light. From the viewpoint of eternity, as Hugo sees things, minor events (such as 1832) as well as major ones (such as 1830) may reveal the intentions of Providence. The self-sacrifice of Enjolras and his friends will serve to mobilize others. Like Berthold Brecht, Hugo does not want to serve up a cathartic, triumphalist (as the French say) vision of history: he prefers to imply that much work remains to be done.

Conclusion: Hugo in Music and Popular Culture

Hugo's writings survive thanks to his dramatic flair, his gift of creating his own legend as a defender of democracy, and his enormous influence on Western literature. At the end of the nineteenth century, he was considered by far the greatest French poet. He continued to speak from beyond the grave. Following the advice of the spirits who spoke to him during the seances of 1853 to 1855, he held back one quarter of his work from publication: edited by pious executors of his literary estate, it was released every few years for decades following his death.[1]

Since the 1950s, in intellectual circles, Mallarmé, Rimbaud, and especially Baudelaire have eclipsed Hugo as a poet. Both modernism and postmodernism dramatize authors who are calculating and controlled—not instinctual and inspired as was Hugo. Moreover, few of us live in the country any longer: today Baudelaire's and Rimbaud's poetry of urban life speaks more readily to our circumstances than does Hugo's pastoral verse (often composed, of course, in Paris).[2] But many of Hugo's short, simple lyrics lent themselves to the French tradition of memorizing texts in school. Thus they became part of a common cultural heritage once secular primary education became mandatory in 1882 (Robb, 512). And Hugo's novels and plays still live on vibrantly in popular culture. Often distorted beyond recognition, in recent years they have enjoyed a widespread renewal of interest. If one overlooks the complex moral evolution of his characters, the calculated digressions that point toward a hidden unity, his wordplay and artistic self-consciousness, and his rich sense of a social network, then his simplified schemes of character interrelationships lend themselves readily to treatment by the musical theater, opera, television, and film.[3]

Franz Liszt (1811–1886) was inspired by *La Légende des siècles* to compose the symphonic poem "Mazeppa," and Benjamin Britten (1913–1976) set two of Hugo's poems to music together with two of Verlaine's in the "Quatre Chansons Françaises." But Hugo himself was tone-deaf, and unenthusiastic about the idea of musical settings for his plays and novels. Berlioz and Meyerbeer each asked Hugo in vain for permission to make *Notre-Dame de Paris* into an opera. Hugo finally wrote a libretto only as a favor to a friend's ailing daughter, because she wanted to compose a score.[4]

Donizetti created a noteworthy operatic version of Hugo's play *Lucrèce Borgia* the same year that it was first staged. His *Lucrezia Borgia* opened at la Scala in Milan on 26 December 1836 (for a comparison, see Descotes, 106–15). Verdi transformed *Hernani* into an opera— *Ernani*—in 1844, but his *Rigoletto* (1851) has been perhaps the most enduring operatic treatment of Hugo's work.[5] Verdi adapted the play as an opera for the Theatro La Fenice in Venice on 11 March 1851. The opera traveled to England in 1853 and finally reached New York in the late 1940s, drawing large audiences. It remains a classic in the operatic repertory. It draws on Hugo's play *Le Roi s'amuse (The King's Diversion)*. The deformed jester Rigoletto helps his king seduce, betray, and abandon many women. Meanwhile, he hides his daughter Gilda, jealously preserving her virtue. When the king discovers and seduces her too, Rigoletto plans revenge. He hires an adventurer to capture the king, who is sneaking about incognito, and to deliver him to Rigoletto in a sack to be stabbed and drowned. But after the jester stabs a body in a sack, he discovers it is his daughter. Despairing, he commits suicide.

Like concert audiences or sports fans, opera audiences want to see virtuoso performances by stars. The triumphant bravura of opera stars is profoundly at odds with Hugo's historical vision of painfully slow progress guided by Providence, but frequently reversed for a time. Musical-theater audiences, in contrast to opera audiences, go more often to be entertained by sentiment and spectacle. Plot coherence and clarity are unimportant in either opera or musicals. Starting in 1980 at the Palais des Sports in Paris, and then transformed by British (1985) and American versions (the latter opened at the Kennedy Center on 28 December 1986), the musical version of *Les Misérables*, affectionately known as "Les Miz," has enjoyed unprecedented success.[6] By 1989, retranslated from the English version into French, the show returned to Paris for the bicentennial celebration of the Revolution. At that time, there were 17 productions worldwide, opposed to only 13 for the immensely popular *Cats*. A sketch of the orphan girl Cosette as a big-eyed waif became the instantly recognizable logo of the show.

"Les Miz" is through-sung, like an opera, with nonstop music in the background. The chiaroscuro lighting "sculpts the stage with light and shadow" corresponding to the moral polarities of good and evil that form the surface of Hugo's fictional universe. A reviewer comments that "John Napier's giant Erector set scenery—two Louise Nevelson–like sculptures that inch in from the wings to form the junkshop barricade over which the students scrambled during the 1832 Paris uprising," forms an imposing backdrop. As a whole, the production exemplifies "event theater," a manufactured stage success.[7] The Broadway production spawned promotions of record albums, bath towels, posters, and wristwatches, won eight Tony Awards, and was named Best Musical of 1986 to 1987 by the New York Drama Critics' Circle.

Among 28 songs, the musical has 11 ensemble numbers. The producers' primary concern with entertainment and the medium itself— live actors on stage rather than a text—inevitably reinterprets a personal drama of redemption (emblematic of the progress of democracy) as a social event. The isolated character Valjean dominates the novel, but the musical transforms the story into a hymn to revolution. You can reconcile these two strains—spiritual versus political heroism—by recognizing that Hugo's is a mystical, symbolic novel.

The musical seeks dramatic concentration by eliminating digressions and by cutting off the beginning and ending of the story. It adds comedy in treating the Thénardier couple, who are more purely villainous in the novel. Finally, the musical becomes a hymn to a revolution from which God is absent. Onstage, you don't see the initially "satanic" Jean Valjean of the novel, or the moral risks he runs throughout his life through his very devotedness to others: becoming embittered or selfish, and abandoning the good.

Owing to their compelling chiaroscuro effects, their interplay of night, light, and shadow, and their dramatic shifts in visual perspective, Hugo's novels in particular inspired cinematic versions as early as 1905, when Les Misérables became the first full-length feature film produced in the United States. The dominant French sponsor of these films was the Société Pathé, and the director Albert Capellani. Capellani was strongly influenced by André Antoine, who had founded the important, experimental Théâtre-Libre (1887–1894) and become director of the Odéon (1906–1914). Antoine introduced major new German and Scandinavian plays to France. He pioneered in adopting a naturalistic style in which theater showed a "slice of life." Capellani filmed Les Misérables (1912), the play Marie Tudor (1912), Quatrevingt-treize (1914), and Les Travailleurs de la mer (1918), with extraordinary photography by Paul Castenet. The latter two films were made in collaboration with Antoine.

After World War I, Pathé lost exclusive rights to Hugo's works. Producers throughout the world began to adapt them: in Egypt, India, Italy, Japan, Mexico, the Soviet Union, and the United States. Among the most noteworthy silent film versions outside France are *The Hunch-*

back of Notre-Dame de Paris (1924), directed by W. Worsley, with Quasimodo acted scrupulously by Lon Chaney; and *The Man Who Laughs* (1928), directed by Paul Leni, with Conrad Veidt, an outstanding German expressionist actor, as Gwynplaine.

Talkies were introduced in the 1930s. *Les Misérables*, the most popular film subject, was eventually produced in more than 30 versions. The 1934 version directed by Raymond Bernard (Pathé-Nathan), with scenarios by André Lang and score by the famous composer Arthur Honegger, was a monumental classic. Others among the most important talking films included *Lucrèce Borgia* by Abel Gance (1935); *Ruy Blas*, with adaptation and script by the famous Jean Cocteau, and featuring Danielle Darrieux and Jean Marais as the romantic leads (1947); and *Notre-Dame de Paris*, with Anthony Quinn playing Quasimodo opposite Gina Lollobrigida as La Esmeralda (1966). The enduring fascination with Hugo was emphasized in 1975 when *Adèle H.*, the story of the daughter who went mad, was filmed by François Truffaut, starred Isabelle Adjani, and received the Grand Prix du Cinéma Français. To the motif of the difficult life of a child overshadowed by a parent's genius, *Adèle H.* adds the feminist implications of a woman destroyed by her desperate yearning for attention in a man's world.[8]

Finally, in 1996, the Walt Disney Corporation created an animated version of *Notre-Dame de Paris*. It is filled with droll changes. Frollo adopts Quasimodo initially only because another priest shames him into doing so. When alone with Quasimodo (whose deafness is conveniently forgotten), three of the gargoyles come alive and are his friends; two of them are named "Victor" and "Hugo." Claude Frollo is no longer a reclusive priest searching for the alchemists' secret for making gold, but rather the fearsome provost (chief executive officer, comparable to a mayor) of Paris. His major ambition is to exterminate the Gypsies, who are hiding in the catacombs of Paris. La Esmeralda becomes an assertive feminist heroine. As she is dueling the captain of the guard, Gaston Phœbus, to a standstill, he admiringly remarks: "You fight almost as well as a man!" "Funny," La Esmeralda replies, "I was just about to say the same about you." The shallow, self-centered Phœbus becomes a likable hero. At the end, Quasimodo symbolically unites him with La Esmeralda and renounces his own hope for her love by joining their hands. The story is a flashback, retold to two children by the Gypsy king disguised as a puppeteer with a stall just outside the cathedral.

Before we hasten to condemn Disney for betraying Hugo's vision, we should realize that Hugo was among the first to betray it himself. In

1836 he wrote the libretto for an operatic adaptation, *Esmeralda*, in which the gypsy and Phœbus truly love each other. Instead of uniting them in Disney's happy ending, however, Hugo makes typical romantics of them: they commit suicide, for no very good reason, at the end.

Television, as well as film, provides a congenial medium for Hugo's works. Adaptations have brought to life some plays never successful on the stage: modern sets and photographic technique can finally convey the grandeur of Hugo's vision. (You will recall the discussion of his essentially cinematic visual imagination in the chapter on *Notre-Dame de Paris*.) Technology has caught up with his genius. Recently, the outstanding experimental Théâtre de la Jeune Lune in Minneapolis has staged highly successful adaptations of both *Notre-Dame de Paris* and of *Les Misérables*. Having 40-some vertical feet to play with, their sets can convincingly simulate a cathedral or a city. Two of the best TV versions have revitalized the plays *Les Burgraves* (1968) and *Torquemada* (1976).

Finally, Hugo has received the ultimate compliment, in popular culture, of being rendered into comic books. Gilberton Publishers of New York issued *Les Misérables* (1945), *Toilers of the Sea* (1949), *The Man Who Laughs* (1950), and *The Hunchback of Notre Dame* (1966) in their Classics Illustrated series. Academic Industries [sic] reissued *Notre-Dame de Paris* as a comic in 1984, and Smithmark (titled *The Hunchback of Notre-Dame*) as a Classic Comics in 1991. Fernande De Felipe's comic-strip version of *The Man Who Laughs*, originally in Spanish, was translated in an issue of *Heavy Metal* in 1994.

The variety of forms of recognition that Hugo has received shows his vast popularity. The chronology at the beginning of this volume mentions some of them. To recall a mere sampling: a geranium named after him won a prize at a flower show in 1877. The Cao Dai Buddhist religious cult in Vietnam today venerates him as a saint—some of its priests are believed to be reincarnations of Hugo and of his sons—and has a thousand shrines and two or three million followers dedicated to his memory.[9] The ending of the movie *Batman* is filled with tongue-in-cheek allusions to the ending of *Notre-Dame de Paris*.[10] Referring to Graham Robb's 1998 biography, a full-page portrait of Hugo appeared on the cover of the 15 February 1998 *New York Times Book Review* (review by Peter France, 7). Hugo currently is featured on many Web sites where you can communicate with other fans. Because he appeals so strongly to both the academic and the popular imagination, his fame today is more widespread—and may be more enduring—than that of other masters of

nineteenth-century French literature such as Balzac, Baudelaire, and
Flaubert. Hugo's flair as a storyteller gives his work broad appeal; his
passionate advocacy of humanitarian causes gives him depth. His growing reputation may still surprise us all. Tony Harrison recently wrote a
well-received reworking of *Le Roi s'amuse*, called *The Prince's Play* (London: Faber and Faber, 1996). And as I write (March 1998), yet another
American film version of *Les Misérables* is being publicized.

Aside from Hugo's genius, the major secret of his great success is our
psychic projections. Here comments by the critics of "Les Miz" are quite
revealing. They find his work simple, elemental. They fall into the same
trap as do most of Hugo's characters and his earlier readers: seeing only
the spectacular surface, they translate his moral universe into black and
white. The British producer John Caird claimed that "nothing has been
lost in transferring *Les Misérables* [a 1,200-page novel] to the stage. . . .
'I mean, you can tell the story without being disrespectful in two or
three sentences. If you try to do that with any Dickens novel it would
take at least two hours and you still would be dissatisfied with the
result.' "[11] (In this book, the plot summary runs 3,000 words.) Another
critic interpreted the novel as a "chase story between good and evil—
with good ironically represented by a runaway convict and evil by a
zealot of a policeman."[12] But anyone who knows the novel well realizes
that both Javert and Valjean are morally complex. The flawed humanity
that makes possible Valjean's ambiguous rehabilitation and Javert's
anguished forgiveness of him is lacking from the "event theater" stage,
where two forces must contend in stark opposition. And the successive
political and moral awakenings of the young hero Marius cannot be represented in a musical. The same leveling affects lesser characters. For
example, Thénardier onstage is merely comic, whereas in the novel he
degenerates morally. Yet as a novelistic villain, he more than once unwittingly serves the designs of Providence. Initially we may be drawn to
Hugo by his blatant sentimentality and by what seems a melodramatic
imagination contrasting pure good with pure evil. But whereas "Les
Miz" rushes to judgment, *Les Misérables* urges us to suspend judgment,
to ponder the complexities of character, of history, and of Providence. As
our craving for simplicity attests, the melodramatic imagination may be
more ours than Hugo's.

Notes and References

Preface

1. Gide's response to a survey in *L'Hermitage,* 2 February 1902, 139.
2. See Graham Robb, *Victor Hugo* (New York: Norton, 1998), 7. Hugo's maternal great-grandfather was an aide to the notorious war criminal Carrier, who ordered mass executions of royalists; his maternal great-aunt was Carrier's mistress.
3. Victor Hugo, *Œuvres poétiques,* vol. 2, *Les Châtiments; Les Contemplations,* ed. Pierre Albouy (Paris: Gallimard, 1967), 482. This and all translations throughout the book are mine.
4. Robb points out that the 11 short plays and dramatic poems posthumously published as *Le Théâtre en liberté* in 1886 anticipate the modernism of Brecht, Ionesco, and Beckett: "Their settings range from a cloister on the Isle of Man to a railway track, and the characters include a talking stone and a 100-year-old woman in a sack" (431).

Chapter One

1. In October 1812, the execution of Lahorie, the lover of Hugo's mother, ended her career as a Republican conspirator. During the Restoration, she espoused the constitutional royalism advocated by Chateaubriand. See Graham Robb, *Victor Hugo* (New York: Norton, 1998), 41, 49.
2. Named after the medieval *Romance of the Emperor Alexander,* which is written with such versification, the alexandrine was the dominant formal French verse rhythm from the Renaissance until the early twentieth century. The English equivalent is iambic pentameter (10-syllable lines), now equally outmoded.
3. Robb, 54–57. Compare the artist Picasso, whose first word was supposedly *piz* (for *lápiz,* "pencil"). In their facility, versatility, intense sexuality, and egomania, the two figures are not dissimilar.
4. Freud's 1917 essay "Mourning and Melancholia" usefully distinguishes normal grieving that the mourner gradually overcomes after a loss from pathological melancholia. The latter is intractable because the bereaved person remains angry at the loved one for "abandonment" (even if the loved person has simply died), and turns that anger against the self. The suicide of Goethe's Young Werther illustrates this condition well.
5. For background on the ode, see Margaret Gilman, *The Idea of Poetry in France from Houdar de la Motte to Baudelaire* (Cambridge, Mass.: Harvard Uni-

versity Press, 1958), 17–18, 86–88, 148–89; John Heath-Stubbs, *The Ode* (London: Oxford University Press, 1969); and Carol Maddison, *Apollo and the Nine: A History of the Ode* (Baltimore, Md.: Johns Hopkins University Press, 1960).

6. For a fuller treatment of how the French romantics recreated neoclassic verse genres in more acutely self-conscious forms, see Laurence M. Porter, *The Renaissance of the Lyric in French Romanticism* (Lexington, Ky.: French Forum, 1978).

7. Pierre Albouy, ed., *Victor Hugo: Œuvres poétiques,* vol. 1, *Avant l'exil, 1802–1851* (Paris: Gallimard, 1964), 312–13. Hereafter cited as *OP* 1. This and all translations throughout the book are mine.

8. Condensed and paraphrased from a traditional folk ballad with varying titles, this motif was readopted in the Broadway tune "Our Love Is Here to Stay."

9. Other writers who reinforced Lamennais's influence on Hugo at that time were Joseph de Maistre, Saint-Simon, Ballanche, and Baron Eckstein. The last introduced Hugo to the idealist philosophy of Fichte, Schlegel, and Schelling. See Bernard Guyon, *La Vocation poétique de Victor Hugo: Essai sur la signification spirituelle des "Odes et ballades" et des "Orientales" (1818–1828)* (Gap, France: Louis-Jean, 1954), 42.

In 1870, at the moment when France was most severely weakened politically, the proclamation of the doctrine of papal infallibility when speaking *ex cathedra* on faith and morals climaxed the Vatican's efforts toward reasserting papal power over the French church, an authority severely compromised when Napoleon had crowned himself emperor in 1804 with the pope present.

10. For countless examples, see Christ's Beatitudes in the Sermon on the Mount, the story of Christ's humiliation and crucifixion ending as a redemptive triumph ("And with His stripes we are healed"), or the Christian topos of the *felix culpa* or "fortunate fall" (humanity had to fall from innocence into sin before reaching the higher state of salvation). William Blake illustrates the negative form of Inversion in "The Marriage of Heaven and Hell" (what seemed an enlightened angel proves to be a spiritually blinded devil).

11. English behaves differently: there the juxtaposition of two nouns—houseboat, boathouse; cornfield, field corn; cable TV, TV cable—is so frequent that some computer programs for translating from English have lumped English nouns and adjectives together into one class, "nadjes."

12. As Albouy explains (*OP* 1, 1240), "[Gaules] refers to the ancient France of [the Druid priestess] Velléda, in [Chateaubriand's] *Les Martyrs,* and also to that of Charlemagne and the Middle Ages in Marchangy's *La Gaule poétique* (Poetic Gaul)."

13. Republished in *Littérature et philosophie mêlées,* in *Œuvres complètes: Edition chronologique,* ed. Jean Massin, vol. 5, 160–73, esp. 160–62.

14. Robb plausibly argues that Ordener's ardent professions of love are coded messages from Hugo to Adèle; both families had forbidden the young people to see or write to each other (88–91).

15. The bear's name suggests a confusion of the animal with the human that will reappear throughout Hugo's career, for example in the Satyr (half-goat, half-man) of *La Légende des siècles*, or in the pair of Homo ("Man") the Wolf and Ursus ("Bear") the Man in *L'Homme qui rit*. At once visionary and intensely sexual, Hugo is keenly aware of his nature as *homo duplex*, a compound of the physical and the spiritual.

16. "Sur l'abbé de Lamennais à propos de 'L'Essai sur l'indifférence en matière de religion' " (July 1823), in *Littérature et philosophie mêlées, OC* 5, 135.

17. Kathryn M. Grossman, *The Early Novels of Victor Hugo: Towards a Poetics of Harmony* (Geneva: Droz, 1986), 52.

18. "Sur Lord Byron: A propos de sa mort," in *Littérature et philosophie mêlées, OC* 5, 140–41.

19. See also Hugo's poem "A mon père" of August 1823, in *Nouvelles Odes* (*OC* 1, 346–48), and Grossman 1986, 61.

20. Victor Hugo, *Bug-Jargal ou la révolution haïtienne: Les deux versions du roman (1818 et 1826),* ed. Roger Toumson (Fort-de-France, Martinique: Désormeaux, 1979), 156.

21. The situation recalls and may have inspired Alfred de Vigny's *Servitude et Grandeur Militaires* (1835), tales of career soldiers enslaved by their sense of honor.

22. For additional parallels with later works, see Richard Grant, *The Perilous Quest* (Durham, N.C.: Duke University Press, 1968), 22–24.

23. Concerning this theme see Servais Etienne, *Les Sources de "Bug-Jargal"* (Brussels: Palais des Académies, 1923), 17–39.

24. Grossman 1986, 104; see also Bernard Mouralis, "Histoire et culture dans *Bug-Jargal*," *Revue des Sciences Humaines* 149 (1973): 47–68.

25. "But de cette publication" (The Goal of This Publication), in *Littérature et philosophie mêlées, OC* 5, 38–40.

Chapter Two

1. Cf. Kathryn M. Grossman, *The Early Novels of Victor Hugo: Towards a Poetics of Harmony* (Geneva: Droz, 1986), 172–73, and Jeffrey Mehlman, *Revolution and Repetition: Marx/Hugo, Balzac* (Berkeley: University of California Press, 1977), 83. Quasimodo may in part represent Hugo himself. After bearing four children, and exhausted by her husband's frequent sexual demands, his wife Adèle had recently refused ever to have sex with him again. He is rejected, but it is he who loves her best. Ironically, "La Esmeralda," "the emerald," traditionally represented chastity, but she like her historical counterpart Adèle throws herself at a vain, uncaring rival (Phœbus/Sainte-Beuve).

2.   In this sequence, the characters appear to correspond to the five stages of evolution Goethe describes in his poem "Urworte, Orphisch" (Primal Words, Orphic) of 1817 to 1818 and its commentary in 1820. (See Johann Wolfgang von Goethe, *The Collected Works*, vol. 1, *Selected Poems*, ed. Christopher Middleton [Princeton, N.J.: Princeton University Press, 1994], 230–33.) The five stages are *daimon* (spirit), corresponding to La Esmeralda; *tyche* (chance), corresponding to Gringoire; *eros* (physical love), corresponding to Phœbus; *ananké* (necessity), corresponding to Frollo; and *elpis* (hope), corresponding to Quasimodo. Charles Dédéyan asserts that Hugo repeatedly praised the German poet from 1830 on; Frollo's search for alchemical knowledge echoes Goethe's Faust myth; La Esmeralda recalls Mignon in Goethe's *Wilhelm Meisters Lehrjahre* (Wilhelm Meister's Apprenticeship). Hugo's admiration was not, however, reciprocated. See Dédéyan, *Victor Hugo et l'Allemagne*, 2 vols. (Paris: Minard, 1964–1965), vol. 2, pp. 286–87, 289, 312, 320.

3.   References from *Notre-Dame de Paris: 1482* are taken from Léon Cellier's edition (Paris: Garnier-Flammarion, 1967) because of its availability and low cost. Hereafter cited in the text by book, chapter, and page.

4.   On Gringoire as a parody of the poet figure, see Grossman 1986, 178.

5.   Cf. 274–76, 455–56, 475–78, and the ironic mention of Gringoire's ultimate success, 507.

6.   Suzanne Nash traces Hugo's ambivalence toward revolution throughout his career. See "Writing a Building: Hugo's *Notre-Dame de Paris*," *French Forum* 8, no. 3 (May 1983): 122–24; four important earlier articles by Victor Brombert on the same theme are cited on Nash, 131 n. 1.

7.   Inspired by Sir Walter Scott's historical novels in general, and by his foray into French history with *Quentin Durward* in particular, Hugo repeatedly emulated Scott. "With *Notre-Dame de Paris* . . . Hugo finally meets in full the challenge presented by Scott, combining historical fiction, melodrama, and Gothic terror with substantial reflections on art, culture, law, and politics" (Grossman 1986, 207; see also 161).

8.   See Richard B. Grant, *The Perilous Quest: Image, Myth, and Prophecy in the Narratives of Victor Hugo* (Durham, N.C.: Duke University Press, 1968), 49–64. Grant interprets this image of religious truth (the rose window) as a *leurre* (a red herring, or misleading clue), but it is more accurate to say that from Hugo's point of view the mistake would be to presume to reach religious truth unaided, and during our mortal life. Compare the last line of Hugo's *Dieu:* the poet must die before he can know God.

9.   Compare the poem "Puissance égale bonté" (Power Equals Kindness) in *La Légende des siècles* (The Legend of the Ages), where the Islamic devil Iblis tries to rival God in creation but can make only a spider. God then transforms the spider into a sun. Recall also Captain Ahab's golden guinea nailed to the mast in Melville's *Moby Dick*.

10.   In a felicitous phrase, John Porter Houston calls the cathedral "a misleading book of wisdom" (*Victor Hugo*, rev. ed. [Boston: Twayne, 1988], 27).

11. See Stirling Haig, "From Cathedral to Book, from Stone to Press: Hugo's Portrait of the Artist in *Notre-Dame de Paris*," *Stanford French Review* 3 (1979): 343–50. Gothic fantasy topping Romanesque mass "*shows* liberty succeeding despotism" (347).

12. As in Greek tragedy, Grossmann points out, "Paquette la Chantefleurie's fervent prayer that her child [La Esmeralda] might be [restored] to her if only for an hour is . . . perversely taken at face value" (1986, 188 n. 37); she dies as her daughter is dragged to the scaffold.

13. Within his plot, Hugo further transcends the limitations of a single vision through his hypercreativity, a characteristic he shares with Balzac. He imagines and evokes many different possibilities for either the causes or the outcomes of events, beyond those pursued in the main line of action. On the first page, he suggests six different reasons for the excitement of the Paris crowds on 6 January 1482, only to reject all of them (1.1.38). Two pages later, he proposes three different explanations for a fire before concluding ironically: "Whatever you may think of this threefold explanation, political, physical, and poetical, for why the Palais de Justice burned down in 1618, the fact that is unfortunately certain, is the fire" (1.1.40–41).

14. Compare Hugo's extraordinary impressionistic account of his first train ride in a letter to his wife on 22 August 1837, in Jean Gaudon, Sheila Gaudon, and Bernard Leuilliot, eds., *Victor Hugo: Correspondance familiale et écrits intimes. II: 1828–1839* (Paris: Laffont, 1991), 420–24. See also how Hugo finds hieratic letters in landscapes ("Voyage de 1839. Albums. 'De Genève à Aix,' 24 July 1839," in *OC* 6, 715–16). The most telling instance of impressionistic vision in *Notre-Dame de Paris* is Hugo's description of the crowd at the *mystère* as "a human kaleidoscope" (1.5.73).

15. On such incomplete hybrid forms, which correspond to Hugo's aesthetic concept of his novel, see Victor Brombert, *Victor Hugo and the Visionary Novel* (Cambridge, Mass.: Harvard University Press, 1986), 51–56.

16. Compare Jehan Frollo's remark, whimsically anticipating the great poem "Magnitudo Parvi" (The Vastness of Little Things) of the *Contemplations*: "The bourgeois are lighting their candles, and the good Lord, His stars" (9.1.377).

Chapter Three

1. See Charles Affron, *A Stage for Poets: Studies in the Theatre of Hugo and Musset* (Princeton, N.J.: Princeton University Press, 1971), 3–115.

2. Michel Butor concludes a three-part article, "Le Théâtre de Victor Hugo" (*La Nouvelle Revue Française* 13 [January 1965]: 105–113), by defending Hugo's medley of dramatic styles as anticipating a "total theater" unappreciated because ahead of its time.

3. Near the end of his career, Shakespeare adequately worked out the problem of achieving a just revenge only in the two fantasy plays with plots

entirely invented by him—*A Midsummer Night's Dream* and *The Tempest*. See Bernard J. Paris, *Bargains with Fate: Psychological Crises and Conflicts in Shakespeare and His Plays* (New York: Insight, 1991). Hugo's affinity with Shakespeare, to whom he devoted a book-length essay (his most substantial study of any author), partly depends on their common thematic interests. Traditional Freudian critics would call such situations "Oedipal": the king is "the father of his country," and the rebel, like a son (younger, less powerful, not yet legitimized), opposes this symbolic father.

4.   One immediately recalls Corneille's play *Cinna, ou la clémence d'Auguste*. The difference is that Corneille's Augustus is from the beginning a legitimate and worthy emperor; Hugo's Cromwell is illegitimate, and his Don Carlos is initially unworthy.

5.   Anne Ubersfeld, *Le Roi et le bouffon: Etude sur le théâtre de Hugo de 1830 à 1839* (Paris: Corti, 1974), 605; hereafter cited in the text.

6.   See Jean Gaudon, *Victor Hugo et le théâtre: Stratégie et dramaturgie* (Paris: Suger, 1985): 28–34; hereafter cited as Gaudon 1985.

7.   Anonymous review in the royalist *La Quotidienne*, 19 November 1838, quoted in Gaudon 1985, 36. Regarding *Ruy Blas*, Gaudon (36 n. 1) reproduces an even more pointed passage: "You can understand that respectable society is disgusted by this queen rolling on the ground beside the corpse of a valet in livery, while those spectators in workers' smocks and caps marvel at a lackey who orders great lords about, insults them, and manages to be loved by a queen" (review in *Le Moniteur*, n.d.).

8.   The recurrent motif of the rivalry of three men for the love of one woman may reflect Hugo's personal situation: his older brother, Eugène, and later his best friend, Sainte-Beuve, both loved Adèle passionately.

9.   Victor Hugo, *Hernani*, ed. Denis Canal (Paris: Larousse, 1991), 1.2.5.155. All references in the text to individual lines come from this edition, chosen for its availability and modest cost. The same reasons dictated the choice of the edition of *Ruy Blas* used here (hereafter *Ruy Blas*, ed. Claude Eterstein [Paris: Larousse, 1995]).

10.   Allan H. Pasco's innovative study *Sick Heroes: French Society and Literature in the Romantic Age* (Exeter, U.K.: University of Exeter Press, 1997) finds the origins of such psychopathology in "the unrocked cradle," that is, widespread abuses of wet-nursing and child labor—the former continuing in France until later than in England and Germany. A skeptical feminist thesis—romantic males' "sick role" is a devious way of maintaining control over women—is brilliantly argued by Margaret Waller in her book *The Male Malady: Fictions of Impotence in the French Romantic Novel* (New Brunswick, N.J.: Rutgers University Press, 1993).

11.   See André Maurois, *Olympio ou la vie de Victor Hugo* (Paris: Hachette, 1954; English translation: New York: Harper, 1956), 174–77; the French edition (translations mine) is hereafter cited in the text. In the tradition of classical theater, all fighting and violent death had to occur offstage.

12. Gaudon (1985, 165–85) deciphers, reproduces, and analyzes Hugo's marginal comments written in the margins of his play during performances (specific comments are found in Gaudon's appendix, 179–85).

13. To this day, right-wing French people may use *vous* even within the family, whereas the intimate *tu* can mark Socialist or Communist leanings—cf. the implications of the English word "comrade." For a thorough, careful study of forms of address in instances other than those discussed here, see Michel Grimaud, "Tutoiement, titre et identité sociale: Le système de l'adresse du Cid au Théâtre en liberté," *Poétique* 77 (1989): 53–75 (on *Hernani*, 64–69). He even argues convincingly that "*Hernani* . . . is largely constructed around acts of naming" (70).

14. Concentrating on *Marion de Lorme* and *Marie Tudor*, Timothy Raser offers an important, characteristically lucid analysis of the defective speech acts in Hugo's theater: the characters frequently give orders, make vows, and issue decrees that misfire or are retracted. Such performatives "occur under circum stances where it is impossible to determine their felicity," circumstances that reflect the confusion regarding the location and prerogatives of legitimate authority in the France of Hugo's time (397). See Raser, "The Limits of Performative Language in Hugo's Theater," *Romanische Forschungen* 105, nos. 3–4 (1993): 392–98.

15. George Moskos, "(En)gendering Power in Victor Hugo's *Hernani*," *Neophilologus* 78, no. 1 (January 1994): 55. This is a groundbreaking feminist/homosocial analysis of the play.

16. See Barbara Cooper, "Parodying Hugo," *European Romantic Review* 2, no. 1 (Summer 1991): 23–38.

17. Ubersfeld rightly observes that valets disguised as masters were not uncommon in the eighteenth-century theater of Marivaux and Beaumarchais (316). Mazarin, a servant, had become the husband of Anne d'Autriche in seventeenth-century France, but such mesalliances were rare.

18. Jean-Marie Thomasseau, "Le Jeu des écritures dans *Ruy Blas*," *Revue des lettres modernes* 693–97 (*Victor Hugo* 1, 1984): 55–80.

Chapter Four

1. Should there be any doubt about the connection between Middle Eastern poetic topics and abandonment of monarchical themes, Goethe dispels it in his *West-Östlichen Diwan (The Parliament of West and East)* of 1814 to 1818:

> North and West and South are breaking,
> Thrones are bursting, kingdoms shaking:
> Flee, then, to the essential East,
> Where on patriarch's air you'll feast!
> There to love and drink and sing,
> Drawing youth from Khizr's spring.

("Hegira" [1814], in Johann Wolfgang von Goethe, *The Collected Works,* vol. 1, *Selected Poems,* ed. Christopher Middleton, 202–5 [Princeton, N.J.: Princeton University Press, 1994].)

2. For contrasts with other French poets, see Laurence M. Porter, *The Renaissance of the Lyric in French Romanticism* (Lexington, Ky.: French Forum, 1978).

3. William Blake, "Auguries of Innocence," in *English Romantic Poetry and Prose,* ed. Russell Noyes (1956; New York: Oxford, 1969), 222–23, vv. 10–13; hereafter cited in the text.

4. Pierre Albouy, ed., *Victor Hugo: Œuvres poétiques,* vol. 1, *Avant l'exil, 1802–1851,* 725 (untitled). Hereafter cited in the text as *OP* 1.

5. For a capable discussion of the other, more predominant side of the *Orientales*—descriptive "pure poetry" leading to the Art for Art's Sake movement led by Théophile Gautier—see John Porter Houston, *Victor Hugo,* rev. ed. (Boston: Twayne, 1988), 11–19.

6. Elizabeth Barineau, " 'Les Feuilles d'automne': l'intime et l'universel," *Modern Philology* 58 (1960): 22–23.

7. See Lamartine's *Méditations* (1820) and his "La Mort de Socrate" (The Death of Socrates, 1823). Platonism was also inherited from the Renaissance poetry popularized by Sainte-Beuve.

8. See Etienne de Ullmann, "La Transposition dans la poésie lyrique de Hugo des *Odes et Ballades* aux *Contemplations,*" *Le Français moderne* 19 (October 1951): 282–86.

9. Hugo liked to claim that he had been conceived near the summit of Mont Blanc—like him majestic, international, and famous. In fact, he may at best have been conceived on the more modest Donon, where a monument to the event was later erected as a practical joke. See Robb, *Victor Hugo,* 3–6.

10. By comparison, one can see the relative weakness of Baudelaire's overrated "Correspondances" ("La nature est un temple où de vivants piliers / Laissent parfois sortir de confuses paroles" [Nature is a temple; living columns / Sometimes allow some faint words to emerge].

11. The notion that his mother influenced him by being a devout Catholic, however, seems unfounded. He was not even baptized. See Robb, 10.

12. A modern, scientific equivalent to the idea of an omnipresent spark of soul would be the presence of DNA in every cell of every living thing. DNA is simultaneously a unique signature in each organism and a universal principle of life.

13. Earl R. Wasserman offers an excellent brief discussion of this concept, situating it firmly in the history of ideas, in *The Subtler Language* (Baltimore, Md.: Johns Hopkins University Press, 1959), 53–61 (part of a reading of Sir John Denham's "Cooper's Hill"). See also Susanne K. Langer's superb reading of a passage from Oliver Goldsmith's "The Deserted Village" in her *Feeling and Form* (New York: Scribner's, 1953), 231–33.

14. To clarify, in these seven nested chiasmuses we have:

1, 2, 2, 1: name A, name B, name B, name A
3, 4, 4, 3: adjective, noun, noun, adjective
5, 6, 6, 5: adverbial, name, name, adverbial
7, 8, 7, 8, 7: adverbial, description, adverbial, description, adverbial
9, 10, 10, 9: noun, adjective of color, adjective of color, noun
11, 12, 12, 11: adjective, noun, noun, adjectives
13, 14, 14, 13: pronoun, verb, verb, pronoun

15. Hugo's depiction of this second death by being forgotten anticipates Jules Romains's "unanimist" novel of 1901, *Mort de Quelqu'un*.

16. See, for example, the text with the editorial title "Voyage de 1837"
(*OC* 5, 1265–1323), 1305–8. In the first section, the poet wonders whether
the dead think of the living as we think of the dead.

Chapter Five

1. Graham Robb, *Victor Hugo* (New York: Norton, 1998), 117.

2. See Jules Michelet, *Mon Journal, 1820–1823* (Paris, 1888), 12–13.
This and related references are found in Gustave Charlier's valuable "Comment
fut écrit 'Le Dernier Jour d'un condamné,' " *Revue d'histoire littéraire de la France*
22 (1915): 321–60.

3. Charlier, 322 and 360. Capital punishment remains a profoundly
controversial issue today.

4. He also voted in favor of a military expedition to protect the Vatican from being overrun by Austrian troops, but he spoke against subverting
that mission by maintaining the temporal power of the papacy, an aim that
Catholic conservatives managed to add (19 October 1849). Saved by the French
army, the pope flouted the wishes of the French Republicans who had sent it.
He promptly issued a bull, *Motu Proprio* ("By Our Own Decision"), that denied
civil liberties to his subjects.

5. See Guy Rosa, "Comment on devient républicain," *Revue des Sciences
Humaines* 156 (1974): 653–71.

6. Victor Hugo, *Œuvres complètes, édition chronologique*, ed. Jean Massin,
vol. 7, *Carnets, Albums, Journaux* (Paris: Le Club Français du Livre, 1967–1971),
1214; hereafter cited as *OC*. For this reference, and for much of the discussion
of Hugo's political role under the Second Republic, I am indebted to Guy Rosa,
"Comment on devient républicain."

7. Madame de Staël anticipated the idea of a Franco-Prussian pact in
De l'Allemagne (On Germany), the greatest manifesto of French romanticism
(1813; the printer's plates for the first edition were smashed by Napoleon I's
police in 1810). Hugo had earlier suggested an accord based on the return of
the Left Bank of the Rhine—lost in 1815—to France. See chapter 16 in his *Le
Rhin, lettres à un ami* (The Rhine), *OC* 6, 535–36.

8. Victor Hugo, *Les Misérables*, ed. René Journet, 3 vols. (Paris: Garnier-Flammarion, 1967), part 5, book 1, chapter 5, 215–18. The substance of

the two foregoing paragraphs comes from Angelo Metzidakis, "Victor Hugo and the Idea of a United States of Europe," *Nineteenth-Century French Studies* 23, nos. 1–2 (Fall 1994–Winter 1995): 72–84. For additional background, see Pierre Renouvin, *L'Idée de la fédération européenne dans la pensée politique du dix-neuvième siècle* (Oxford: Clarendon, 1949), and Georges Gusdorf, "Quel horizon on voit du haut de la barricade," in *Hommage à Victor Hugo* (Strasbourg: Bulletin de la Faculté de Lettres de l'Université de Strasbourg, 1962), 175–96.

9. Victor Hugo, "À Juvenal," in *Victor Hugo: Œuvres poétiques*, ed. Pierre Albouy, vol. 2, *Les Châtiments, Les Contemplations* (Paris: Gallimard, 1967), 6.13.170–76; hereafter cited in the text as *OP* 2.

10. A literary provocation for Hugo's rebuttal of the notion that the military person's integrity consists in absolute obedience to authority can be found in Alfred de Vigny's three novellas of army life, *Servitude et grandeur militaires* (1835). On the latter, see Stirling Haig, "Conscience and Antimilitarism in Vigny's *Servitude et grandeur militaires*," *PMLA* 89 (January 1974): 50–56.

11. Cf. Jean-Marie Gleize and Guy Rosa, " 'CELUI-LA': Politique du sujet poétique: Les 'Châtiments' de Hugo," *Littérature* 24 (December 1976): 97.

12. Ibid., 86, 90, 96. The critics refer particularly to poem 6 (of 13) in book 4 (of 7), "La Religion est glorifiée." This text, "Écrit le 17 juillet 1851, en descendant de la tribune" (written 17 July 1851 while coming down from the speaker's platform) expresses Hugo's scorn for the representatives who approved revising the constitution so as to give the future Napoleon III absolute power. Hugo's famous speech denouncing the change was interrupted 111 times, and the president of the assembly joined the deputies of the Right in shouting down and condemning Hugo.

13. Pierre Barbéris, "A propos de 'Lux': la vraie force des choses (sur l'idéologie des *Châtiments*)," *Littérature* 1 (1971): 92–105.

14. It was Hugo, incidentally, who popularized the dialectal word *la pieuvre* for octopus, replacing the standard French *la poulpe*. *La pieuvre* probably appealed to him because of its phonic resemblance to *l'épreuve* (the ordeal).

15. John Porter Houston, *Victor Hugo*, rev. ed. (Boston: Twayne, 1988), 145–46.

16. Jacques Body, "Préface" to *Quatrevingt-treize*, by Victor Hugo (Paris: Garnier-Flammarion, 1965), 12–14. Further references are to this edition.

Chapter Six

1. See Albert O. Lovejoy, *The Great Chain of Being: A Study of the History of an Idea* (Cambridge, Mass.: Harvard University Press, 1936); Jacques Roos, *Les Idées philosophiques de Victor Hugo: Ballanche et Victor Hugo* (Paris: Nizet, 1958); Denis Saurat, *La Religion de Victor Hugo* (Paris: Hachette, 1929); Gustave Simon, *Les Tables tournantes de Jersey, Procès-verbaux des séances* (Paris: Conard,

1923); Auguste Viatte, *Les Sources occultes du romantisme, illuminisme, théosophie, 1770–1820,* 2 vols. (Paris: Champion, 1928); and Charles Villiers, *L'Univers métaphysique de Victor Hugo* (Paris: Vrin, 1970).

2. Victor Hugo, *La Légende des siècles; La Fin de Satan; Dieu,* ed. Jacques Truchet (1962; Paris: Gallimard, 1981), 830; hereafter cited in the text as *Légende.*

3. Pierre Albouy, *Victor Hugo: Œuvres poétiques,* vol. 2, *Les Châtiments, Les Contemplations* (Paris: Gallimard, 1967), 485; hereafter cited in the text as *OP 2.*

4. This motif of expiatory reincarnation appears earlier in *Les Contemplations,* in "Saturne" (3.3). The planet traditionally associated with melancholy is imagined as a prison world.

5. An author must treat visionary subject matter to qualify as one of Hugo's geniuses. Shakespeare may be considered an exception—he has a vision of supreme justice, but not of the Supreme Being but Goethe does not qualify: despite *Faust,* Hugo dismissed Goethe as merely very talented. *Faust* was too playful and satiric for Hugo to consider it truly prophetic.

6. As a psychopomp, or spiritual guide, she recalls the silent, smiling muse in Mallarmé's "Prose pour des Esseintes." Mallarmé's poetry, at first glance so different, has rightly been described as "sublimated Hugo." Compare "Un coup de Dés jamais n'abolira le hasard" to Hugo's *Dieu* to see how much Hugo inspired Mallarmé.

7. See Elisabeth Kübler-Ross, *On Death and Dying* (New York: Macmillan, 1969), and John Bowlby, *Loss: Sadness and Depression* (New York: Basic, 1980).

8. In the next book, "Paroles sur la dune" (5.13.695–96: Words Spoken on the Dunes) provides one of Hugo's most moving expressions of despair. It contrasts the ironically joyful beauty of nature with the poet's despondency.

9. Compare the ironic light at the conclusion of Alfred de Vigny's "Le Mont des Oliviers" (The Mount of Olives) in *Les Destinées.* Christ's disciples have abandoned Him by falling asleep. Anguished in the darkness, He tries to speak to God but receives no reply. "Et puis il vit rôder la torche de Judas" [And then He saw approach Judas's torch] in the last line, announcing the betrayal.

10. See Leo Spitzer, *Linguistics and Literary History* (1948; Princeton, N.J.: Princeton University Press, 1967), 207 (hereafter cited in the text as Spitzer 1967); and his *La Enumeración caótica en la poesía moderna* (Chaotic enumeration in modern poetry) (Buenos Aires: Coní, 1945).

11. Jean Gaudon provides a richly informative account of the genesis of *Les Contemplations* in his *Le Temps de la contemplation* (Paris: Flammarion, 1969), 192–269.

12. In French, such a device can be called an *embrayeur,* by analogy with the gearshift on a car.

13. This description derives from but modifies Jacques Seebacher's "Sens et structure des 'Mages,' " *Revue des Sciences Humaines* 111 (July–September 1963), 347–70, especially 353, 360, and 369.

14. Suzanne Nash, in *"Les Contemplations" de Victor Hugo: An Allegory of the Creative Process* (Princeton, N.J.: Princeton University Press, 1976), 58–60, 63, misleadingly claims to find aspects of Léopoldine in all women in Hugo's "Aurore" (book 1 of the *Contemplations*). It is more accurate to recognize that all women, including Léopoldine, serve Hugo as embodiments of the feminine principle.

Chapter Seven

1. For the most vigorous, influential expression of such conservative Catholic views, see Joseph de Maistre, *On God and Society: Essay on the Generative Principle of Political Constitutions and Other Human Institutions,* ed. Elisha Greifer, trans. Laurence M. Porter (in French, 1809; Chicago: Regnery, 1959; 3d printing, 1967). This work parallels Edmund Burke's classic *Reflections on the Revolution in France* (1790).

2. The mystical philosophy of illuminism has inspired a vast critical literature. See, for example, Laurence M. Porter, "La Pensée de Nodier," chap. 1 of "Le Style et l'art narratif de Charles Nodier dans les *Contes*" (Ph.D. diss., Harvard University, 1965), 15–63, and two works by the leading French historian of romanticism, Paul Bénichou: *Les Mages romantiques* (Paris: Gallimard, 1988) and *Le Temps des prophètes: Doctrines de l'âge romantique* (Paris: Gallimard, 1977). In English, a masterful summary by Frank Paul Bowman appears in Peter France, ed., *The New Oxford Companion to Literature in French* (Oxford, U.K.: Clarendon, 1995), s.v. "Illuminism" (399; see also the cross-references from that entry). Among literary works, see Honoré de Balzac, *Louis Lambert* and *Séraphîta;* Gérard de Nerval, *Aurélia.*

3. For a more detailed discussion of romantic epiphanies, see Laurence M. Porter, "Writing Romantic Epiphany: *Atala, Séraphîta, Aurélia, Dieu,*" *Romance Quarterly* 34, no. 4 (November 1987; special number, "Perspectives on French Romanticism," ed. James S. Patty): 435–42.

4. On Lautréamont, see Laurence M. Porter, *The Literary Dream in French Romanticism* (Detroit, Mich.: Wayne State University Press, 1979); on Rachilde and Mirbeau, see Porter, "Decadence and the *fin-de-siècle* Novel," in *The Cambridge Companion to the French Novel from 1800 to the Present,* ed. Timothy Unwin (Cambridge: Cambridge University Press, 1997), 93–110.

5. Italo Calvino's playful postmodernist *Cosmicomics* (1965) delightfully parodies the epiphany genre.

6. The image is not new to Hugo: in his 1834 essay "Sur Mirabeau" (On Mirabeau [a famous French revolutionary orator and ruthless politician]), Hugo writes: "To anyone who has studied that [revolutionary] period, it is obvious that the Convention [1792–1794: it voted the execution of King Louis

XVI and promulgated the Terror} was contained in the Constituent Assembly
{1789–92} as early as 1789. It was there like a dormant seed. . . . '93, in a
word, a black speck in the blue sky of '89. Everything was already inside that
black speck." Victor Hugo, *Œuvres complètes,* ed. Jean Massin, vol. 5 (Paris: Le
Club Français du Livre, 1967–1971), 215; hereafter cited as *OC.*

7. *Le Rhin, Lettres à un ami,* letter 4, *OC* 6, 221. See the entire passage
where Hugo contemplates the sky, 220–21.

8. In the political unconscious of romantic visionaries, syncretism
(combining insights from diverse religions into a single system) betrays
repressed nostalgia for a lost social unity in a bygone age when class conflict,
viewed retrospectively, seemed less acute.

9. Richard B. Grant, "Progress, Pessimism, and Revelation in Victor
Hugo's *Dieu,*" *Nineteenth-Century French Studies* 17, nos. 1–2 (Fall 1988–Winter
1989): 45, 46, 54.

10. Jacques Delille (1738–1813) and Charles Millevoye (1782–1816)
were among other influential precursors. For additional background on the
petite épopée, or *poëme,* see René Jasinski, *A travers le dix-neuvième siècle* (Paris:
Nizet, 1975), 9–64; Laurence M. Porter, *The Renaissance of the Lyric in French
Romanticism* (Lexington, Ky.: French Forum, 1978), 47–74; and Joseph Sun-
golowsky, *Alfred de Vigny et le dix-neuvième siècle* (Paris: Nizet, 1968), 173–211.

11. Victor Brombert would rightly express reservations here. To conclude his study *Victor Hugo and the Visionary Novel* (Cambridge, Mass.: Harvard
University Press, 1984), 242, he cites a sentence from Hugo's draft for "L'Infini
dans l'art" (1862–1863): "Evil, in nature as well as in destiny, is a dark beginning of God continuing beyond us into the invisible" (*OC* 12, 356). "The sentence reveals with particular clarity," Brombert comments, "the inadequacy of a
naive reading of Hugo as the reassuring bard of progress, of light, of redemptive love, and of Satan's ultimate salvation." He invokes the octopus of *Travailleurs de la mer* as an instance of primordial evil in nature. But I must protest
that the octopus does not make moral choices; moreover, it serves as the providential instrument for punishing the villain Clubin.

12. Convenient summaries of the main structures of *La Légende des siècles,* with brief commentaries, are found in Paul Berret, *"La Légende des siècles" de
Victor Hugo* (Paris: Mellottée, 1957), 76–183; and in Paul T. Comeau, " 'Le
Satyre' dans *La Légende des siècles* de Victor Hugo," *French Review* 39, no. 6 (May
1966): 849–61.

13. See Charles Baudouin, *Psychanalyse de Victor Hugo* (Geneva: Editions
du Mont-Blanc, 1943), 114–23; Bernard Guyon, *La Vocation Poétique de Victor
Hugo: Essai sur la signification spirituelle des "Odes et Ballades" et des "Orientales"
(1818–1828)* (Gap: Louis-Jean, 1954), 28–29, 35–36, 42; and Paul Zumthor,
Victor Hugo, poète de Satan (Paris: Laffont, 1946), 116.

14. See André Maurois, *Olympio ou la vie de Victor Hugo* (Paris: Hachette,
1954), 358–493.

Chapter Eight

1. Should this detail seem too melodramatic and far-fetched, we should recall the fate of a California man recently sentenced to life in prison under the "three strikes" law. He had stolen a slice of pizza.

2. On the concept of the hypogram, see Michael Riffaterre, *Semiotics of Poetry* (1978; Bloomington, Ind.: Indiana University Press, 1984), 26–46, 94–99.

3. For sources other than Hugo's early work, see Paul de Kock's *La Laitière de Montfermeil* (The Milkmaid of Montfermeil), discussed by Richard B. Grant in *The Perilous Quest* (Durham, N.C.: Duke University Press, 1968), 154–55, hereafter cited as Grant 1986; and Jean Pommier, "Premiers pas dans l'Etude des 'Misérables,' " in *Centenaire des Misérables (1862–1962): Hommage à Victor Hugo* (Bulletin de la faculté des lettres de Strasbourg, 1962), 33–35.

4. Originally called "Les Misères" when composed between 1845 and 1848, at the height of Hugo's political activity in the House of Peers, the work was expanded by about 60 percent and retitled between 1860 and 1862. See René Journet and Guy Robert, *Le Mythe du peuple dans Les Misérables* (Paris: Editions Sociales, 1964), 22–56; hereafter cited as Journet and Robert.

5. Victor Hugo, *Les Misérables,* ed. René Journet, 3 vols. (Paris: Garnier-Flammarion, 1967). Further references in the text are to this edition, in the form part-book-chapter-page. Prepared by an excellent Hugo scholar, this edition has been chosen because of its affordability.

For a splendid analysis of a parallel statement by a contemporary "inner exile" who had remained in Paris where his home, the artists' and writers' neighborhood around the Carousel, was being razed by Baron Haussmann's urban renewal projects, see Richard Terdiman's "Baudelaire's 'Le Cygne': Memory, History, and the Sign," chapter 4 of Terdiman, *Present Past: Modernity and the Memory Crisis* (Ithaca, N.Y.: Cornell University Press, 1993), 106–47. An abridged, simplified version will appear in Laurence M. Porter, ed., *Approaches to Teaching Baudelaire's "Fleurs du Mal"* (New York: MLA, 1999).

6. See Simon Schama, *Citizens: A Chronicle of the French Revolution* (New York: Random House, 1989), 3–5.

7. On this essential topic, see Georges Piroué, *Victor Hugo romancier ou les dessus de l'inconnu* (Paris: Denoël, 1964), 47–84; and Journet and Robert, *Le Mythe du peuple dans "Les Misérables,"* 43–50.

8. See Grant 1968, 158–76, and Victor Brombert, *Victor Hugo and the Visionary Novel* (Cambridge, Mass.: Harvard University Press, 1986), 86–139.

9. Two inconsistent details in the text reflect Hugo's preoccupation with a rhetoric of pathos at the expense of a plausible plot. First, although Valjean is always described, after his release, as incomparably strong, the baker whose loaf Valjean has stolen catches him and easily detains him; Hugo seems to be trying to represent here the fatal power of social inequity. Second, after his release, Valjean can never find his sister and her children again. He makes no

particular efforts to locate them, nor even thinks of them later; they are episodic characters who help set in motion a plot where poverty struggles with grace.

10. Hugo draws similar parallels between individual destiny and national history in his unfinished poem *La Fin de Satan*.

11. Cosette remains totally marginal even when idolized by Marius and Jean Valjean. See Nicole Savy's pungent feminist analysis of "Cosette: un personnage qui n'existe pas," in *Lire "Les Misérables,"* ed. Anne Ubersfeld and Guy Rosa (Paris: Corti, 1985), 173–90.

12. Kathryn Grossman offers a detailed analysis of Thénardier as a fictional character in her *Figuring Transcendence in "Les Misérables": Hugo's Romantic Sublime* (Carbondale: Southern Illinois University Press, 1994), 16–25. Fritz Peter Kirsch examines many individual characters, the chronotope (the represented time-space continuum), and the narrators of Hugo's novels in his *Probleme der Romanstruktur bei Victor Hugo* (Vienna: Austrian Academy of Science, 1973).

13. In popular culture, *Les Misérables* quickly became the focus for celebrations of new sewer construction (not a trivial matter in a city that wealthy people left in warm weather to avoid the stench). Prints and figurines inspired by the novel were sold widely even before its publication had been completed. See Fred Radford, "A Cloacal Obsession: Hugo, Joyce, and the Sewer Museum of Paris," *Mattoid* 48 (1994): 66–85, esp. 76–80. See also Alain Corbin, *The Foul and the Fragrant: Odor and the French Imagination* (Cambridge, Mass.: Harvard University Press, 1986), and Lawrence Wright, *Clean and Decent: The Fascinating History of the Bathroom and the Water Closet, and of Sundry Habits, Fashions, and Accessories of the Toilet, Principally in Great Britain, France, and America* (New York: Viking, 1960).

14. Concerning Valjean's renunciation of his role as a parent, see Galya Gerstman, "Fictional Fathers and Fathers by Fiction: The Surrogate Father as Novelist in the Work of Victor Hugo," *Nineteenth-Century French Studies* 24, nos. 3–4 (Spring–Summer 1996): 370–80.

15. Thus he realizes the evil dream of prosperity in America cherished by Balzac's arch-criminal Vautrin in *Le Père Goriot (Old Goriot)*.

16. On Balzac's novel, see Laurence M. Porter, "Nuance in the Novel: Teaching *Old Goriot* in a French or World Context," and other materials in Michal Peled Ginsburg, ed., "Approaches to Teaching Balzac's *Le Père Goriot*" (New York: MLA, in press).

17. See Juan Cirlot, *A Dictionary of Symbols* (New York: Philosophical Library, 1962), s.v. "Inversion"; and Gilbert Durand, *Les Structures anthropologiques de l'imaginaire: Introduction à l'archéotypologie générale*, 3d ed. (Paris: Bordas, 1969), 317.

18. A satiric form of negative inversion appears at the Champmathieu trial when the prosecuting attorney claims that this ignorant man became a

criminal monster under the influence of romanticism, baptized by its enemies "l'école satanique" [the satanic school] (see 1.7.8.298). French has a proverb for such situations where pretensions to the ethereal turn sour: "Qui veut faire l'ange, fait la bête" [The person who tries to act like an angel will end up acting like a beast].

19. See Angelo Metzidakis, "On Rereading French History in Hugo's *Les Misérables*," *French Review* 67, no. 2 (December 1993): 187–95, with a useful bibliography.

20. See William Blake, "The Marriage of Heaven and Hell," in *The Poetry and Prose of William Blake*, ed. David V. Erdman (New York: Doubleday, 1965), plate 9, line 57, p. 37; and Johann Wolfgang von Goethe, "The Prologue in Heaven," in *Faust*, trans. Walter Arndt, ed. Cyrus Hamlin (New York: Norton, 1976), 8–9, vv. 299–343.

21. Concerning the aesthetic function of digressions and enumerations in Hugo's fiction, see Michel Butor, "Victor Hugo romancier," in Butor, *Répertoire II* (Paris: Minuit, 1964), esp. 215–24.

22. On the organic worldview cosmology, see René Wellek, "The Concept of Romanticism in Literary Scholarship," *Comparative Literature* 1 (1949): 1–23, 147–72.

23. Naomi Schor, *George Sand and Idealism* (New York: Columbia University Press, 1993).

24. As many critics have observed, Jean/Val/jean's name itself reflects the novel's general movement of spiritual descent (*val* means valley), enlightenment, and redemption. This structure has, for Hugo, political and spiritual parallels. The rise of democracy follows the bloody revolution; the redemption of Satan follows his revolt and fall.

25. Among other biblical parallels, see an allusion to the parable of Martha and Mary, an allusion to the apostles' Gift of Tongues at Pentecost, and a stylized use of the parable form itself (1.1.1.27; 1.1.4.37; 1.2.8.122).

26. The motif of the two-phased spiritual conversion is commonplace: consider, for example, Saint Augustine (converted first to Manichaeism and then to Christianity) or Malcolm X (converted first to the Black Muslims and later to the international Islamic faith), as Marius is converted from Royalist to Bonapartist to Republican.

27. Karen Masters-Wicks, *Victor Hugo's "Les Misérables" and the Novels of the Grotesque* (New York: Lang, 1994), 101.

28. Gavroche recalls the street urchin in Delacroix's painting *La Liberté guidant le peuple* (Liberty Leading the People, 1830).

Conclusion

1. Graham Robb, *Victor Hugo* (New York: Norton, 1998), 509, 534.

2. See Laurence M. Porter, ed., *Approaches to Teaching Baudelaire's "Fleurs du Mal"* (New York: MLA, 1999) for information on the present state of Baudelaire studies.

3.   Much detail concerning Hugo's posthumous triumphs in popular culture, and many splendid illustrations and photographs, are available in the folio compiled by Jean-François Barrielle, *Le Grand Dictionnaire Victor Hugo* (Paris: Flammarion, 1985). There are some inaccuracies.

4.   Maurice Descotes, "Du drame à l'opéra: les transpositions lyriques du théâtre de Victor Hugo," *Revue d'Histoire du théâtre* 34, no. 2 (April–June 1982), 103–4.

5.   Descotes provides detailed comparisons of Verdi's *Ernani* and *Hernani* (115–25); Verdi's *Rigoletto* and *Le Roi s'amuse* (125–39); and Amilcare Ponchielli's *La Gioconda* (1876), adapted from Hugo's play *Angelo, tyran de Padoue* (*Angelo, tyrant of Padua,* 1835) (139–55). Jules Perrot's ballet *La Esmeralda* opened in 1844.

6.   Adapted by Alain Boublil and Claude-Michel Schönberg, with lyrics by Herbert Kretzmer and music by Schönberg.

7.   The quoted remarks, although not the context in which they are embedded, come from Hilary Devries's review in the "Arts–Leisure" section of *The Christian Science Monitor,* 18 December 1987.

8.   Here the story of the brilliant sculptor Camille Claudel, sister of the writer Paul Claudel and for a time mistress of the sculptor Rodin, comes to mind.

9.   Robb, 539–40; see also Gabriel Gobron, *Histoire et philosophie du Caodaïsme: Buddhisme rénové, spiritisme vietnamien, religion nouvelle en Eurasie* (Paris: Dervy, 1949).

10.   Thanks to Professor Ilinca Zarifopol-Johnston, who demonstrated the parallels to us in her October 1997 talk at the national Colloquium on Nineteenth-Century French Studies.

11.   Cited in David Kaufman's review in *Horizon* (March 1987): 39.

12.   William A. Henry III, "An Epic of the Downtrodden," *Time,* 5 January 1988.

Selected Bibliography

PRIMARY SOURCES

English Translations

The Distance, The Shadows: Selected Poems. Vancouver, B.C.: Anvil, 1981.
Hernani. New York: Fertig, 1987.
History of a Crime. New York: Fertig, 1993.
The Hunchback of Notre-Dame. New York: Bantam, 1981; New York: Random House, 1995.
The Last Day of a Condemned Man. New York: Oxford University Press, 1992.
The Man Who Laughs. Lafayette, Colo.: Atlantean, 1991.
Les Misérables. Modern Library, 1992; New York: Random House, 1992; New York: Knopf, 1998.
Napoleon the Little. New York: Fertig, 1992.
Ninety-Three. Mattituck, N.Y.: Amereon, 1976.
Notre-Dame de Paris. New York: Oxford University Press, 1993; Mineola, N.Y.: Dover, 1995; New York: Penguin (film and TV tie-in edition), 1996; New York: Viking Penguin, 1997.
Three Plays: Hernani, Ruy Blas, The King Amuses Himself. New York: Fertig, 1995.
Toilers of the Sea. Lafayette, Colo.: Atlantean, 1993.
The United States of Europe. New York: Garland, 1973.

Collected Works

Œuvres complètes. Ed. Jean Massin. 18 vols. Paris: Club français du livre, 1967–1970. Chronological. Also issued in 36 vols. Includes 153 often outstanding essays by numerous scholars of Hugo's life and works. Overall the best edition.
Œuvres complètes de Victor Hugo. Ed. Jacques Seebacher and Guy Rosa. 16 vols. Paris: Laffont, 1985 –1990. Inexpensive paperbacks; respectable scholarship.

Individual Works

(See also the expensive "Pléiäde" editions published by Gallimard, and the inexpensive editions in the "Garnier-Flammarion" and in the "Livre de Poche" series.)

L'Âne. Ed. Pierre Albouy. Paris: Flammarion, 1966. Valuable introduction on Hugo's view of history.

Les Contemplations. Ed. Léon Cellier. Paris: Garnier, 1969. Valuable notes on critical debates and on genesis (that is, on how the poems were inspired and composed).

Dieu: Le Seuil du gouffre et l'Océan d'en haut. Ed. René Journet et Guy Robert. 2 vols. Paris: Nizet, 1960–1961. The second part has been called Hugo's poetic masterpiece.

La Légende des siècles; La Fin de Satan; Dieu, ed. Jacques Truchet. 1962; reprint, Paris: Gallimard, 1982. Useful notes and variants.

Promontorium Somnii. Ed. René Journet and Guy Robert. Paris: Les Belles Lettres, 1961. Originally planned as part of *William Shakespeare.* Important exposition of Hugo's intellectual history and ideas.

Ruy Blas. Ed. Anne Ubersfeld. 2 vols. Paris: Les Belles Lettres, 1971–1972.

SECONDARY SOURCES

Bibliography

Grimaud, Michel, Patricia Ward, Bernadette Lintz-Murphy, Nicole Mallet, Claire-Lise Rogers, Elliott M. Grant, and Richard B. Grant. "Victor Hugo." In *A Critical Bibliography of French Literature 5: The Nineteenth Century,* ed. David Baguley, vol. 1, pp. 208–31. Syracuse, N.Y.: Syracuse University Press, 1994. Authoritative; coverage through 1989.

Biographies, Correspondence, and Reputation

Barrielle, Jean-François. *Le Grand Dictionnaire Victor Hugo.* Paris: Flammarion, 1985. Much detail on Hugo's posthumous triumphs in popular culture; splendid illustrations and photographs. Some factual inaccuracies.

La Gloire de Victor Hugo. Paris: La Réunion des musées nationaux, 1985. Hugo's fame and influence. Strong on adaptations and on artists' interpretations of Hugo's works.

Hugo, Adèle. *Victor Hugo raconté par Adèle Hugo.* Ed. Anne Ubersfeld and Guy Rosa. Paris: Plon, 1985. A critical edition of his wife's "as told to" biography, *Victor Hugo raconté par un témoin de sa vie.*

Laster, Arnaud. *Pleins feux sur Victor Hugo.* Paris: Comédie-Française, 1981. A valuable encyclopedia, including chapters on theatrical parodies and on film and television adaptations.

Maurois, André. *Olympio ou la vie de Victor Hugo.* Paris: Hachette, 1954; trans. G. Hopkins, New York: Harper, 1956. Standard but now frequently corrected by Robb.

Robb, Graham. *Victor Hugo.* New York: Norton, 1998. Definitive.

Wytteman, Jean-Pierre. "Présentation." In *Victor Hugo: Œuvres complètes,* vols. 15–16, ed. Jean Massin, 1205–35. Paris: Club Français du livre, 1967–1970. Indispensable account of Hugo's political career from 1870 to 1885.

General Studies of Hugo's Art and Ideas

Albouy, Pierre. *Mythographies.* Paris: Corti, 1976. Important posthumous collection of articles, particularly illuminating concerning Hugo's view of the hero.
Baudouin, Charles. *Psychanalyse de Victor Hugo.* 1943; rev. ed., Paris: Colin, 1972. A classic.
Bénichou, Paul. *Les Mages Romantiques.* Paris: Gallimard, 1988. On the French romantic poets' self-assumed roles as seers and prophets. This book won four literary prizes.
Butor, Michel. *Répertoire II,* 199–42; *Répertoire III,* 185–239. Paris: Minuit, 1964, 1969. Speculative examination of Hugo's versification, of *Notre-Dame de Paris,* of Hugo's theater, and of Hugo's criticism.
Cellier, Léon. "Hugo lu par Baudouin et Mauron." *Circé* (Chambéry, France) 1 (1970): 81–131. A major evaluation of the psychoanalytical criticism.
Lectures de Victor Hugo, ed. Mireille Calle-Gruber and Arnold Rothe. Paris: Nizet, 1986. An important colloquium in Heidelberg.
Levaillant, Maurice. *La Crise mystique de Victor Hugo.* Paris: Corti, 1954. Essential study of the relationship between Hugo's spiritualist seances and his visionary art in the middle 1850s.
Poulet, Georges. *La Distance intérieure.* Paris: Plon, 1952; translated as *The Interior Distance,* Baltimore, Md.: Johns Hopkins University Press, 1959. Masterful essay on Hugo's spatial imagery on pp. 153–81 in the English edition.
Riffaterre, Michael. *La Production du texte.* Paris: Seuil, 1979; translated as *Text Production,* New York: Columbia University Press, 1983. On humor in *Les Misérables* and on "Ecrit sur la vitre d'une fenêtre flamande" in *Les Rayons et les Ombres.*
Swinburne, Algernon Charles. *A Study of Victor Hugo.* London: Chatto and Windus, n.d. Also published as Swinburne's *Prose Works,* vol. 3. The most sensitive and comprehensive study of Hugo during his lifetime, by a famous English poet.
Ubersfeld, Anne. *Paroles de Hugo.* Paris: Messidor-Editions sociales, 1985. Eleven wide-ranging studies.

Hugo's Poetry

Chambers, Ross. "De la marge à la marge: Le poème 'Le Pont' et 'Eclaircie.' " In *Hugo dans les marges,* ed. Lucien Dällenbach and Laurent Jenny, 118–38. Geneva: Zoé, 1985.

Gaudon, Jean. *Le Temps de la contemplation: l'œuvre poétique de Victor Hugo des "Misères" au "Seuil du gouffre" (1845–1856)*. Paris: Flammarion, 1969. The major study of the visionary poetry.

Grant, Richard B. "Progress, Pessimism, and Revelation in Victor Hugo's *Dieu*." *Nineteenth-Century French Studies* 17, nos. 1–2 (Fall 1988–Winter 1989): 44–57.

Guyon, Bernard. *La Vocation poétique de Victor Hugo: Essai sur la signification spirituelle des "Odes et Ballades" et des "Orientales" (1818–1828)*. Gap: Louis-Jean, 1954. Essential.

Houston, John Porter. *The Demonic Imagination: Style and Theme in French Romantic Poetry*. Baton Rouge: Louisiana State University Press, 1969. The Romantic rebel in context, approached through poetic imagery.

———. *Victor Hugo*. Rev. ed. Boston: Twayne, 1988. Pages 11–19 capably discuss *Les Orientales* as pure poetry.

Nash, Suzanne. *"Les Contemplations" of Victor Hugo: An Allegory of the Creative Process*. Princeton, N.J.: Princeton University Press, 1976. Several sensitive close readings, and intelligent comments on the structure of the collection.

Porter, Laurence M. *The Renaissance of the Lyric in French Romanticism: Ode, Elegy, and "Poëme."* Lexington, Ky.: French Forum Monographs, 1978. How Hugo transforms the traditional treatment of the sublime in the ode.

———. "Writing Romantic Epiphany: *Atala, Séraphîta, Aurélia, Dieu*." *Romance Quarterly* 34, no. 4 (November 1987): 435–42. Places the visionary genre and its conventions in a broad context.

Seebacher, Jacques. "Sens et structure des 'Mages.' " *Revue des Sciences Humaines* 111 (July–September 1963), 347–70. Outstanding analysis of a key poem.

Ullmann, Etienne de. "La Transposition dans la poésie lyrique de Hugo des *Odes et Ballades* aux *Contemplations*." *Le Français moderne* 19 (1951): 277–95. Studies synesthesia, which became frequent in the *Contemplations*.

Hugo's Novels

Charlier, Gustave. "Comment fut écrit 'Le Dernier Jour d'un condamné.' " *Revue d'Histoire littéraire de la France* 22 (1915): 321–60.

Etienne, Servais. *Les Sources de Bug-Jargal*. Brussels: Palais des Académies, 1923.

Grant, Richard B. *The Perilous Quest: Image, Myth, and Prophecy in the Narratives of Victor Hugo*. Durham, N.C.: Duke University Press, 1968. Has worn very well; perceptive comments on many novels and plays.

Grossman, Kathryn M. *The Early Novels of Victor Hugo: Towards a Poetics of Harmony*. Geneva: Droz, 1986. Includes an inspired reading of *Han d'Islande*.

———. *"Les Misérables": Conversion, Revolution, Redemption*. New York: Twayne, 1996. Clear, intelligent overview.

Lire "Les Misérables." Ed. Anne Ubersfeld and Guy Rosa. Paris: Corti, 1985.

Mouralis, Bernard. "Histoire et culture dans *Bug-Jargal.*" *Revue d'Histoire littéraire de la France* 149 (1973): 47–68.

Petry, Sandy. *History in the Text: Quatrevingt-treize and the French Revolution.* West Lafayette, Ind.: Purdue University Monographs in Romance Languages, 1980. Rich, lucid, and informative.

Pommier, Jean. "Premiers pas dans l'étude des 'Misérables.' " In *Centenaire des Misérables (1862–1962): Hommage à Victor Hugo,* 29–37. Strasbourg: Presses Universitaires, 1962. Pioneering study of the sources.

Savy, Nicole. "Cosette: un personnage qui n'existe pas." In *Lire "Les Misérables,"* ed. Anne Ubersfeld and Guy Rosa, 173–90. Paris: Corti, 1985. How the heroine is erased by Hugo.

Hugo's Theater

Gaudon, Jean. *Victor Hugo et le théâtre: Stratégie et dramaturgie.* Paris: Suger, 1985 (updates his 1955 study).

Glachant, Paul, and Victor Glachant. *Un laboratoire dramatique: Essai critique sur le théâtre de Victor Hugo.* 2 vols. Paris, 1902–1903.

Moskos, George. "(En)gendering Power in Victor Hugo's *Hernani.*" *Neophilologus* 78, no. 1 (January 1994): 45–56. Groundbreaking feminist/homosocial analysis.

Ubersfeld, Anne. *Le Roi et le bouffon: Etude sur le théâtre de Hugo de 1830 à 1839.* Paris: Corti, 1974. Richly varied approaches, including the indispensable study of audience reception at the height of Hugo's career as a playwright.

Index

179

The Author

Laurence M. Porter studied at Harvard University. Since 1963 he has taught French, comparative literature, African studies, and critical theory at Michigan State University, where he received the Distinguished Faculty Award in 1995. His main interests include romanticism, poetry, feminism, fantasy, and psychoanalytic theory. He has coedited *Aging in Literature* (International Book Publishers, 1984) and *Approaches to Teaching Flaubert's "Madame Bovary"* (MLA, 1995) and edited *Critical Essays on Gustave Flaubert* (Hall, 1986) and *Approaches to Teaching Baudelaire's "Fleurs du Mal"* (MLA, 1999). His monographs include *The Renaissance of the Lyric in French Romanticism: Elegy, Ode, and "Poëme"* (French Forum, 1978), *The Literary Dream in French Romanticism: A Psychoanalytical Interpretation* (Wayne State, 1979), *"The Interpretation of Dreams": Freud's Theories Revisited* (Twayne, 1987), and *The Crisis of French Symbolism* (Cornell, 1990, nominated for the James Russell Lowell Prize of the Modern Language Association of America). He has held an NEH Fellowship for University Teachers in 1998. He currently serves on the editorial boards of *Nineteenth-Century French Studies* and *Studies in Twentieth Century Literature*.

The Editor

David O'Connell is professor of French at Georgia State University. He received his Ph.D. in 1966 from Princeton University, where he was a National Woodrow Wilson Fellow, the Bergen Fellow in Romance Languages, and a National Woodrow Wilson Dissertation Fellow. He is the author of *The Teachings of Saint Louis: A Critical Text* (1972), *Les Propos de Saint Louis* (1974), *Louis-Ferdinand Céline* (1976), *The Instructions of Saint Louis: A Critical Text* (1979), and *Michel de Saint Pierre: A Catholic Novelist at the Crossroads* (1990). He has edited more than 60 books in the Twayne World Authors Series.